Intimacy

Intimacy

Personal Relationships in Modern Societies

LYNN JAMIESON

Polity Press

First published in 1998 by Polity Press in association with Blackwell Publishers Ltd.

2 4 6 8 10 9 7 5 3 1

Editorial office:
Polity Press
65 Bridge Street
Cambridge CB2 1UR, UK

Marketing and production:
Blackwell Publishers Ltd
108 Cowley Road
Oxford OX4 1JF, UK

Published in the USA by
Blackwell Publishers Inc.
350 Main Street
Malden, MA 02148, USA

ISBN 0–7456–1573–2
ISBN 0–7456–1574–0 (pbk)

A CIP catalogue record for this book is available from the British Library and has been applied for from the Library of Congress.

Typeset in 10½ on 12 pt Palatino
by Ace Filmsetting Ltd, Frome, Somerset
Printed and bound in Great Britain by MPG Books Ltd, Bodmin, Cornwall

This book is printed on acid-free paper.

To all my friends and family, particularly Sarah, Stuart, Tom, those with whom I've lived and worked as well as loved, and to the memory of Alison Freeman, 1952–88.

———————

Contents

Acknowledgements

Thanks to the many lively and thoughtful students who have taken my Intimate Relationships (previously Primary Relationships) course in the Department of Sociology at the University of Edinburgh. Thanks also to the following for helpfully reading a draft of the manuscript: Colin Bell, Gill Jones, David Morgan, David Pearson, Sue Scott, and, in the case of particular chapters, Claude Fischer, Claire Toynbee and Judy Wajcman. Thanks to Denis Marsden and Jean Duncomb, Sharon Hays, Stevi Jackson and Sue Scott, Graham Allan and Graham Crow and to Jeff Weintraub for sending me material which was not yet published. Thanks to Sarah Price for proofreading. Thanks to the University of Edinburgh for my sabbatical and the departments of Sociology in Berkeley and in Wellington for my periods as a visiting scholar.

CHAPTER 1

Introduction

A Story of Intimacy?

Ten years ago this book might have been called 'personal relationships' or 'primary relationships'[1] since it is mainly about family, friendship and sexual relationships; relationships which are often described as the 'most important' to people. However, this book is called *Intimacy* because it critically examines the notion that *intimacy* is at the centre of meaningful personal life in contemporary societies. Intimacy has become a fashionable word both in the social sciences and in popular self-help books advising on the art of good relationships. What is meant by intimacy is often a very specific sort of knowing, loving and 'being close to' another person. The self-help books advocate talking and listening, sharing your thoughts, showing your feelings. This is the type of intimacy I call 'disclosing intimacy'. The emphasis is on mutual disclosure, constantly revealing your inner thoughts and feelings to each other. It is an intimacy of the self rather than an intimacy of the body, although the completeness of intimacy of the self may be enhanced by bodily intimacy. Mutually shared intimacy of this type typically requires a relationship in which people participate as equals. In other words, intimacy across genders, generations, classes and races can only take on this character if the participants can remove social barriers and transcend structural inequalities. Some authors argue that this type of intimacy is more sought after than in previous historical eras because of the specific social conditions of the late twentieth century. At the century's end, there is then, a new story of the nature and significance of intimacy. One of the tasks of this book is to consider whether this type of intimacy is in fact commonly found or found at all in people's personal lives. Another task of the book is to ask what the evidence is for a late twentieth-century transformation of intimacy? Both these questions are addressed by a review of academic and mainly sociological research on personal, 'primary' and perhaps intimate relationships: parent–child relationships, relationships with friends and kin, sexual relationships and couple relationships. Each of these types of relationship is the topic of a separate chapter.

The academic research reviewed in this book is largely about the European and North-American societies and the Euro-North American influenced societies of Australia and New Zealand.[2] While the end of the twentieth century is the central focus, the next chapter considers a much wider time frame. This historical approach is essential to understanding the emergence of 'the intimate relationship' as an idealized version of personal life which gains ground previously dominated by a particular idealized version of 'the family'. Clearly this is a contested shift resisted by those who promote 'family values'. Does research show that this shift in ideals is reflected in the practices of private lives? Do people act as if having 'good relationships' is more important than being part of 'a family' or following a family career from son or daughter to grandfather or grandmother? The reader is warned at the outset that the evidence is equivocal. Change is undoubtedly occurring but how to characterize the nature and significance of the change remains deeply contested. Although stories told about personal life emphasize disclosing intimacy to an unprecedented degree, there is no clear evidence that disclosing intimacy is increasingly the key organizing principle of personal lives.

The Wider Significance of Intimacy in Personal Life

If a new quality of intimate relationship is increasingly dominating personal life, the effects may be wide reaching. A diverse array of sociological traditions agrees that personal relationships have profound social consequences. Personal relationships are a key form of social cohesion. Family and friendship relationships of childhood are critical in the production of socially competent adults, for structuring the gender and sexual identities of individuals and thus for helping sustain societal patterns of sex/gender difference. Personal relationships are also crucial in maintaining social divisions. They can provide training in hatred as well as love and in dominance and submission as well as co-operative efforts. In highly hierarchical or segmented societies, extreme social divisions can block not only close association, but also the potential for empathy, creating the conditions for the dehumanizing of 'the other'.

Sociologists have long argued that it is the innate potential and highly developed social ability to see things from the other person's point of view, to put yourself in the place of the other (Max Weber's (1904) *'verstehen'*; George Herbert Mead's (1927) 'generalised other'[3]), to anticipate and understand how the other reacts, which distinguishes humans from other animals. Indeed, societies would not be possible if people ceased to make sense of and anticipate the actions and reactions of others. Community, friendship, all co-operative relationships rely on the human capacity for and interest in building shared knowledge and understanding with others. For the theoretical traditions referred to as symbolic interactionism (Mead, 1927) and phenomenology (Schutz, 1932), all that is known and taken for granted as how things are done, is the product of social interaction. The phenomena which inhabit our world are apprehended and constructed through symbols – words, language, gestures and meaningful actions. A sense of a solid unchanging world, a stable society and a stable self can only be achieved through intense, face to face, sustained interaction. Personal relationships are a key site of socially and personally constructive interaction. The term 'significant others' (Berger and Luckmann, 1966) is used to describe those intimates who have a particular significance in and commitment to the shaping of a self. Personal relationships, then, have a particular significant both for the individual and for society.

In a psychoanalytic account, early emotional attachment is assumed to be highly significant for subsequent relationships. For psychoanalysts, early emotional life is characterized as a violent psychological struggle. In the classic psychoanalytic account of Sigmund Freud, (1856–1939), the infant is preoccupied with the erotic pleasures of the body and desires to possess and control their source, the mother or main carer. The term Freud used to describe the way the infant focused his or her emotional/sexual energy on the carer has been translated in English as 'cathexis', derived from the Greek verb 'to hold fast', 'to retain'. The infant has to learn that the carer is a separate being with an independent will which cannot be wholly controlled. Psychoanalysis is the theoretical tradition which most emphatically conceptualizes sex and intimacy as inherently linked. Through clinical studies, Freud concluded that an individual's sexual and emotional make-up are profoundly shaped in the first few years of life. A person's original complex of desires and feelings remain represented as part of their psychological make-up in their subconscious. How the individual approaches all subsequent relationships depends on the patterning of the subconscious. Both a person's capacity for intimacy and their sexuality can only be understood by unravelling how they have managed infantile attachments and desires. Contemporary psychoanalytic accounts continue to trace adult intimacy to the infant's emotional and erotic tie to his or her primary carer. Without taking on board all of Freud's understanding of the stages of this psychosexual development, many authors nevertheless accept that the mother–child bond is the template for subsequent sexual love relationships. For example, 'Attachment between lovers is rather similar to that between infants and mothers, and indeed uses some of the same kinds of baby-talk and bodily contact. Perhaps one is derived from the other?' (Argyle, 1991, p. 136).

Contemporary authors influenced by psychoanalysis vary in their optimism concerning the typical legacy of the intimate relationships of early childhood for the emotional life of the adult. It has been argued that war and destruction stem from unmanageable shame and anger rooted in a failure to establish a secure sense of a bond with others in childhood (Scheff, 1990). The range of optimistic and pessimistic positions is illustrated in British sociology by the views of Anthony Giddens and Ian Craib. Giddens (1991) stresses that the typical end-product of early childhood is 'ontological security', a secure sense of one's own being, and a 'basic trust' in the project of life. Because of this 'basic trust', adults can operate in a world which they know to be risk-ridden without being overcome by anxiety. Moreover, they have the capacity for trusting others sufficiently to form committed close relationships (1991, pp. 38, 51, 186). Ontological security and 'basic trust' are only absent when carers have failed to provide a quality of care which enables children to invest trust in them. However, according to Ian Craib this denies the contradictory feelings and fears that are the psychological inheritance of all adults not just the unfortunate few (Craib, 1994). Craib argues that infancy leaves a legacy in every person of contradictory emotional needs.

Infant learning about boundaries between self and others, and of the power of others, leads to, on the one hand, fears of loss and abandonment and, on the other, fears of being swallowed up by others. This leaves adults with highly contradictory needs, both seeking and fearing emotional intimacy and a sense of merging with others.

These different views of the legacy of infancy all take for granted that children need care and devotion but precisely how children should be loved is an area of debate. For some authors the details are not critical; on the one hand, children grow into adults with a secure sense of themselves unless they have highly neglectful parents and, on the other, even children of utterly devoted parents will be wracked with contradictory feelings. For other authors, the details of parent–child interaction are crucial. In the 1950s psychologists talked of the importance of natural 'maternal instinct' (Bowlby, 1953) but now the psychologically important dimensions of love are defined more specifically as attentive, responsive interaction and approval, generating a sense in the child of being highly valued by another or others (Trevarthen, 1993). Both expert advice to parents and the actual practices of parents have varied considerably over time and place.

In some times and places, parents' love for their children has varied according to the sex of the child. In most contemporary societies, there is evidence of parents valuing rather different qualities in boys and girls. From sociological perspectives which emphasize how the world is socially constructed, gender differences are largely created by the different ways of interacting with people on the basis of their sex. A number of feminist or feminist-informed authors have attempted to document how childhood interactions educate boys in being aggressive and self-assertive while discouraging girls away from confident assertiveness towards being decorous, considerate, pleading and pleasing (Belotti, 1975; Jackson, 1982; Gagnon and Simon, 1973; Sharpe, 1976). For psychoanalysis, differential treatment of boys and girls is not the key issue but rather the typical way in which boy and girl infants cope with the discovery of biological differences between men and women while grappling with powerful emotional and sexual feelings. Freud developed the notion of an Oedipus complex (after the story of Oedipus, who grows up not knowing his parents then unwittingly kills his father and marries his mother) from clinical observations of boys (Freud, 1924, 1925). Freud argued that boy infants had strong feelings of hatred and jealousy towards their fathers as rivals disrupting their own desires for cathexis with their mother. But he alleged that the discovery of anatomical differences between boys and girls, results in the abandonment of overt sexual pleasure until adolescence. Infants, Freud believed, react to the anatomical difference of the sexes by believing that girls have been castrated. Hence, he argued, boys suppressed their sexual desires for their mother for fear of castration and became resolved to be men not women. A girl, on the other hand 'develops, like a scar, a sense of inferiority' and sees her future in terms of relationships with men. This particular version of events is no longer given much credence but the psychoanalytic project of making sense of masculinity and femininity by looking at the psycho-emotional dynamics of early childhood has never been abandoned.

The extent and nature of gender differences in the capacity to sustain intimate relationships remains deeply contested. Some academics believe that there is a causal relationship between structural gender inequalities and the capacity for intimacy. Historically in Euro-North American societies, the systematic dominance of men over women, sanctioned by law, state and church, and rendered a material reality by different access to property, income, wealth, education, business and pleasure, coincided with stereotypes of men as independent beings, distanced from emotions and of women as dependent, emotional creatures. For many feminist authors commenting on contemporary heterosexual relationships, if men apparently pursue intimate relationships less than women do, this is one facet of a much bigger picture of persistent inequalities between men and women. It has long been argued that women's weaker economic position, particularly their disadvantages in the labour market, ensured their greater dependence on marriage for economic survival, which in turn gave men the advantage in the marriage market as well as the labour market (Engels, 1972). Divisions of labour, which allocated to women the responsibility for child care and domestic work, made marriage an occupation for women in a way that it was not for men, while the exclusion of women from many occupational spheres severely limited women's possibilities of living independently of marriage. The idea that women needed marriage more and were more focused on marriage was the corollary of divisions of labour which allocated high-status full-time employment to men and child care and domestic work to women. Portrayals of marriage as an exchange in which men looked after dependent women financially while women physically and emotionally cared for men and brought up their children, concealed the overwhelming advantages to men (Delphy and Leonard, 1992, Pateman, 1988; Walby, 1989, 1990). Since men had the upper hand in the marriage market as well as the labour market, it was men who had the power to make the rules of sexual conduct. Hence women must guard their sexual reputations and attach themselves through a romantic relationship to one particular man.

The relationship between gender, sexual behaviour and intimacy remains a matter of debate. Some contemporary public stories depict women as wanting and needing commitment (what Hollway (1984a, b) calls the 'to have and to hold' discourse which has its roots in Christian views of marriage) and men as wanting and needing sex (the 'sex drive' discourse). The realities of men and women's lives are typically more complex and contradictory. Nevertheless, these stories encourage men to downplay and women to exaggerate their emotional needs, undermining women's power in heterosexual relationships while maximizing men's (Cancian, 1987; Hollway, 1984a, b). The persistent public story of men's sex drive fits with cultural stereotypes of macho man. Seeing the male body and its distinctive appendage, the penis, as a tool or weapon, fits with a macho male sexuality in which sex is a performance, like violence, confirming masculinity. This is a view of sex which reduces women to objects for conquest. Feminists have argued that in many times and places men have routinely and successfully represented women as the lesser 'other', to the point of denying women human subjectivity (de Beauvoir, 1972, Kappeler, 1986). The notion of the lesser 'other', whether it be women or peoples of other classes, ethnic groups or religions, is a legitimating representation of the world created by those who are trying to dominate or to maintain their more favourable position. It blocks mutual understanding and permits the use or abuse of the 'other' by the powerful.

Dimensions of Intimacy

Is there some fundamental level of intimacy which is a basic human need? The ways and degrees of being intimate vary enormously within and between human societies. First it is worth noting that many societies are not or have not been characterized by 'disclosing intimacy'. It is only relatively recently that talking about yourself, disclosing, 'sharing' are generally advocated as part of an individual's emotional well-being and of good relationships. The virtues of 'keeping yourself to yourself' and 'not wearing your heart on your sleeve' have been and still are extolled in some strands of Euro-North American cultures. It is possible to imagine a silent intimacy. For example, clearly affection for and feelings of closeness to another person are not necessarily accompanied by a dialogue of mutual disclosure. A loving couple who believe they 'mean the world to each other' but yet are typically people of few words, may be as deserving of being called intimate as those who incessantly check out each other's feelings. Disclosing intimacy is by no means the only type of intimacy to be found in primary or personal relationships.

Arguably, only a very minimal sort of intimacy can be found universally. If intimacy is defined as any form of *close association* in which people acquire familiarity, that is *shared detailed knowledge* about each other, then it is impossible to conceive of a society without intimacy. Sharing a hearth and home would be sufficient to ensure such intimacy. There is no society in which all forms of close association between adults are avoided. Moreover, growing up and the process of becoming a member of a society typically involves close association between a child and one or more specific adults, giving children the social place and cultural knowledge required to be a participant in the society. Growing up with a sibling, bringing up a child, spending years sharing a house with a partner provide people with a *privileged knowledge* of each other which nobody else has. In some circumstances, people in close association feel emotionally close to each other even if they say little to each other. For this to be possible they must sense they share a common view of the world and/or mutually benevolent views of each other.

Close association and privileged knowledge may be aspects of intimacy but perhaps are not sufficient conditions to ensure intimacy as it is more generally understood. It is possible to imagine people who live side by side and yet have no sense of closeness fostered through privileged knowledge of everyday details. Rather they may feel trapped together as strangers who know nothing of each other's inner worlds. The contemporary usage of the terms *knowing* and *understanding* suggests not just cognitive knowledge and understanding but a degree of sympathy or emotional understanding which involves deep insight into an inner self. The term 'empathy' partially captures this deep knowing but only partially because some degree of empathy with another person is possible without being acquainted, through imagining yourself in their situation. Imagining is easier if a common culture or attributes are shared between the imagined and the imaginer. The more basic and emotional the human situation –

death or rescue from death of self, a loved one, health or home – the less common culture is needed to make the imaginative shift to the other's point of view. In contemporary Euro-North American culture, it is assumed that intense interaction with a person is required to 'really' know and understand them. 'Really knowing' is privileged knowledge to an inner self only permitted to those who are loved and trusted. *Trust*, faith that confidences will not be betrayed and privileged knowledge will not be used against the self, is perhaps a more fundamental dimension of intimacy than knowing and understanding as these terms are now used. However, it is deep knowing and understanding which particularly characterize disclosing intimacy.

The cliché 'my wife does not understand me', makes reference to possible divergence between close association and understanding. When used jokingly, this cliché also acknowledges the possibility of cynically playing with a public story about how private life should be. The cliché takes for granted the pervasive public story that marriage is an intimate relationship in which spouses should understand each other. This sets up the publicly sanctioned view that a marriage has failed if a wife does not understand her husband hence giving him permission to move on to another relationship. However, joking use also recognizes the possibility of the cynical use of the personal story of 'not being understood' by the sexually predatory adulterous husband who is pursuing sex not intimacy. In doing so, it is also drawing on another public story about differences between men and women, sex and intimacy. In this story men seek sex and women seek intimacy. Communicating with and understanding other human beings are fundamental aspects of being human but the cultural baggage carried by current usage of 'understanding' goes far beyond this. Clearly such statements as 'my wife does not understand me' are complex social constructions that have to be heard in specific historical and cultural contexts.

Loving, caring and *sharing* are also dimensions of intimacy which have taken on different meanings over time. What people want, expect and feel they need in terms of love throughout their lives is a complex social construction which varies historically and culturally. Men and women brought up in the first decades of this century describe happy childhoods in which their parents never cuddled them or told them they were loved. This, of course, does not mean the emotional bond was absent but rather that visible displays of affection were not an expected part of their culture. Ideas and practices of being a 'good' parent and of 'natural' affection have changed in the course of this century. A contemporary child faced with such undemonstrative parents might come to feel they lacked the love and care they needed, possibly with profound consequences for their sense of self and approach to subsequent relationships.

Just as expectations of demonstrative parental love have changed, similarly people's expectations of 'falling in love' or having loving relationships as adults have changed historically. One version of true love is a willingness to do anything for the loved one and to put their needs and interests above one's own. This is the version of love which Luhmann refers to in his assertion that 'marriages are made in heaven and fall apart in the automobile' (1986, 35), when he describes how the passenger's perception of risk-taking by the driver unnerves the former's visions of the latter's love. Such a version of love typically involves idealizing the loved one rather than embarking on a mutual project of endlessly getting to know every facet of each other's being. In popular usage, loving is often linked with caring. To care can mean to watch over, look after or assist in practical ways as well as to feel attachment and fondness. Love and care in the more practical sense need not go hand in hand. A love which idealizes the other may leave too much unknown and unsaid for effective practical caring to be possible. Mutual disclosing intimacy cannot be sustained if forms of care are felt to be needed by one or both participants but not received. However, disclosing intimacy may occur in relationships in which some forms of care are separated off from the relationship. For example, practical assistance and social support may be sought elsewhere. People may feel they are expressing love through acts of care but analytically, feelings of love and actions of care are quite distinct. Paid carers may care in practical ways but they may not love and some associates feel a deep affection for each other that they call love but yet do little caring.

Stories and Story Tellers

Throughout this book, there is an awareness of a separation between public stories about personal life and the life that is lived. Stories always present a particular view rather than everything that could be said. When story tellers seek an audience beyond a personal circle, they invariably have an interest in telling a particular version of events. Academic stories claim to be more considered, more grounded in evidence and more open about their limitations than everyday stories. But all stories may have unanticipated consequences as they are reinterpreted in the hearing and retelling. The deconstruction of public stories, whether of other academics, of politicians, moral entrepreneurs or the media, is an important type of academic work. This book draws on the efforts of a number of academics who have scrutinized public discussions of personal life. For example, the next chapter refers to analysis of how Victorian medical, educational and scientific experts, predominantly male, white and middle-class, largely supported a sexist, racist and classist Victorian view of family and sexual relationships.

For a number of reasons it is important to know and consider the pervasive public stories that are being told in our own time. Ours is a time of unprecedented exposure to public stories through the mass media. Some commentators claim we are not only more exposed but more susceptible to their influence than in previous eras. Everyday face to face relationships now rarely sustain clearly defined and detailed views of how personal life should be conducted, hence allowing public messages to be heard by more open minds. Public stories about personal life are both cause and consequence of a lack of separation between public and private life. Cumulatively, pervasive stories are inevitably consequential for both private and public life. They become representations that people cannot avoid working with at both a deep and surface level. Pervasive stories are a stock of narratives that anyone can draw on or distance themselves from when telling their own story. They are a repertoire of themes, stereotypes and judgements concerning mothering, fathering, parenting, befriending, sex, dating, marrying, loving and the like for recycling or adaptation when making sense of, justifying or glamorizing personal life. At the deeper level, public stories may be taken 'to heart' and profoundly shape personal identity. Stories also feed into both public and private lives when they coalesce into official views shaping public policies, laws and the distribution of resources. For example, who is legally recognized as 'next of kin' and who is denied such recognition is a consequence of public views on personal life.

The most pervasive public stories are typically produced and reproduced by people occupying positions of power and authority, that is, they operate from and on behalf of powerful institutionalized structures. Their stories are never 'just stories'. Stories are not free-floating but produced and reproduced by people who are located in networks of social relationships. Stories often become part and parcel of sets of practices and ways of doing things, which are in themselves consequential for private lives. To take a dramatic example, the story told by certain religious leaders and other moral crusaders about abortion as maternal child murder is associated with political actions including lobbying for legislative prohibitions, distributing pictures of aborted foetuses, picketing abortion clinics and violently attacking clinic staff. These acts are sometimes highly consequential for those on their immediate receiving end and they become widely known as expressions of views which have to be navigated by women considering abortion.

For practical, methodological reasons there is also no choice but to listen to stories, public and private. The lives that everyday people live (rather than the academic, political and moral public stories that are told about personal life) are often only known through stories that people tell about themselves. Personal stories told by ordinary people to researchers are, of course, also not the whole or only possible story. This is not suggesting an inevitable contradiction between the story and the reality, but refers to a more complex relationship between stories and lives. Degrees of complexity have already been identified: the fact that people may recycle public stories when speaking of themselves; the fact that stories are not 'just stories' but associated practices; the difficulty, and some would argue impossibility, of separating out 'the real me' and the story of the self, as the latter is implicated in the former. Nevertheless, it is the case that sometimes lives look very different through evidence other than the story. A common theme in contemporary research on heterosexual couples for example, is the gap often found between the equality and fairness some couples speak of and the extent to which they act out mutual responsibility for maintaining a happy domestic and personal life. However, although actions may speak louder than words, it is not often possible for researchers to observe how people usually act towards each other in personal relationships. Detailed questioning about ways of doing things can balance a picture derived from more packaged stories that people tell about themselves. Good research is typically aware of the relationship between personal and public stories and the possible gaps between story and action, and looks for ways of going behind glib presentations of the self.

The term 'story' has not typically been used in academic writing, although there are exceptions (Plummer, 1995). I use it because 'story' does not signal a particular theoretical approach and can be read without prior theoretical baggage. The more abstract and complex construct 'ideology' was the preferred term until it was ousted by the now more frequently used term 'discourse'. Ideology has been used neutrally to describe sets of beliefs associated with particular people or activities and negatively to describe ideas which cover the nasty reality lurking beneath (Thompson, 1984). In the classic Marxist account, the ideas of the ruling class provided an ideological smoke-screen which protected the *status quo* by concealing how capitalism served their interests. 'Discourse' is frequently used in current sociological work to encompass both what is said and written in public stories about a particular topic and associated sets of practices around the topic. The prevalence of the term partly stems from the popularity of the work of the French theorist Michel Foucault (1926–1984). Foucault argued that discourse makes and shapes reality rather than conceals it and that the powerful are not the only makers of reality. Even when and if the powerful are the dominant voices there are always reactions, resistances and unintended consequences. In a Foucauldian analysis of discourse, an association between doing and thinking is taken for granted: talking and thinking about things in particular ways constitute sets of practices and rules for doing things, including practices and rules of resistance. However many contemporary users of the terms 'discourse' and 'ideology' employ them in ways that are effectively interchangeable.

Conclusion

This book scrutinizes several stories of intimacy but in particular the notion that a specific and new form of intimacy is increasingly dominating personal and private life. However, the complex relationship between public stories and everyday personal lives complicates the task. It can be said at the beginning that many more types of intimacy are theoretically possible than the disclosing intimacy favoured in the story. A number of different dimensions of intimacy have been suggested and it is clear that not all need to be present for some form of intimacy to be maintained in a relationship. Of the dimensions discussed, disclosing intimacy must include close association, privileged knowledge, deep knowing and understanding and some form of love, but it need not include practical caring and sharing. If intimate relationships are being transformed as the story of disclosing intimacy suggests then, according to theorists from a number of different theoretical traditions, this would necessarily be connected with significant changes in both social divisions and social cohesion, particularly in inequalities and differences between men and women.

CHAPTER 2

From 'The Family' to Sex and Intimacy

This chapter maps public stories about the history and the future of personal life which some academics have produced and other academics have deconstructed. Until very recently the orthodox historical story was one of the long-term emergence of companionate marriage and a particular type of child-centred, emotionally intense, privacy seeking, nuclear family household with an acute division of labour between a husband/father and a mother/wife. This is the type of family household, for example, in which mothers 'stayed at home' and devoted their lives to the happiness of their children and husband. The orthodox story was that marriage and the gendered family household centred on children emerged as *the* main sites of intimacy within capitalist industrial societies. It is now recognized that some features of this type of family household have a long history (like gender divisions and inequalities between husband and wife) but others (like child-centredness) do not. The deconstruction of the story has demonstrated that this idealized happy nuclear family now seen as more common in the 1950s–1970s, had a relatively short history. The trends which are denounced by some moral commentators as evidence of the impending collapse of the family – married women increasingly entering the labour force and rising divorce – had already begun at this time. Even in the 1950s, there were, of course, many other types of family household. Not everybody followed the conventional life course of moving from a family-household where they were a son or daughter to a household formed by marriage in which they brought up children. Moreover, in all historical periods deeply unhappy and abusive relationships have been documented within the idealized nuclear family household structure and in the 1970s the Women's Movement subjected this idealized family to considerable critique.

The story of the emergence of companionate marriage and the gendered, emotionally intense, private, child-centred family (the conventional family, for short) often draws a contrast between pre-industrial, 'pre-modern' family households and the 'modern'. It has become standard to describe the societies which were first to become capitalist industrialized nation states in terms of a 'modern' or industrial period and a 'pre-modern' or pre-industrial period. If used loosely and interchangeably with pre-industrial then the pre-modern era extends right up to the 18th century, despite the fact that for many historians the pre-modern period ends and 'modern' history begins in the mid fifteenth century. In sociological accounts the disjuncture between 'modern' and 'pre-modern' typically involves much more than the presence or absence of capitalist industrial forms of organizing economic life. Those who have been regarded as 'the founding fathers' (Emile Durkheim, 1858–1917; Karl Marx, 1818–83; Max Weber 1864–1920) of sociology grappled to theorize this disjuncture and variously discussed new forms of social cohesion, new social divisions, a new ethic of individualism and loss of tradition. Contemporary retelling of such accounts often stress that the faith in tradition and 'knowing your place' of the 'pre-modern' era is replaced by faith in scientific rationality, 'progress', respect for individual achievement and recognition that each individual is equal under the law.

Recently this story has been superseded by that of a new form of society that has emerged towards the century's end. Anthony Giddens has recently argued that tradition managed to persist into the early 'modern' period and that until recently people rebuilt traditions as modernity dissolved them. He now speaks of a 'post-traditional society' (Giddens, 1994). His is one of many efforts to label Euro-North American societies at the century's end as distinctive from 'modern' societies. 'Postmodern' is the most popular term but other labels include 'reflexive modernity' (Beck, 1994), 'high modernity' (Giddens, 1990, 1992) and now 'post-traditional society' (Giddens, 1994). Other academics argue that the period of modernity is not over but is simply in a particular and distinctive phase (Bauman, 1987, 1990). This distinctive recent period, contentiously named as 'postmodern', is part three to the previously two-part story. A story of transformations in personal life is contained within tales of 'pre-modern', to 'modern' to 'postmodern' society. These presentations of the past are a part of how 'intimacy' is constructed in the present. Some commentators suggest that the 'old days' were the bad days because personal life lacked intimacy in contrast to the present. Others argue that the late twentieth century is as lacking in intimacy as the pre-industrial period and lament the passing of the 'good old days' in the more recent past of 'modern' society. These accounts of each period are briefly summarized below and the remainder of the chapter subjects these stories to further scrutiny.

Pre-modern/pre-industrial period

In the story of the pre-modern period, by modern standards, intimacy was attenuated. People maintained relationships with kin, family, neighbours and friends because they were bound together by necessities and tradition. Privacy was in short supply and little valued. While members of a household were in close association and had privileged knowledge of each other, household composition and lack of privacy meant that this was not restricted to members of the nuclear family. Moreover, the intimacy of close association did not necessarily result in empathy, because this was a highly stratified social world in which each knew his or her place in the social order. While most people lived in family households, many never married or had children, but all had some part in the round of traditional festivals of community life. Love and care between parents and children, and between spouses was tempered by the social distance between generations and genders. Children were treated as little adults at an early age and were often sent off to live as apprentices or servants in the households of others. Marrying and having children were economic arrangements and the relationships which resulted were ones in which men were assumed to rule and own women and children. This was sanctioned by religion, law and community norms. The church preached the restriction of sex to the marriage bed (for procreation not as an expression of love). Intimacy between friends was also tempered by the struggle for survival. Death constantly stalked life.

Modern/industrial period

When the term is used interchangeably with 'industrial', the 'modern' period had its roots in the eighteenth century but was not established until the nineteenth century. In the story of the emergence of this modern period, intimacy in personal life was heightened greatly, with the family-household at its core. The family household became a private domain in which intimacy – close association and privileged knowledge, empathy and understanding, love and care – blossomed. Fear of loss through death no longer overshadowed relationships between the living to the same degree (although even by the late twentieth century the rich still live longer than the poor) and individuals were not tightly bound by religion, necessity and a common community life. Relationships of marriage and parenthood became more emotionally intense. The rule of men over women in marriage no longer had the unequivocal support of religion, law and community norms. However, love and care between spouses was a more important dimension of intimacy than knowing and understanding an inner self. Divisions of labour between men and women became more extreme with the separation of private homes (the site of women's unpaid domestic work) from public places of employment (the modern means of ensuring survival through waged labour) and continued men's objective advantages over women, who were their financial dependants. As the twentieth century proceeded, marriage became highly romanticized and by the mid-twentieth century the emphasis placed by experts on love, sex and the relationship implied equality, mutuality and deep understanding between spouses. In the same period, children were increasingly protected from the adult world and remained dependent on their parents for much longer. By the second half of the twentieth century, devoting a great deal of time, attention and affection to children was a taken for granted aspect of being a parent, and particularly of being a mother. At the beginning of the century the 'good mother' loved and cared for her children but by the second half of the century she also empathized with and understood them. Youth as a stage of semi-independence between childhood and adulthood, between being a dependant in a parental household and forming a new household on marriage, grew in significance. Young men and women increasingly chose to marry for love and to protect their relationship with privacy and distance from others. Home became a private sanctuary; an appropriate setting for intense intimacy between its inhabitants. For the majority, home meant a family-household of a couple of parents and their children. A common community life had all but disappeared and only a very small minority did not form their own family households.

'Postmodern' period

There is not yet one story of the so-called postmodern period. Stories can be summarized as one of two versions, optimistic or pessimistic.

In the optimistic story, intimacy is intense and intimate relationships remain the crux of private life but 'the family' based on marriage is losing or has lost its centrality as the norm and ideal. One or more good relationships (ideally encompassing a good sex life) are at the centre of personal life, not 'the family'. The good relationship is a relationship of disclosing intimacy, a mutual relationship of close association between equals in which really knowing and understanding each other are the crux of the relationship rather than more practical forms of 'love and care'. Conventional gendered divisions of labour are breaking down. The late twentieth century growth in the labour market in the number of married women with children was the beginning of the end of the division between male 'breadwinner' and female 'housewife'. Sex is no longer harnessed to marriage-like arrangements and couples negotiate their own rules of sexual conduct on a we-will-do-what-we-enjoy basis. Relationships are more fragile but they are also potentially more mutually satisfactory. Although people continue to choose long-term intimate relationships, including marriage-like relationships and parenting relationships, a diversity in styles of personal life inevitably blossoms.

The proponents of the pessimistic version of postmodernity lament the loss of the vestiges of the economic, religious and normative underpinnings of marriage which survived in the modern period. Their fears regarding the collapse of family life echo those of commentators on the emergence of the 'modern' family who have spoken of its collapse for over a century. The pessimistic story of 'postmodernism' deplores the further flourishing of individualism which in the modern period encouraged a free choice of partner in love and is now thought to undermine commitment to a partner. In this vision of postmodernity, intimacy is again becoming attenuated not because people are re-absorbed into a pre-modern type of communal life but because mass consumer culture promotes a self-obsessive, self-isolating individualism which is incapable of sustaining anything other than kaleidoscopic relationships. Love, care, empathy and understanding are not sustained when long-term projects of marriage-like relationships and parenting are in constant jeopardy. A particular variant common among moral commentators on the political Right blames the welfare state for encouraging these trends.

Whether contemporary societies are postmodern or not, an image of a conventional family arrangement as the happiest way of life is still produced by popular culture in Australia and New Zealand, Europe, and North America. In 1982 British sociologists Michèle Barrett and Mary McIntosh talked of the persistence of familial ideology, the pervasive focus on 'the family' as the emotional centre of life, and of familism, the organization of society on the assumption that the once 'modern' and now traditional type of family household – a husband earner/provider and a housekeeping, child-caring wife – is the basic unit of society. Barrett and McIntosh noted that familism and familial ideology persisted despite the reality of a whole array of family types, rising divorce, rising cohabitation, the marked increase in the labour force of married women with children, and the onslaught of feminist and radical critiques of the family. In the 1990s, nostalgia for a mythical past in which people lived in conventional stable happy families is acute, particularly in the United States (Coontz, 1992; Skolnick, 1991). One explanation for the rise of nostalgia is that personal life in general, and intimate relationships in particular, are in crisis or at least unsettled. This makes the gender-stereotyped, mother, father and happy family images of a past in which everybody knew the rules highly attractive (Skolnick, 1991).

The Making of the Conventional Modern Family

In this section the story of 'the modern family' is scrutinized. Under the heading 'Victorian sexual morality and the Victorian family', the appropriateness of contrasting the moral uprightness of the Victorians and the allegedly degenerate permissiveness of the present is questioned. This is followed by examining strands of a more complex academic story of change in the relationship between sex, marriage and the family.

Victorian sexual morality and the Victorian family

In the late twentieth century a number of political figures, including the former British Prime Minister, Margaret Thatcher, have called for a return to Victorian values. The assumption that Victorian val-

ues add up to a greater good involves a reckless disregard for the
detailed histories of the period which have documented wide gaps
between public values and private practice. For example, historians
have long exposed the fact that many respected Victorian men made
extensive use of prostitution and pornography while exhorting total
sexual abstinence outside of monogamous marriage (Pearsall, 1969).
A theoretical reworking of the notion of the Victorian era as a time of
sexual repression comes from the intellectual traditions of symbolic
interactionism (Gagnon and Simon, 1973) and the philosophy of
Michel Foucault (1978). This was the period in which new sex experts, new forms of sexual perversion and a new sense of sexuality
as the essence of identity emerged. While for Victorian moral entrepreneurs only the 'Malthusian couple' (the married couple controlling their family size by abstinence) were conducting their sexual
lives properly, the same 'experts' were obsessed with sex in a way
which was historically unprecedented. The normality of heterosexual
genital sex within marriage was affirmed by the naming, describing,
denouncing, warning against and attempting to reform so-called
perverse sexualities. Foucault argued that rather than clamping down
on existing sexual categories, the new concerns with sex were creating new sexualities for the first time. A similar argument was made
by Gagnon and Simon concerning the Freudian notion of childhood
sexuality. They argue that children were newly sexualized and
pathologized by the 'discovery' of childhood sexuality. The middle-
class Victorian fear of masturbation is often taken as an example of
these consequential effects of so-called sexual repression. As efforts
at combating the dangers of childhood masturbation intensified, a
new, albeit fearful and guilt-ridden, sense of its forbidden pleasures
was created. Hence it is argued that the so called sexual perversions
of this era were an inextricable complement of the 'normal' Victorian family (Walkowitz, 1980; Weeks, 1981).

In Victorian society the possibilities for sexual expression and intimacy were structured by the harsh inequalities of class, gender, and
race. The apogee of the double standard in sexual conduct, the middle-class white Victorian Englishmen's view of the world, has been
deconstructed by the historian Leonore Davidoff (Davidoff, 1983;
1986; Davidoff and Hall, 1987). These were men who consolidated
and justified their position in the world through powerful stories
about themselves and others. As Davidoff puts it they 'had the resources as well as the need to propagate their central position'. Getting others to do their dirty work for them was normalized by seeing

these others as intrinsically dirty and polluting. In their sexist and racist world view, domestic servants, working-class people in general, foreigners, non-whites, 'natives' of the colonies were suited to their place by being closer to dirt and nature, that is less civilized, less pure, more sexual and potentially polluting. While a good middle-class man struggled manfully against his sexual instincts, he viewed good middle-class women as aiding his moral salvation. The asexuality and purity of a 'good woman' could help his reason triumph over his baser nature. On the other hand there were fallen, sexualized 'bad women' who were potentially corrupting and with whom men succumbed to their baser instincts. The good woman was pure in thoughts and deed, virginal, sexually innocent on marriage, accepting sex as a conjugal duty thereafter. Her mental purity was accompanied by physical weakness: she needed protection from too much physical or mental exertion in order to preserve her energies for reproduction. This idealized femininity justified women's dependence and subordination. It offered little possibility of women exploring the potentials for pleasure of their own bodies or of negotiating sexual pleasure with their partner. These idealized versions of masculinity and femininity severely constrained the possibilities of intimacy between men and women. Clearly, intimacy between husband and wife was not precluded. Indeed, devotion, consideration and shared understandings were expected. They were regulated, however, by particular patterns of mastery and dependence. Shared understanding was based on each 'knowing their place' rather than through mutually negotiated knowledge of each other.

Similar ideologies justified class, race and gender privilege in all Euro-North American societies in the nineteenth century. Such views made it possible for the less circumspect middle-class man to romanticize or dehumanize working-class and non-white sexuality precisely because it was seen as closer to nature – as rich, racy and exotically lacking in inhibitions – or as animal rather than human. Indeed middle-class men could readily create opportunities to observe voyeuristically and to use the victims of their fantasies sexually. This sexual voyeurism is often betrayed in nineteenth-century philanthropic perceptions of the moral dangers lurking in the mines (Humphries, 1981) and factories in which working-class women laboured (Gilding, 1991, 100). The term 'scrubber', still used in Britain and one of many insults to describe women of alleged promiscuity, carries the classist assumptions which rendered previous generations of resident domestic servants a close-to-home target for attempts at sexual adventure. The racist assumptions of white society in the south of the incipient United States, legally and socially sanctioned white men's sexual use of black slaves, and versions of their white racist fears and fantasies about black sexuality live on into the present (Collins, 1991; D'Emilio and Freedman, 1988; Staples, 1982).

Marriage, love and sex

The public story that marriage is the natural outcome of a loving and sexually charged relationship between a man and a woman has a relatively short history in comparison to religious and legal injunctions restricting sexual behaviour, particularly that of women, to the conjugal duties of marriage. While love and sex may have been regarded as a legitimate part of marriage for the past two centuries, the public story for much of the period has been that marriage comes first and then love and sex follow. Historians who have documented the dominant Christian religious ideas which significantly influenced the lives of Europeans in previous centuries, suggest a series of logical shifts from marriage as an economic arrangement in which sex was a marital duty, to an emphasis on companionship and compassion in marriage which paved the way for marriage based on love, and then for the view of sex as an expression of love.[1] For the middle-class Victorians, marriage was both a taken for granted vocation and a privileged calling, which men of sufficient means and women virtuous and fortunate enough to be asked entered into naturally. Happiness was assumed to follow from a good marriage. While marriage for love surfaced increasingly in novels, 'suitability' was the guiding principle in the choice of a partner. Those intending to marry spent limited and chaperoned time together prior to marriage. If they did feel themselves to be 'in love', then love was often necessarily based more on an imagined than a known other. Courtship was a formal and public statement about intention to marry, not a process of testing out a relationship by getting to know each other's inner self.

The history of the shift from marriage as a patriarchal institution to marriage which is a relationship – between equals, resulting from a freely made choice, based on love, and not love-at-a-distance but love developed in a relationship – is one that floats uneasily in time. While some historians speak of these shifts as having roots in the eighteenth century, the notion of marriage as a partnership of equals was not a dominant public story until after the Second World War. (Finch and Summerfield, 1991; Morgan, 1991). Speaking of Britain, Janet Finch and Penny Summerfield (1991) note that the term 'companionate marriage' could be found in the 1920s but was not widely used until after 1945. However, despite the currency of the concept in the post-war decade, public discussions of birth, motherhood, sexuality, women's employment and girls' education all stressed gender-segregated traditional roles. Moreover, their review of studies of family life of the 1950s led these authors to suggest a profound dissonance between the post-war ideology of companionate marriage and the lived experience (Finch and Summerfield, 1991, p. 31).

Sociologists of the 1950s, such as Talcott Parsons (Parsons and Bales, 1956, 1959), talked optimistically about complementarity between men and women while acknowledging that men and women did not fall in love on equal terms. In keeping with their different positions of power, men chose marriage partners, women worked at being chosen by the man of their choice. The language of equality rather than complementarity is not part of the academic account until the 1960s. After this the expectation that men and women will come together as equal partners in intimacy is more commonly expressed. It was in the 1960s that sociological accounts of ideal-typical marriage began to describe something like 'disclosing intimacy' between men and women (Berger and Kellner, 1964): the ideal marriage partner was then seen as a best friend, and confidante, as well as a responsive sexual partner. Intimacy now meant working at empathy and understanding and mutually working out how to please each other rather than following traditional patterns of delivering love and care.

Academic accounts describe how the pervasive public story of love as the basis of marriage gave birth to a new popular story in which love is a basis for sex. This is presented as a series of logical shifts which were embraced and acted out by populations of Euro-North American youth this century. As love became the basis for marriage, and marriage was the context in which pleasurable sex was anticipated by both men and women, then increasingly a degree of sexual contact before marriage was tolerated for both men and women. Hence, some sexual behaviour, at least kissing and often a great deal more, became a normal part of 'dating'. The late 1960s and early 1970s are often seen as the key 'permissive moment' but social historians argue that a trend of sexually charged behaviour prior to marriage was already well established (Weeks, 1981). The 1920s can be characterized as a decade of sexual revolution in the US (D'Emilio and Freedman, 1988). Recreational dating, involving kissing and 'petting', developed around such sites as dance halls and cinemas for working-class youth, and through college entertainment for middle-class youth. So love and sex within marriage became love and sex before marriage, but, for women at least, only with the partner you planned to marry. Academic accounts agree that women's behaviour changed more in the course of the twentieth century than men's. A double standard in sexual conduct had always allowed men 'rules for breaking the rules' and even when religious and moral commentators declared sex outside of marriage as morally inappropriate for men as well as women, a strand of popular culture celebrated sexual adventures for men. The causes of the growing gap between age of first heterosexual 'experience' and age of first marriage in the twentieth century are still debated (D'Emilio and Freedman, 1988; Lewis, 1994; Weeks, 1981) but the permissible order of events certainly shifted in the portrayals of popular culture, much expert advice and in practice. The summing up by the historians J. D'Emilio and E. Freedman of the state of play in the USA, spelled out what would have been seen as a chaos of fornication and adultery by conservative moralists of the time: 'By the late 1960s the belief in sex as the source of personal meaning had permeated American society. The expectation that marriage would fulfil the quest could no longer be sustained' (D'Emilio and Freedman, 1988).

The 1960s have often been described as the decade when sexual behaviour definitely ceased to be harnessed to marriage. However, broad sweep accounts tend to exaggerate the pace and pervasiveness of change. Studies of married couples in the 1960s still found men and women who married believing that sex was a duty suffered by women and enjoyed by men. For example, for some of the British coal-miners' wives, interviewed by Norman Dennis and his colleagues, a good husband 'Didn't bother me much' (Dennis et al., 1969). Their testimony suggested neither 'disclosing intimacy' nor sexual pleasure featured greatly in their relationship either before or after marriage. Medical texts and advice books for the newly marrieds of the time continued to suggest that men had a stronger sexual drive than women and these texts had not yet wholly embraced the notion that a good relationship involves mutual sexual pleasure. Moreover, the physiological facts were still being misrepresented to portray women as if they could only gain sexual pleasure in penetrative genital heterosexual intercourse (Koedt, 1991; Scully 1973/4;

Jackson, 1994). In fact, changes in young people's sexual behaviour in the 1960s were arguably less dramatic than the sexualization of commodities and proliferation of sexual imagery generally. The sexualized aspects of youth culture made highly visible through television were suggestive of more dramatic change than the picture revealed by research into young people's behaviour. Youth culture as a highly visible mass media phenomenon which transcended national boundaries was in itself new and, for conservative moralists, disturbing. Post-war baby booms, relative affluence, the extension of the availability of secondary and tertiary education to larger proportions of young people, near full employment among school leavers, mass production of consumer products, and the increased availability of television, all set the scene for the massive expansion of spontaneous and commercialized youth and student culture in the 1960s (Brake, 1985; D'Emilio and Freedman, 1988; May, 1992)

The moral panic of the 1960s and 1970s largely focused on the higher levels of sexual activity among young people. But, gradually a new public story was circulated by many medical and therapeutic experts and by popular culture. Sex in the context of loving relationships was natural and healthy. It was casual and careless sex which was a problem because it risked psychological harm, pregnancy and disease. As before, the underlying rules were more rigorously applied to women than men and the old story of men needing sex more than women also continued to be told. Less radical religious figures and the moral Right continued to voice grave doubts about the separation of sex and marriage.

Child-centred family households?

By the 1970s, there was considerable consensus among North American and European social scientists writing about the development of the 'modern family', now thought of as the 'traditional' or 'conventional' family. A number of high profile, respected authors shared the view that the nuclear family household of a heterosexual married couple and their children had inexorably come to monopolize and reshape intimacy and emotional life by the twentieth century (Jamieson, 1987). Authors of the 1970s often saw the causal factors as located in the nineteenth or the eighteenth centuries but a number of subsequent critics argue that the key changes were much more recent (Gittins, 1982; Harris, 1983, Jamieson, 1987), and now the 1950s is treated as an exceptional period rather than as a culmination of a long slow change.[2]

In the 1970s, depictions of personal life at the beginning of the twentieth century often overstated the extent of child-centredness (Jamieson, 1987). Oral history in a number of industrialized countries has since indicated considerable variation in the extent to which adults had child-centred, home-based, privatized family lives at the beginning of the twentieth century. In Britain, Australia and New Zealand until the mid-century, parent–child relationships were not as a rule highly emotionally intense with family life orienting around children's needs (Jamieson and Toynbee, 1990; Reiger, 1985; Toynbee, 1995). Here, and arguably also in North America, it was only in the 1950s that motherhood was generally perceived in terms of an emotionally intense relationship, with mothers carrying responsibility for the psychological well-being of their children rather than simply caring through good housewifery. It could be argued that the material circumstances of family life limited the possibilities of intimacy between many parents and children until the relative affluence experienced by industrial societies after the Second World War. At the beginning of the century, larger family sizes, poorer health, the more common loss of family members through death, the more labour-intensive nature of housework and longer hours in paid employment were significant constraints on family time, particularly in poorer households where the daily efforts to make ends meet consumed all energies. However, middle-class households were not necessarily characterized by more intimate parent–child relationships until after the demise of the employment of domestic servants. In the early decades of this century upper middle-class children were often brought up by nannies and governesses and hence spent very little time with their parents. While there was considerable variation, many parents and adults were unashamedly superior to children who were required to be obedient and subservient. Only the exceptional few talked to children as if they were potential equals. In the USA the ethos of parents and children being pals may have been established somewhat earlier (Mintz and Kellog, 1988, p. 113). Certainly in Britain in the first decades of the twentieth century most parents did not yet want to be a friend to their children; nor did they consider family life to consist of doing things with the children (Jamieson and Toynbee, 1990; Thompson, 1977; Vigne, 1975). By contemporary standards parents from a range of social backgrounds remained distant from their children.

> My mother, you know, never had charge of us. She liked to see us but then when we got rather obstreperous we were banished again. . . . Then at the age of eleven I went to boarding school. We all went to boarding school. My mother said it was the happiest day of her life when we went to boarding school. (Caroline, born 1910, mill owner/manager's daughter)

> I don't know if you know the golden rule 'Children should be seen and not heard'. You were not to talk back to elders. You never joined in the conversation at the tea-table. You were never allowed at the tea-table if there were visitors in. Children were kept apart. (Angus, born 1902, tailor's son)

Contrast these statements of elderly people remembering their childhood in the first decades of the twentieth century (Jamieson, 1983) with what British mothers say about the relationship between themselves and their seven-year-old children in the 1970s.

> Well, it's a strange sort of rudeness disrespectful rudeness. . . . I would never dreamt of talking to my mother like that; not even thinking that way! I've just come to the conclusion that children today are like this, you know – all the children down the street are like this. (Quoted in Newson and Newson, 1976, p. 364)

> If I felt she was treating me really disrespectfully, I wouldn't tolerate it. But I like her to think of me as another human being. (Quoted in Newson and Newson, 1976, p. 364)

The British mothers quoted by John and Elizabeth Newson are reflecting on the loss of traditional authority and the reduction in social distance between parents and children. The first mother notes that since her own childhood, the hierarchy between parents and children has contracted, if not collapsed where once a mother could expect deference she must now accept rudeness. The second mother is expressing a tension between her desire for respect from her child and the desire to be 'like another human being'. In so far as respect means deference then it requires hierarchy and social distance whereas the desire to be human implies a closer relationship. Many studies find post-war parents wanting to be closer to their children than their parents were to them. The quoted men and women born 80 to 100 years ago can claim a happy childhood without needing to present themselves as having been 'pals' with their parents. They generally took their parents' love for granted unless exceptional brutality had proved otherwise. People of this generation remember automatic deference to the traditional authority of parents. Hence, they use 'obedience' and 'respect' as key terms for making sense of their childhood. For parents in the second half of the century, 'obedience' and 'respect' are not typically taken for granted as automatic entitlements in this way and parents have to work at being loved and loving.

Gendered divisions of labour

Non-feminist authors of the 1970s typically assumed a natural division of labour between men and women, underpinning any particular gendered division of labour. For example it was assumed that women 'staying at home' was a logical corollary of the separation of home and paid employment since women are child bearers and the natural carers. Talcott Parsons, for example, needed no elaborate explanation for the following: 'The isolation of the nuclear family . . . focuses the responsibility of the mother role more sharply on the one adult woman' (Parsons and Bales, 1956, p. 23). Many authors never make their underlying assumptions of a natural division of labour explicit because these were so taken for granted. Feminist authors argued that men collectively engaged in a patriarchal project of subordinating women; gendered divisions of labour reflected this project; and the history of the 'modern' family cannot be understood without recognizing this process. So, for example, Roberta Hamilton (1978) explained why the historical separation of home and work, production and consumption resulted in women at home and men at work by reference to patriarchal religious ideas about women's place which predated these separations. Feminist historians have documented the active exclusion of women from many industries and the development of bars against the employment of married women (Tilly and Scott, 1978). Marriage bars allowed men to protect their positions at the expense of women both directly, by excluding women, and indirectly by upholding a particular model of the family-household in which women were the dependants of men who earned a 'family wage'.

The story of the fight for a 'family wage', allowing a male worker to support a full-time housewife and children, has been told in terms of men consolidating their power as workers and as husbands over women (Barrett and McIntosh, 1980). However, there are also feminist dissenters from this view who suggest the historical picture can be read as working-class men and women struggling together to protect their class from the super-exploitation of capitalism. Jane Humphries (1977, 1981; Mark-Lawson and Witz, 1990) argued that working-class men and women both fought for a family wage, sometimes drawing on sexist assumptions about natural divisions of labour, in order to preserve a family life beyond the reach of the exploitative capitalist labour relations. The specific conditions which made the division of labour between a husband/earner and a full-time housewife a strategy for working-class survival have now changed. These conditions involved much toil for both husband and wife. Long hours in paid work did not earn a comfortable living without the full-time efforts of a wife who mobilized all her domestic skills to decently feed and clothe her large family in a clean home, in spite of the low level of amenities and the labour-intensive nature of all domestic work.

Rising standards of living including better wages, better housing and domestic utilities, shorter working hours in employment, greater acceptance of 'family planning' and improved accessibility to contraception transformed these material conditions by the 1950s. But the 1950s are remembered as the heyday of conventional families. In this post-war period gendered divisions of labour were reasserted and given a new dimension with respect to intimacy. Home took on a new emotional resonance after the displacements and disruptions of war. In Australia, Britain, New Zealand and North America, the state propaganda machinery which had enlisted the services of women war workers now incited them to return to the home. Industries that had been diverted to war work switched to mass producing for a civilian market. The good housewife was recast from the person who 'makes down' and mends old things on behalf of her family to the purchaser of new things to make her family happier (Gittins, 1982). Domestic technology was bought and used without reducing the burden of housework to a minimum. Ruth Schwartz Cowan (1989) has documented how products such as vacuum cleaners and washing machines meant higher standards rather than radically less work: floors were cleaned and clothes were washed more often. If standards of housework were changing, then the task of mothering changed more radically still to the intensive mothering of the late twentieth century.

In the public story of the 1950s, happy families were created by a devoted, home-based wife and mother. The academic version of this view was provided by Talcott Parsons. In the Parsonian ideal-typical family, married women stayed out of the labour force in order to take the lead in the expressive work of child rearing and stabilization of adult personalities. This meant more than delivering cuddles, cooking and clean clothes; it also encompassed subtle techniques of emotional manipulation, psychological management directed towards ensuring a harmonious household. Family intimacy, Parsons theorized, involved at least the mother in empathy and understanding as well as love and care. In contrast, Parsons depicted husbands as taking the lead in the instrumental work of bread winning. He argued that this division of labour avoided contaminating the intimacy of the family home by over-exposure to the competitive rational world of work. Several decades later, sociologists (Morgan, 1991) noted that post-war governments drew on the notion of the happy conventional family as a unifying placatory ideology which papered over differences of gender, class and race. Elaine Tyler May suggests that emphasis on the family and domestic harmony fitted with the political aims of the post-war US state. 'With security as the common thread, the cold war ideology and the domestic revival reinforced each other. The powerful political consensus that supported cold war policies abroad and anti-communism at home fuelled conformity to the suburban family ideal. In turn, the domestic ideology encouraged private solutions to social problems and further weakened the potential for challenges to the cold war consensus' (1988, 208).

However, divisions of labour between men and women were not frozen in time. Contemporary married women are often earners as well as mothers, a trend which has accelerated sharply in recent decades. Although the 1950s were the crescendo of the public story of happy families based on a complete division of labour between men and women, the trends that make this story seem dated and less plausible as a summary of most adult lives had already begun: married women's entry into the labour force and the increase in divorce. There is no dominant romanticized image of a dual-earner household to replace the once dominant image of the happy family with the full-time mother at home. There are regular public debates about who has gained and who has lost in the process of change. In 1993 Naomi Wolf claimed that men and women were on the verge of a new and ultimately mutually beneficial equality in Britain and the US: the ground had been prepared by unrecognized gender quakes in divisions of labour and distributions of power; all that was still holding women back was the patterning of their emotional attachments (which she blamed on early childhood socialization). Perceptions of the shift in the gender order are generally more modest. The 'stalled revolution' is the phrase that Arlie Hochschild (1990) has used to describe the fact that married women and women with children have entered the labour force without men's sharing the physical and emotional responsibilities of housework and child care. Hochschild argues that men's failure to share emotional and domestic labour is key cause of much of women's anger and frustration with their marriage; men's refusal to share the double burden militates against the 'sharing' and 'mutuality' of intimacy. Her work can be read as suggesting that men's lack of participation becomes a failure of intimacy for women, who sense a neglect of love and care and a blindness to or disregard for empathy and understanding.

Some authors depict men as enduring their own particular suffering, a crisis of masculinity precipitated for some men by married women's entry into the labour force. It has long been argued that employment is at the core of many men's sense of themselves as men. 'A man disciplined himself to earn money for himself or his family, and the extent of hardship suffered to this end was an expression of his manhood' (Wight, 1993b, p. 106). A sense of being a man through the sacrifice of work is potentially disrupted by the equal participation of women in this sacrifice. The conventional male ways of expressing intimacy, caring by being the provider, expressing love by giving gifts, for example, fit with the position of greater earning power. A number of authors of varying political persuasions cite the undercutting of men's earner/provider role as incompatible with stable marriage and two-parent families (Staples, 1982; Murray, 1984, 1990, 1994). In the more right-wing variants, welfare provisions to single parents are blamed for further undermining the role of father/provider, and social disorder ranging from crime to riots is blamed on fatherless families. Some illustrations of these arguments are presented in the next section.

Visions of the Future

In the 1980s and 1990s rates of marriage have fallen and age of first marriage has increased in the majority of 'Euro-North American' societies. While most people continue to plan to marry at some point, a common pattern is to live with a partner prior to marriage (for Britain see Haskey, 1995). Cohabitation is the norm before first marriage and is even more common prior to a second marriage. One interpretation of the increase in cohabitation is that as marriage has moved from an institution to a relationship then the formal legal arrangement ceases to be important to people. Cohabitation then does not mark an increased casualness in relationships and cohabiting partners look pretty much like married partners (Burgoyne, 1991; McRae, 1993). A similar 'there-is-no-big-change' interpretation of divorce has been routinely offered by sociologists: high incidence of divorce is a reflection of the heightened importance of having a good marriage. In other words people are not giving up on the search for life-partners with whom they will live happily-ever-after, but they are not prepared to put up with relationships that do not work out. Expectations of marriage are high and the quality of the relationship is the key test of the marriage. Giddens takes this a step further in suggesting that the type of intimacy increasingly sought in relationships is inherently fragile. In practice women sue for divorce more often than men and this would fit with a view of women as seeking and valuing intimacy to a greater degree than men. This conclusion is often reached too glibly, however. For financial and practical reasons, women often need legal recognition of marital breakdown to a greater extent than men. Hence the figures concerning who initiates divorce proceedings contain an unknown number of cases in which women initiate the legal tidying up, after their partner has initiated the breakdown of their marriage.

However, there are also authors who emphasize the more profoundly disintegrative effects of high divorce rates. This is precisely because a marriage or a marriage-type arrangement is not just a relationship but a key node in a web of financial and domestic arrangements and social networks. The dissolution of a particular couple disrupts each member's social networks and that of any children. Some research suggests that in about half of cases involving children, children lose not only a parent but a set of grandparents, aunts and uncles and other friends they were connected with through the lost parent (Cherlin and Furstenberg, 1988; Furstenberg and Cherlin, 1991). Women and children left together after divorce are typically significantly poorer financially than they were before. Besides these serious disruptions to the social fabric there is also evidence that a high incidence of divorce is transforming attitudes to marriage. People marrying today do not necessarily expect to be together for ever, and from the start they have the possibility of divorce in mind (Wallerstein et al., 1989).

A number of authors, particularly in the US suggest that the high rate of divorce and separation is evidence of degenerating moral fibres – weakening commitment to marriage and children, the devaluation of love and the sapping of morality. To take two contrasting examples, Robert Bellah et al. speak with regret about the loss of the nineteenth-century conventional modern family (Bellah et al., 1985, pp. 88–89) and Arlie Hochschild talks of the subversion of the feminist goal of women's independence into magazine images of women on their own using their purchasing power to please themselves as they need nobody else (1994).

The European sociologist Zygmunt Bauman, drawing on an early version of this type of analysis (that of the US social scientist Richard Sennett), contrasts the social cohesion of an earlier period, provided by tradition and enforced through the scrutiny of public life, with the disintegration of the present. He describes how social skills become undermined by excessive concern with individuality and the compulsive consumption incited by the market forces of late capitalism:

> Unable to cope with the challenges and problems arising from their mutual relations, men and women turn to marketable goods, services and expert counsel; they need the factory produced tools to imbue their bodies with socially meaningful 'personalities', medical or psychiatric advice to heal the wounds left by previous – and future – defeats, travel services to escape into unfamiliar settings which it is hoped will provide better surroundings for solution of familiar problems, or simply factory-produced noise (literal and metaphorical) to 'suspend' social time and eliminate the need to negotiate social relations. (Bauman, 1987, p. 164)

The scientific rationalizing faith in 'progress' that accompanies the development of market capitalism has also been blamed for stripping people of their social skills. Christopher Lasch (1977) has written of the proletarianization of parenthood, a process by which parents are deskilled by child care 'experts' in much the same way as management imposition of the assembly line deskills workers. Rationality did not stay outside the door of the modern family household. Some historians have attempted to provide documentation of the effects of the ideas and practices of scientific rationality on domestic and sexual life. One of the most comprehensive accounts is Kereen Reiger's history of the impact of the medical, welfare, educational and architectural professions on Australian family households and the resulting 'disenchantment of the home'. The claimed combined negative effects of individualism and State intervention have become part of a questioning of welfare policies in the writings of a number of authors much cited by right-wing political opponents of welfare provisions (see chapter 3).

Andrew Cherlin, a US commentator on the family and social change, emphasizes individualism more than market forces without the same negative emphasis on welfare provision or state intervention:

> The family values of the 1950s contained elements of a more individualistic ethos that would help transform family life again a generation later. Under that ethos, which has gained force throughout the West since the emergence of commercial capitalism, individuals increasingly have sought meaning in life through self-fulfilment and intimacy. The family form celebrated in the 1950s was the isolated nuclear family consisting of only parents and children. It fits the ethos by providing a more private setting for personal life. . . . But there is no reason why individualism should stop with the nuclear family – after all, obligations to spouses and children can conflict with personal desires as well. Since the mid-1960s, the quest for self-fulfilment and intimacy has taken an even more individualistic tone; increasingly what counts is one's own emotional satisfaction, even if it clashes with the needs of spouses and children and even if it leads to the break-up of a marriage. (Cherlin, 1992, p. 38)

While there is a sense of possible dangers in Cherlin's account, he stops short of a depiction of rampant individualism in which people have degenerated into self-obsessed incompetents. A similar balance of danger and optimism is found in Swidler's analysis of love in American culture. Drawing on contemporary films and novels as well as historical material, she argues that changes in the meaning of love reflect shifts in how the life course is structured and how the self is understood. The 'true self' is now defined in impulsive behaviour performed outwith institutions rather than through membership of institutions. The institutional affiliations of contemporary adulthood, to a particular employer, to a marriage partner, to children are no longer assumed to be ideally 'for life'. While stability in adult life has not necessarily been a feature of the past, the expectation that marriage lasted a lifetime meant that a sense of 'being settled' once accompanied marriage. Now a marriage is not taken for granted as the threshold of a settled adulthood; rather adulthood is seen as a phase of life which requires constant struggle.

> Identity, commitment, self-realisation, and intimacy, once achieved,
> were simply supposed to last a life-time. Moral meaning lay in
> being able to stick to what one had chosen, to be animated by the
> commitments one had made. But in the contemporary period, the
> valence of the love myth is shifting – in ways which often seem
> regressive. . . . our culture now seeks moral significance in acts of
> choice, in attempts to discover, clarify, or deepen the self, whether
> or not these choices lead to or remain within a commitment.
> (Swidler, 1980, p. 143)

Accounts such as those of Cherlin and Swidler suggest the possibility of either moral degeneracy or a benign evolutionary increase in
the degrees of individualism tolerated and encouraged in Euro-North
American societies. Benign because greater individualism means
more opportunities to value people for themselves, for the unique
qualities that they possess, and more opportunities for self-expression, including expression of emotion. Each of these aspects of individualism opens up possibilities for greater intimacy and particularly
'disclosing intimacy'.

The British anthropologist Marilyn Strathern takes issue with this
view of a progressive increase in individualism, suggesting rather
that what is meant by individualism has changed. For Strathern, the
modern period has been characterized by a middle-class English tendency, if not a general Euro-North American tendency, to see each
generation as if it were more individual than the previous generation, to conceive of children as more individual than their parents, to
equate parents with natural ties and convention and to equate children with choice (1992a, pp. 15–19). In Strathern's view, however, this
English mind set has spiralled into a hyper-individualism which loses
all sense of the individual's relationship to and responsibility for
others.

> We have lost the relational facility for making a partial analogy
> between nature and society work as the context for the way we
> think about individuals. . . . The individual vanishes not just from
> a surfeit of individuality. It vanishes when it no longer seems rel-
> evant to talk about its environment and thus – as Mrs Thatcher
> discovered – about 'its relationship' to society. (1992a, p. 150)

In the previous mind set of the modern era, the world was rich in
cultural and natural diversity which allowed degrees of freedom
without fragmenting the world into pieces. This is captured in the

modernist English view of kinship: 'Kinship delineated a developmental process that guaranteed diversity, the individuality of persons and generations of future possibilities' (1992a, p. 39). Kinship also expressed the subtleties of thinking about relationships between individual and society, nature and culture: 'In the modern epoch, kinship and family could play either nature to the individual's cultural creativity, or society to the individual's natural spirit of enterprise' (1992a, p. 43). Much of the comfort of this world view is now lost to the post–pluralist. New reproductive technologies render kinship more problematic as a way of thinking about, representing and constructing relationships between individual and society, nature and culture.

> 'More choice seems less choice': with the engineering of genetic stock, the potential for long-term future variation may be reduced rather than enhanced. When diversity seems to depend literally on the vagaries of human individuals, it suddenly seems at risk. . . . Procreation was a natural fact of life. But the 'natural' image has lost its obviousness in a world where couples can seek assistance to beget offspring without intercourse. So too have the 'cultural' conventions of the union. The otherwise lawful connection of husband and wife may conceivably subsume a contract with a birthing mother or an agreement to obtain gametes by donation. (1992a, p. 43)

A quite opposite interpretation of the consequences of the possibility of sex without reproduction and reproduction without sexual intercourse is made by Anthony Giddens. Giddens suggests this disengagement of sex and reproduction has helped pave the way to 'the pure relationship' and 'plastic sexuality', in his relatively optimistic account of gender, intimacy and social change (1992).

Giddens suggests that rapid social change is forcing a shift towards a particular type of more intensely intimate relationship in personal life in ways which undermine inequality between men and women. The speed and nature of change forces people to become self-reflexive, consciously working on sustaining a sense of who they are and self-consciously considering what kind of personal relationships they want (Giddens, 1991, 1992). Men as well as women are forced to self-reflexively confront their emotional needs. Greater self-awareness heightens the need for self-affirming connections with others and makes possible new depths of knowing and understanding. This is deeper than empathy based on pre-given shared understandings of a common culture. It is a knowing which is 'discovered' or created through intense interaction. Giddens predicts that a growing number of individuals will seek a type of love relationship characterized by 'disclosing intimacy' which he calls 'the pure relationship'. The 'pure relationship' is 'pure' in the sense of having no *raison d'être* over and above an appreciation of the relationship itself. For Giddens, a pure relationship is by definition a relationship between equals. In so far as people pursue heterosexual relationships, the ascendancy of the 'pure relationship' will necessarily involve greater equality between men and women. The dimension of intimacy emphasized above all is knowing and understanding, rather than more practical forms of caring:

> A pure relationship is one in which external criteria have become dissolved: the relationship exists solely for whatever rewards that relationship can deliver. In the context of the pure relationship, trust can be mobilised only by a process of mutual disclosure. (1991, p. 6)

> It [a pure relationship] refers to a situation where a social relation is entered into for its own sake, for what can be derived by each person from a sustained association with another; and which is continued only in so far as it is thought by both parties to deliver enough satisfaction for each individual to stay within it. (1992, p. 58)

These same characteristics of the relationship also make it inherently fragile. It cannot hold without mutual satisfaction.

Giddens claims that the trend towards 'the pure relationship' is paralleled by the emergence of a more responsive and creative form of sexuality which he calls 'plastic sexuality'. The term 'plastic'[3] is a shorthand for the late twentieth-century heightened awareness of the plasticity of sexuality – that is, of the fact that there is no essential pre-given way of being sexual. 'Plastic sexuality is decentred sexuality, freed from the needs of reproduction' (1992, p. 2). 'Plastic sexuality' involves freedom from preconceived notions about what is typical or appropriate: 'a revolution in female sexual autonomy', that is in women finding sexual pleasure in ways which are not dictated by men, and 'the flourishing of homosexuality' (1992, p. 28) are manifestations of this shift.

An important causal factor underlying the ascendancy of the pure relationship and plastic sexuality concerns the heightened sense that individuals have of their own creativity and their own limitations in the business of producing their social world. The deep-rooted changes which underlie the transformation of intimacy are those detailed in Giddens's earlier work on the development of 'high modernity' (1990, 1991): globalization, disembeddedness, risk, dominance of experts and abstract systems, reflexivity. The pace of social change is such that traditions are more profoundly swept away than ever before (1994). The revolutions in communication technology and transport penetrate every part of the globe, promoting both the homogenization of culture and a sense of choice, reducing cultures to alternative lifestyles disembedded from their time and place. More and more aspects of life are visibly dependent on complex expert systems beyond our comprehension. Pre-modern faith in tradition was only briefly replaced by faith in the scientific fact. Facts are now known to be socially constructed such that today's right answer is tomorrow's mistake. The processes of change have sensitized people to the fragile and arbitrary nature of the social world, heightening a sense of risk and lack of control on the one hand, and a creative ability to construct ourselves on the other.

> Where large areas of a person's life are no longer set by preexisting patterns and habits, the individual is continually obliged to negotiate life-style options. Moreover – and this is crucial – such choices are not just 'external' or marginal aspects of the individual's attitudes, but define who the individual 'is'. In other words, life-style choices are constitutive of the reflexive narrative of self. (Giddens, 1992, p. 75)

The phrase 'narrative of the self' emphasizes the ongoing process of self-construction. It is as if in the Euro-North American world of the late twentieth century people cannot avoid being consciously self-reflexive, frequently considering if they are doing things in the right way as they struggle to maintain an identity.

The 'pure relationship' and plastic sexuality are forums in which the individual can intensively and co-operatively explore and construct a narrative of themselves. Men and women need to find 'forms of self exploration and moral construction' (Giddens, 1992, p. 144). The implication is that keeping oneself to oneself and denying emotions is increasingly impossible in what some authors refer to as a 'post modern' world. A successful pure relationship recreates psychological stability by resonating with the ontological security and basic trust developed in childhood (originally derived from the trust placed by children in their 'caretakers') (Giddens, 1991, p. 186).

Side-stepping Strathern's fears about the unsettling psychological consequences of new reproductive technologies, Giddens sees the freedom of the separation of sex and reproduction as part of the room for manœuvre in which people make their own psychological stability. Exploring and discovering sexual pleasure can be part of both the 'narrative of the self' and 'the pure relationship'.

Giddens's vision of a possible future draws selectively from the range of available evidence and only briefly discusses aspects of the wider context which perpetuate inequalities between men and women. Indeed, Giddens seems to underplay the very widespread roots of inequality by suggesting that a transformation of intimacy could undermine the ways in which the wider social context produces gender and power. Moreover, the self-reflexivity which Giddens discusses with optimism is interpreted with pessimism by some authors (Bauman, 1987; Bellah et al., 1985; Hochschild, 1994; Strathern, 1992a,b). For these authors the constant monitoring of the self by the self is part and parcel of a rampant self-obsessive individualism or consumerism which may threaten to destroy all intimate relationships. They fear a future in which concern with self-satisfaction or self-protection renders impossible the necessary compromise involved in commitment to another. Women and men are envisaged as becoming equal in selfishness. Hence all intimate relationships are potentially casualties. The hypothesized diminishing of intimacy in the parent–child relationship is heralded as particularly catastrophic in its consequences. Giddens's use of psychoanalytic work is also selective, ignoring the more pessimistic offerings within the psychoanalytic tradition (see the discussion of Craib, in chapter one).

Like some other British and American commentators, Giddens constructs a positive account of a qualitative rather than simply quantitative shift in individualism. Sociologists have long argued that, in order to be able to get on with their lives, people in every society take what are arbitrary person-made rules for granted, as if they were natural or God-given. Giddens's account of high modernity suggests that less is taken for granted than ever before. And in particular people are more self-reflexively aware that they construct themselves. The American sociologist Arlene Skolnick talks of a similar process using somewhat different language. She refers to people's heightened awareness of 'individuated ways of responding in the world' (Skolnick, 1992, p. 146). The evidence for this type of reflexive individualism is reviewed by Skolnick who notes that as well as a complex set of demographic, structural, and cultural changes that have created a more individualised life course and a heightened sense of self, there is a political dimension, variously described as 'rights revolutions' or the 'democratization of personhood'. At the centre of this shift is the claiming of political and cultural rights for disadvantaged groups – from blacks and other minorities, to women, to children, to gay people, to the handicapped, to the elderly. The democratization of personhood goes beyond the rights of citizenship, extending to all forms of authority and hierarchy. (1992, p. 169)

A number of theorists have observed that the 'democratization of personhood' and the associated reflexive search for identity is only possible at historical moments when sheer toil and the struggle for survival are not the main preoccupations of the majority (Giddens, 1990; Gellner, 1985; Skolnick, 1992). The post-war years of the twentieth century were years of relative affluence for the majority in all industrialized societies, although poverty was never wholly eradicated. Recent decades have seen reversals in fortune for significant minorities in many industrialized countries resulting from high unemployment and cuts in welfare provisions. The psychological revolution may not have stalled but for growing numbers the self-reflexive 'who am I?' questioning must compete with more pressing considerations such as where the next bed and meal is going to come from.

While stories of the past have been deconstructed and subjected to critique, this is also an ongoing if more openly speculative process for stories of the future. The competing nature of these stories, the pessimistic and the optimistic, already indicate mutual criticism. The same present-day events are often cited as evidence in opposing stories of radical change in personal life. For example, trends in cohabitation, divorce and remarriage can be interpreted as either a continuance of a profound commitment to family-type arrangements but with some modification of what counts as 'family', or as leading to the end of 'the family' as a pervasive ideal. Versions of the past are inevitably implicated in visions of the future. Those who speak pejoratively of a phenomenon described as 'rampant individualism' fear the end not just of particular forms of family life, but of all responsibility to others, with children as the main victims. In their version of the past there were limits, constraints, obligations and sanctions which worked for the benefit of all. The same phenomenon is also interpreted as an extension of the 'democratization of personhood' advanced by feminism, civil rights movements and others struggling for more equal societies. Their vision of the past is one of pernicious inequality and unfair impositions. The issue of visions of the future, optimism and pessimism is a theme to which I will return in the final chapter of this book in the context of the interim reviews of empirical research in each intervening chapter.

CHAPTER 3

Parenting and Intimacy

Theoretical and historical stories of intimacy suggest two sets of questions to be asked concerning the parent–child relationship. First, is the balance of parenting between mothers and fathers changing, with profound consequences? From a variety of perspectives, more emotionally involved fathering will create a realignment of gender and intimacy. For example, psychoanalytic accounts link differences in intimacy between adult men and women back to the balance of parenting between mothers and fathers. The balance of parenting is the issue dealt with in the first section of this chapter. Secondly, are parent–child relationships moving towards equality and 'disclosing intimacy' and how should such a shift be evaluated? This issue is dealt with in the second section of the chapter. On both these issues, there are already opposing camps, those for whom more shared caring between mothers and fathers is good and those for whom it is bad, and those for whom greater equality between parents and children is good and those for whom it is bad. Much is written and spoken with limited or no evidence and, of course, all existing evidence involves a process of interpretation.

Mothers *and* Fathers as Intimates

By the late nineteenth century, motherhood had become a matter of public policy and debate in all industrializing nation states. A corollary of the focus on mothers was the marginalization of fathers. Fathers were implicitly irrelevant to the intensive management of children expected from mothers. Much greater intimacy was expected between mothers and children, particularly young children, than between fathers and children. The majority of experts promoting such views were men. The old professions – law, medicine and education – grew and diversified. New disciplines, and new experts emerged with competing claims of relevant knowledge for ensuring the healthy, educated and regulated citizens desired by modern nation states. Drawing on expert knowledge, states increasingly intervened in private lives to foster 'desirable' citizens and to prevent or control 'undesirables'. Racist and classist eugenic concern with the 'stock' of the nation was a common theme of state nationalism in Europe, North America, Australia and New Zealand: 'true citizens' risked engulfment or dilution by less desirable elements. The perceived threats were various: 'yellow peril' in Australia, California, Canada, New Zealand (Price, 1974), the 'lower orders', in Britain and former slaves in the USA. (The early decimation of indigenous peoples in lands settled by white Europeans typically left populations too small to be seen as a threat by the twentieth century.) While mothers perceived to be of 'good stock' were to be encouraged to have children, preoccupation with 'the enemy within' resulted in targeted birth control and surveillance.

By the early twentieth century there were many state and charity initiatives attempting to educate mothers and potential mothers and to monitor the standard of child care. This is well documented for Australia (Reiger, 1985), New Zealand (Toynbee, 1995) USA (Ehrenreich and English, 1979; Hardyment, 1983; Hays, 1996) and the UK (Corr, 1983; Lewis, 1986; Riley, 1983). Initiatives included school medical inspections, domestic science training in schools for girls, medical management of pregnancy and birth, postnatal and infant welfare movements, kindergarten and infant education movements. In Australia, the forced removal of light-skinned 'half caste' babies from aboriginal mothers, in order to 'civilize' them as domestic servants or ranch hands, was ironically justified in the 1930s by the desire to preserve a 'dying race' (Broome, 1982). At any one time, particular states pursued a number of policies, often containing contradictions and lacking coherence, but all modern states became engaged in the business of managing motherhood. A dominant story of the new experts was that parents and particularly mothers are responsible for the construction of the *character* of their children. This notion was not widespread at least among British parents until the mid-twentieth century (Jamieson and Toynbee, 1990), but is now described as 'the domain assumption of modern child rearing' (Harris, 1983, p. 241). Working-class parents, ethnic minority parents and especially mothers, have often been characterized as deficient. Right-wing rhetoric continues to blame under-privileged mothers for the greater and often increasing rates of criminalization suffered by ghetto populations.

The view that children benefit if both mothers and fathers are their intimates only emerged (or re-emerged) as a popular ideal in the late twentieth century.[1] In the initial modern period the content of fatherhood declined as motherhood gained in complexity. Historically the law had privileged fathers' claims to children over those of mothers. In the modern period this was transformed. The law no longer focused on children as primarily potential heirs to men's property and as men's human capital. Children were seen as needing a protected world of childhood, and mothers, not fathers, became the socially accepted best carers. 'Fathering' was commonly used until recently simply to refer to the procreative process involved in becoming a biological father. The ideal of the loving, caring and empathetically involved father was a later and less frequently told story than the pervasive public story of intensive motherhood. Nevertheless, calls for and portrayals of 'the sensitive father' are now commonplace. Experts who advocated involved fathers often focus on the benefits for children (while acknowledging benefits for women and men): these range from ensuring children are not damaged by psychologically overburdened mothers to a positive psychological effect of a strong bond with a male figure. A 'good' of intimacy between fathers and children stressed in popular culture is its humanizing and civilizing effect on men themselves. Men becoming better people through more involved fatherhood has become a recurrent theme and sub-plot of popular films.[2] However, 'the sensitive father' must contend with continued popular disdain for weak men and the looming spectre of the child abuser. Moral commentators often call for a more disciplinarian father figure. Young people helped or put on the right track by the benevolent but disciplinarian father figure is also a theme of popular films.[3]

Theories of good mothering

Sociologists contributed to the ideology of 'the good mother'. The functionalism of Emile Durkheim (1858–1917) provided the starting point for much past sociological writing about the family. Durkheim wrote that, as societies became more complex, complementary divisions of labour between men and women became more acute with women retreating from public life to concentrate on reproductive, familial and domestic functions. His vision of the inevitability of women focusing on mothering to the exclusion of public life was a cultural reading of nature. He assumed the biological facts of reproduction provided the unalterable and determining scaffolding of gender segregation. Therefore, he saw the extreme separate spheres of men and women in his own time (at least in the middle-class) as a predictable evolutionary outcome. Talcott Parsons, who dominated American sociological writing on parenthood, courtship and family life from the 1940s to the 1960s, followed this lead. He argued that bringing up children in the mid-twentieth century required an attuned and dedicated specialist and took it for granted that the task fell to women. It was no longer appropriate to provide children with detailed rules: young people have to be self-directing, autonomous and robust to cope with rapid social change. He argued that a mother used the emotionally intense bond between herself and her child to psychologically manipulate the child into a socialized human being. In his view a separation of the mother, as primary carer, from immersion in paid employment was essential because the competitive values of employment were inimical to the work of socializing children and stabilizing adult personalities which he envisaged women doing at home. In his terms, it was functional if men filled the provider side of the division of labour while women were the primary carers.[4]

Meanwhile, in psychology experimental work on rhesus monkeys (Harlow, 1958) and monitoring of children in institutions and evacuees (Bowlby, 1953; Rutter, 1972) demonstrated the serious effects of 'maternal deprivation'. The research unequivocally demonstrated that monkeys and humans need consistent social interaction with caring others of their own kind in order to thrive. However, authors went further in their interpretation of these findings, valorizing 'natural' maternal love. In his popular writings Bowlby, for example, argued that it was the devoted care of a loving mother which was naturally suited to the task of child rearing and that mothers would naturally love their babies. 'The normal mother can afford to rely on the prompting of her instincts in the happy knowledge that the tenderness they prompt is what the baby wants' (Bowlby, 1953, p. 18 quoted in Richardson, 1993, p. 44). While different countries have had their particularly influential experts,[5] mothers were increasingly spoken to by experts from an orthodoxy which stressed the mother's responsibility for the psychological well-being of the child. The best-selling experts of the late twentieth century, the paediatricians Dr Benjamin Spock, T. Berry Brazelton and the British social psychologist Penelope Leach, all argue that consistent nurture by a single primary care-giver is absolutely crucial. Day-care centres, preschools, spouses, and baby-sitters may help out but they are incidental to the bond the child really needs with an individual adult, usually the biological mother. The increasing entry of mothers into the labour force has not been accompanied by a public story which de-emphasizes the significance of 'mother'. Rather the ideology of intensive mothering 'which holds the individual mother as primarily responsible for child-rearing and that understands the child as sacred, innocent and pure' has heightened the tensions between work and mothering which women must manage (Hays, 1996).

What was expected of 'the good mother' became increasingly demanding and complex, despite reassurances about following instinct. Advice shifted from an emphasis on imposing routine on infants and denying indulgence (Reiger, 1985; Richardson, 1993) to avoiding unnecessary frustration of the child's wishes and an emphasis on the importance of maternal communication with the child (Richardson, 1993, pp. 43–61). There is a late twentieth century consensus among child development experts that 'good mothering' strikes an appropriate balance between permissiveness and restrictiveness, using psychological control and discussion, rather than physical punishment. The emergent ideal is a 'mix of firm control and high demands for competence with warmth and a willingness of parents to communicate with children, listening to their point of view and expressing their own' (Woollett and Phoenix, 1991, p. 31). The stress on listening, discussing and expressing reflects an addition to the previously expected dimensions of intimacy of showing love and care through domestic work; intimacy now encompasses constantly working with the child, to know and understand him or her. Hays refers to contemporary American ideals of mothering as 'intensive mothering' – child-centred, expert-guided, emotionally absorbing, labour-intensive and financially expensive (1996).

A number of authors have observed that expert views of good mothering were often formed with no knowledge of a mother's experience of mothering (Richardson, 1993, Woollett and Phoenix, 1991). Psychologists' views of 'good mothering' are typically inferred from their knowledge of child development. The emergent view of the 'sensitive mother' has involved in some cases a process of negatively judging many working-class, and ethnic minority mothers as 'bad' with no appreciation of the class or culturally specific dilemmas of mothering (Walkerdine and Lucey, 1989). Moreover, psychological literature tends to treat 'mother' as the totality of the child's environment, as if the mother–child were isolated from a wider social world (Riley, 1983). While some experts extolled the virtues of intense mother–child bonding, their colleagues documented the downside of a system which left many women isolated in sole charge of young children, with little social or material recognition for their work. Critiques came from clinicians who believed they were dealing with mothers who were worn down by the burden of mothering (Brown and Harris, 1982; Boulton, 1983) and children damaged by mother–child bonds which stifled the development of an autonomous self (Laing, 1960).

Absent fathers deplored and affirmed

By the late twentieth century, alongside the story of the virtues of the 'sensitive mother', there are stories of the deficiencies of single mothers or motherhood without fatherhood (Lewis, 1986). This is a long-running refrain which was well established in the 1950s. Bowlby, for example, identified single mothers as 'pathologically disturbed' (Hardey and Crow, 1991; Riley, 1983). The pathologizing of single mothers as intrinsically unfit parents, also reasserts the importance of fathers. However, for much of this century father–child relationships were portrayed as a one-dimensional intimacy in which a father's care for children meant financial support. The theorists of 'the good mother' would argue that they never wrote off fathers, rather fathers were seen as complementary figures, who enabled mothers to focus on mothering by being providers. Parsons offered the most thorough account of this complementarity. The Parsonian father was the 'instrumental leader' of the family household and mother was the 'expressive leader'. Fathers were the necessary link between the family and the wider social world, who would help propel children beyond the apron strings. For Christopher Lasch and other champions of patriarchal fathers, such theories were a mask concealing the death of meaningful fatherhood – fathers had lost 'the powerful union of love and discipline' (Lasch, 1977). Lasch's work can be read as a rallying call against sensitive mothering as destroying the authority of fathers.

In the USA the most publicized research which cast doubt on the health of families without fathers concerned black families. This work also referred to the importance of fathers as authority figures. Daniel Patrick Moynihan's 1965 report for the Labour Department read 'Ours is a society which presumes male leadership in private and public affairs . . . and reward(s) it. A subculture, such as that of the Negro American, in which this is not the pattern, is placed at a distinct disadvantage' (quoted in D'Emilio and Freedman, 1988, p. 299). The acknowledgements of the effects of racism and poverty in the report were outweighed by its focus on absent fathers as the crux of disadvantage (Rainwater and Yancey, 1967). Subsequent research in the USA and the UK indicates that the most common disadvantages suffered by children with lone mothers are the poor housing and low income associated with the absence of a male wage. The circumstances in which people are brought up in lone-parent households are arguably more important than the fact of lone parenthood itself. Charles Murray, writing about both the United States (1984) and Britain (1990, 1994) has claimed that a new and potentially morally degenerate 'underclass' is emerging as the result of the increasing proportion of poor family households in which children are brought up without committed fathers. Murray's loose usage of the term 'underclass' has been much criticized (Morris, 1994; Wilson, 1993). But related arguments have been put forward in Britain by a series of authors published by the conservative Institute of Economic Affairs.[6] All of these authors consider an increase in lone-mother families as a symptom and self-perpetuating cause of social disorder. Working-class and ethnic minority boys without fathers are claimed as particularly at risk of becoming socially disruptive. These concerns are folded into a critique of the welfare state, as state provision for lone mothers is accused of relieving fathers of their responsibilities and undermining the work ethic. Murray predicts an increased polarization of society between the better-off who maintain conventional family households, morals and decency and an increasingly degenerate rabble of an underclass (1994). Other authors acknowledging a disassociation of poor, working-class and black young men from family life emphasize economic circumstances beyond the control of individuals and talk in terms of a 'crisis of masculinity' arising from labour market factors which deprive men of the earner/provider role (Anderson, 1990; Campbell, 1993; Staples, 1982). Their hopes for the future are in either the removal of barriers to male employment or the restructuring of masculinity around useful activities other than the role of earner/provider.

Fears have also been expressed that men more generally are making a 'flight from commitment' (Ehrenreich, 1983), a turning away from fatherhood itself. A number of authors interpret the research as suggesting a polarization between men who invest more in family life and particularly fatherhood than ever before and men who choose the freedom of a single existence or uninvolved fatherhood in which they remain physically and emotionally distant from children (Furstenberg, 1988; Jensen, 1995). A proportion of men have always been rendered unavailable to their children by their occupations. There have always been certain predominantly male occupations and patterns of working that entail profound absence from home. There is no clear evidence that membership of occupations which take men or women away from home for long periods is numerically increasing. Even very long distance commuting is not a new phenomenon although it is probably more common now than in the mid-century. At the same time there is a popular perception in Europe and North America that 'greedy' occupations which demand extra hours are becoming more common for both men and women. Rosanna Hertz has suggested that some high-earning dual-career households could be characterized as having two husbands and no wife, with a third person hired to do much of the child care and cleaning. (Hertz, 1986; Hunt and Hunt, 1982). Clearly such couples remain exceptional. However, the constraints of labour markets, housing markets, state benefits systems and working conditions can produce pressures which promote uninvolved fatherhood and/or motherhood. Conflicting stories are told about whether more or fewer men are choosing involved fatherhood.

The increased use of artificial insemination, drawing on medically administered stocks of donated sperm, is resulting in the social construction of a new 'absent father' – the sperm donor. Clearly, the objective of those using artificial insemination by donor (AID) is to have a child, not to acquire a futher or alternative father to that child. However, within the social work profession analogies are being drawn between AID and adoption, where it is argued that children have a right to know their biological/genetic origins. Christine Walby (1990), for example, strongly advocates that children be informed not only of the details of their conception but also that they be provided with the identity of and background information on their genetic father. She argues that sperm donors should be prepared to be contacted by their children because it is lack of knowledge and uncertainty about 'who I am' that has caused problems for some adopted children. In Sweden it is no longer legally permissible for a sperm donor to remain anonymous (Bjornberg, 1995). As yet there are no studies of the effects of such policies on the relationships between donors, social parents and their children.

The public story of the 'absent father' is typically a tale of woe, but how the problem is diagnosed depends on the political project of the story teller. Only a subset of those denouncing absent fathers seek more intimate father–child relationships. Those whose political project is to reduce 'welfare dependency' are primarily concerned that the absent father is not paying up. For those advocating joint parenting as an issue of gender equality, the problem of the absent father is that he is not taking up his share of the work of parenting. If joint parenting is seen as beneficial to child development, the problem is the loss to the child resulting from the father's uninvolvement, although the type of involvement desired varies according to further political nuances. The more conservative advocates want to see fathers as providers and disciplinarians, while others advocate more emotionally involved fathers. For the advocates of the disciplinarian, head-of-the-household, patriarchal father, lone motherhood means no 'natural' division of labour between a 'soft' mother and a 'firm' father, and no masculine role model. The radical version seeks involved fathers not to reinforce traditional gender roles but to smash them. The 'good' father in some of these accounts is not the interested disciplinarian who is ready to step in when needed but the father who wants to maintain the same quality of intimate ties with his children as 'the sensitive mother'. Meanwhile, advocates of children's right to know their genetic origins re-emphasize a definition of fathering which makes reference to procreation rather than the quality of relationships.

Feminist debate over equal parenting

Feminists are divided over the prospects and desirability of the intimate father. Calls for equal parenting are common across a wide range of theoretical traditions, but not all advocate men who mother in the sense of having the same quality of intimacy with children as do mothers. Alice Rossi (1984), for example, uses biological and psychological research to argue that females and males are generally different in the skills in which they excel (she assumes these differences have a genetic base but are exaggerated by learning) such that women are better equipped to deal with infants than men. However, she also argues that if both a father and a mother were to devote a great deal of time and energy to bringing up a child then the child would develop a greater range of skills than if she were brought up simply by the mother. Hence shared parenting would result in more creative and productive people.

The strongest advocates of men who mother are psychoanalytic feminists who suggest that shared parenting can restructure intimacy, putting men and women on an equal footing. Nancy Chodorow, Dorothy Dinnerstein and Carol Gilligan (Chodorow, 1978, 1994; Dinnerstein, 1976; Gilligan, 1982) have each offered accounts that suggest men have a lesser capacity for intimacy than women which can be traced back to early childhood. Chodorow suggests that mothers encourage boys to be independent earlier than girls and in the process cause emotional hardening in the boy which makes intimacy more problematic in adult life. Her account suggests that disclosing intimacy, revealing the self and working at knowing and empathizing with another, will be particularly problematic. According to Chodorow, it is a mother's awareness that boy children have to grow up to be boys, and her lesser affinity with boy children than girls, that results in cutting the boy off from herself earlier. Boys develop stronger 'ego boundaries' in response to their loss. This has lasting consequences, the boy in the man remains cautious about forming close relationships, not wishing to repeat the pattern of deep attachment and loss. Girls, on the other hand, have a longer period of being closely in touch with the needs and feelings of another and hence form less strong ego boundaries. This provides girls with a much stronger foundation for empathy with others in adulthood (and hence mothering) than boys. Gilligan similarly talks of boys' earlier loss of a 'relational world' (1982, Brown and Gilligan, 1992). Dinnerstein suggests that boy and girl infants cope differently with the experience of an all-powerful mother who is the source not only of all satisfaction but of all frustration. Boys create an imaginary good mother and bad mother which then are internalized, buried in their subconscious. The consequences for men are damaging to the possibility of intimate relationships with women, as they alternate between idealizing and denigrating women. This route is not taken by girls because they recognize that they too may become mothers.

It is possible then to read Chodorow and Gilligan as suggesting that if fathers and mothers were both involved carers for infants, then this would cancel out the gender difference in capacity for intimacy generated by mothers' empathetic ties with daughters.

Similarly Dinnerstein can be read as suggesting that if men and women both mothered then the ambivalent feelings of infants towards their carers would not be resolved by boys through splitting women into the good and the bad. In other words, men, not just the odd exceptional man, could further develop their capacities to be empathetic, relational, emotional and nurturing, if only the dominant patterns of how women mother and men father at the moment could be dislodged.

> Men need to share in looking after children to reclaim their tender caring selves . . . If we were cared for from birth by men as well as women, boys and girls would not develop such divergent personalities. Girls would have less trouble becoming separate beings, and boys would not be obliged to repress their soft sides in order to identify with men. As adults, we would not fit so neatly into the system that oppresses women and limits men. (New and David, 1985, p. 236)

Feminists working outside of a psychoanalytic tradition do not necessarily give mothering and fathering this degree of significance. Rather than seeing mothering as causal in the structuring of masculinity and male dominance, the gendered pattern of parenting is often presented as an effect of other structures supporting male dominance. Conventional gendered division of labour in child care and housework 'at home' are clearly interconnected with gender divisions beyond the household: for example, with the different job opportunities for men and women and the different distributions of pay and promotion in many types of employment. If gender division and hierarchy are the result of many interconnected levels of social practice then it is both unlikely that patterns of child rearing can change in isolation and that, even if they did, radical restructuring of gender inequality would follow. For some feminists, shifts towards equal parenting are more a matter of men taking their share of the work than of reshaping men's and women's psychological capacities for intimacy. For example, the writing of the French feminist Christine Delphy (1984, Delphy and Leonard, 1992) suggests equal parenting would end a key way in which men exploit women's labour power.

The observation that mothers are more involved with their daughters than their sons has been interpreted as a consequence rather than a cause of dominant cultural ideas about masculinity and femininity

(McGuire, 1991). McGuire suggests that mothers whom she studied were more involved with their daughters because, having been socialized into conventional femininity, they had definite ideas about appropriate behaviour and appearance of girls. Their involvement with boys was more tentative and tolerant due to less certainty about their ability to communicate appropriate masculinity; a job they believed their husband had to share. For Miriam Johnson, the fact that boys pursue a male identity by making themselves tough, rejecting women and feminine ways is not a consequence of being brought up by women or of the dynamic between the mother and child. Rather the significant factors are the institutionalized practices reproducing male dominance outside of mothering; boys' devaluation and rejection of women is not a reaction to women's mothering but a consequence of taking up the position of the superior male to the inferior female. Rather than seeing mothering as a cause of gender differentiation, Johnson argues that children's early identification with a carer (whether the latter be their mother or not) 'represents the common humanity that both genders share and lays down the capacity for nurturance in both females and males'. But an array of others (fathers and the male peer group in particular) incite boys to repudiate their connectedness to their carer and to women. 'In reality, males are constrained to deny this human connectedness, and later, in a strange metamorphosis, they deny women's humanness by making them into objects' (Johnson, 1988, p. 108).

A minority of feminists, including Miriam Johnson, strenuously argue for keeping fathers and men in general distanced from children. The facts of child abuse, they argue, are sufficient to demonstrate that children are usually safer with women. The social historian Linda Gordon (1988) suggests that the adults who are most likely to abuse children have no empathetic relationship with the child and hence no sense of the child's interests. Mothers are more often thinking from the child's point of view than are fathers. It is those fathers, stepfathers, mother's boyfriends, uncles and the like, who have never identified with the child's interests that are capable of abusing their privileged access to the child. However, if most men are generally less skilled in empathetic intimacy than women, and as Dinnerstein argues, if men are more able to objectify others than women, then men remain more likely to be dangerous to children than women. Johnson makes a case against more involved fathers by noting that fathers are more likely to sexualize children than mothers, reacting more consciously to the sex of their children, and more actively constructing their gender. Unlike Chodorow she sees mothers as typically treating boys and girls as if their children were unsexed and ungendered, while arguing that fathers typically see children as boys and girls who are becoming sexually developed men and women.

> For mothers a child is a child – a mother may get pleasure from breast feeding or stroking the soft bodies of a boy or girl child – this may be an erotic but is not a sexualised or gendered experience. Fathers on the other hand are more likely to sexualise their interaction and flirt with girl children withdrawing from physical contact with boy children. Moreover fathers differentiate in ways which promote male dominance and foster sexual aspects of gender difference. Fathers make more demands of boys, expect little of girls, show more physical affection to girls and react with her as an 'interested' male protecting her from outsiders. . . . Fathers encourage a kind of male-oriented 'darling girl' orientation in daughters and a power-competence orientation in sons. (Johnson, 1988, p. 135)

Arguably Johnson somewhat overplays the gender neutrality of mothers. The mothers observed by McGuire (1991), for example, clearly had some interest in nurturing feminine daughters. Also, although extremely rare in comparison to father–daughter sexual abuse and incest, some mothers do treat their children as sexual objects: mother–son incest is certainly not unknown.

In her more recent work, Chodorow puts greater emphasis on the role of fathers and on patriarchal ideas and practices outside the parent–child relationship which nevertheless impinge on it (Chodorow, 1994, p. 83–84). She notes not only that fathers are more interested than mothers in having feminine daughters and masculine sons but that they also have a tendency to show more interest in sons than daughters. 'This leads to a feminine idealization of men and constraints on assertions of desire. The girl learns to put up with less from him and from men than she really wants' (Chodorow, 1994, p. 87; Sharpe, 1994, p. 37). Fathers who are characterized as fostering conventional femininity in daughters and masculinity in sons do not practice the ideal type of father–child intimacy sought by feminist advocates of equal parenting. Rather, they reinforce the view that mothering is best left in the hands of mothers.

Notwithstanding the complex processes encouraging conventional forms of masculinity and femininity identified by these authors, all fathers are not the same (just as all mothers are not the same). The theoretical accounts discussed in this section are rather too abstracted from engagement with class and cultural differences, the detailed circumstances structuring father–child interaction (such as working away from home for long periods, or being around the house because of unemployment), and the rich variation of emotional biographies that adults bring to parenthood. Categorical theories which speak as if all men were the same but different from all women (who are also treated as if they are all the same) are always unsatisfactory (Connell, 1987). All men are not emotionally hard and all women are not empathetic. In her later work Chodorow is sensitive to this critique, and in responding partially deconstructs her own story of differences in capacity for intimacy between men and women reproduced through mothering. She is careful to emphasize the uniqueness of individual biography on the one hand, and the interaction between personal biography and cultural context on the other. An emphasis on background cultural messages and foreground accidents of biography reduces the distance between her psychoanalytic account and that of other sociological traditions. General statements about fathers and mothers derived from psychoanalytic theory have to be re-evaluated as one pattern among many possibilities.

More Shared Caring between Mothers and Fathers?

When considering social change in fatherhood, and particularly intimacy between fathers and their children, researchers have drawn on a variety of types of evidence. Histories which monitor public stories about fathers generally speak more confidently of change[7] than the literature on the doings of fathers, particularly studies of the divisions of labour between mothers and fathers.[8] At the level of popular culture, fathers have no specific mandate to remain the distant figures of the turn of the century. It seems reasonable to assume that more fathers are more involved with their children since they are *expected* to be more involved with their children. For example, in many Euro-North American societies, fathers are now expected to be and often are present at the birth of their children, whereas they were formerly banished as an irrelevance or hindrance. In general, however, factors which perpetuate conventional gender inequalities work against involved fathering (for example, different employment and promotion opportunities for men and women, the continued celebration of macho masculinity in popular culture, the reinforcement of macho masculinity in men-only social networks (Riley, 1990).

The largest body of relevant sociological research on the contribution of fathers and mothers to child care focuses on white two-parent households with dependent children, covering a variety of class backgrounds and levels of involvement in the labour force. While this research is important it has to be seen in the context of ethnic diversity, the growing number of lone parents (overwhelmingly lone-mother households), and the increasing likelihood of two-parent households being disrupted by divorce. Indeed, there are now bodies of literature covering all of the variations and recent interest in fatherhood, which have produced work on the fate of father–son and father–daughter relationships involving non-custodial fathers (Furstenberg et al., 1985), stepfathers and blended family relationships (Burgoyne and Clark, 1984; Furstenberg and Cherlin, 1991), and a number of pieces of research which deal with the more exceptional lone-parent fathers (Barker, 1994; Grieff et al., 1993).

Lost fathers following divorce

One of the most disturbing findings of the literature on divorce is the high atrophy rate of relationships between children and non-custodial fathers in the years following the divorce. A number of studies suggest that in about half of cases children lose their father and all his kin (Bradshaw and Millar, 1991; Burgoyne et al., 1987; Furstenberg and Cherlin, 1991). Furstenberg and colleagues note that for children who are young when their parents part, over time the vast majority will have little or no contact with their father. By ten years almost two-thirds of children with separated parents (drawn from a representative sample of US children) had had no contact with their father in the previous twelve months: 'the pattern of modest initial contact and a sharp drop-off over time is strikingly similar across studies' (Furstenberg and Cherlin, 1991, p. 36). Some research suggests that fathers who were very close to their children may be equally likely to withdraw completely finding it too painful to sustain a more attenuated relationship (Burgoyne and Clark, 1984). Wallerstein and Blakeslee (1989) suggest that the rising incidence of divorce means a weakening of moral commitment to children, but the practice of parenting after divorce suggests it is men's moral commitment which remains more in doubt than women's.

Earning fathers and full-time mothering

In conventional, father-earner and mother-full-time carer households, ideas about the roles of mothers and fathers have changed more dramatically than actual practice (Ruble et al., 1988). For example, the British middle-class parents interviewed by Backett believed that mothers and fathers should have qualitatively similar relationships with their children while actually having very unequal involvement with their children (Backett, 1982).

> The majority of the couples in fact themselves maintained that being a mother and being a father were essentially similar activities. However, as they talked about their family lives, it became evident that whilst these couples were concerned to sustain their belief in mutual involvement with the children, they were in effect describing two very different kinds of parenthood. (Backett, 1982, p. 62)

Even when both parents were at home, mothers had more contact with children than fathers. The couples had a range of strategies for covering over or squaring this state of affairs with their strong belief in 'fairness'. They told themselves that it was a necessary but temporary phase. While both thought of themselves as experts on the subject of their own children, the mother was the acknowledged expert of experts. They emphasized the fact that the husband/father *could* take over from the mother, even if he never did. And the small ways in which men did express interest in and were involved with their children took on large symbolic importance. 'These developments which were taking place in these families were concerned more with sustaining such beliefs about joint parenthood, rather than actually constituting practical attempts to create objectively equal arrangements' (Backett, 1982).

Backett's study was conducted about the same time as an in-depth American study which was also of white middle-class parents (LaRossa and LaRossa, 1981). These authors found fathers were more likely to treat their babies as 'things' than mothers. Fathers typically reinforced their own assumptions that babies were uninteresting by their limited attention to and efforts with the baby. Fathers did spend time with their infants but more from a sense of obligation than intrinsic enjoyment. Most fathers were found to enjoy the social approval that goes with being a father more than they enjoyed the children themselves. Pushing around a child who is strapped into a stroller/buggy is an ideal situation for enjoying the social approval of parenthood while making minimal interactional effort with the child.

Time-budget work based on large random samples of households provides general confirmation that fathers spend a smaller proportion of their available-if-children-want-them hours with their children than mothers. Such studies also show that when mothers are with children they are often doubling up activities, minding the child and doing other housework tasks (Bittman 1992, Bittman and Lovejoy, 1993). Fathers are not typically doing the difficult juggling acts attempted by the 'sensitive mother' (like turning doing-the-washing-up into an educational game). Qualitative studies of households with older children suggest that many fathers remain less involved than mothers in their children's lives. For example, in the British study of fifteen- and sixteen-year-olds by Julie Brannen et al., mothers were far more likely than fathers to know the friends of their child (1994).

Unemployed fathers at home

A number of studies have investigated whether or not working-class fathers become more involved with domestic routines when they are unemployed (McKee and Bell, 1985; Morris, 1985; Wheelock, 1990). Change in time, content and quality of father–child relationships was not investigated in as much detail as changes in domestic chores. However, there is sufficient evidence to conclude that while unemployment *can* trigger more involved fathering, this was neither necessarily or typically the case. Lorna McKee and Colin Bell found men hardening against doing 'women's' domestic and caring work in order to protect the sense of their masculinity. While Jane Wheelock, in contrast, observed shifts in gender roles, the moves she documented suggest a quantitative shift in housework rather than a qualitative shift in involvement with children. A sense of responsibility, 'having to do something', motivated men who were reluctant participants in household work. A higher level of involvement in domestic routines undertaken in this spirit is not likely to lead to a new depth of relationship with children. Unemployment is only likely to have this result for the minority of men who had always wished to be more involved in their family.

Dual-earner households

From the 1970s to the 1990s, studies show that even when both mothers and fathers are engaged in full-time employment it is the mother who typically carries the major physical burden and the sense of responsibility for child care as 'her job'. Paid help with child care is perceived as coming from her wages. She takes time off work when child care arrangements break down. She spends more time on child-care tasks.[9] Doing their best to fulfil the role of the main earner (whether they earn more than their wife or not) still sums up the business of being a father for many men. Research found men who believed that their children got all the love and care they needed from their partners while mothers reported the stress of struggling to fit children into overburdened timetables (Hochschild, 1990, p. 229).

The exceptionally involved fathers

The literature identifies some fathers who are besotted with their children and want to spend as much time as possible with them. These are not necessarily fathers who strive to take an equal share in the practicalities of cleaning, caring and cooking for their children. Rather they are fathers who talk in romantic terms, as if they have fallen in love with their children (Ehrensaft, 1985, 1987). These men are characterized in the literature as having their wariness of emotional closeness with other adults lowered in the face of a small dependent child, allowing them to discover the rewards of intimacy. At the same time there is a suggestion of an unhealthy loading of all of the father's needs for intimacy onto the child. This pattern of besottedness is not incompatible with the father playing the disciplinarian or seeing fathering primarily in terms of the role of the provider for the family. The aspects of intimacy that are cherished can be ones in which the father gives special treats and creates special times with the child, and need not involve seeking a friendship-like relationship.

On the other hand there are a number of studies which have identified or deliberately sought out men whose relationships to their children were more similar to those of mothers than traditional fathers. Kathleen Gerson's (1993) interview study of New York men led her to suggest a bimodal pattern of some men fleeing the commitments of family life while others sought deeper involvement, a pattern also suggested by Arlie Hochschild (1995). The involved fathers identified by Gerson had come to see their family as a more important source of satisfaction than their work: they were middle-class men who wanted 'off the fast track' or working-class men who had hit a 'dead end'. Moreover, involved fathers commonly regretted their father's lack of involvement in their own childhood. These men would have liked parent-friendly employment which allowed them more time with their children: 'Contrary to the stereotype of the work-obsessed man, most involved fathers preferred to work less and parent more. . . . Were it not for economic necessity, they would have chosen a more flexible or less time-consuming full-time job, a part-time job or no job at all' (Gerson, 1993, p. 245).

In a British study of largely working-class lone fathers Richard Barker (1994) finds fathers who speak positively of the change in their relationship to their children, although they did not set out intentionally to pioneer a new style of fatherhood. Becoming a lone father was not typically a process of choice but the result of the death or desertion of their partner, although some had forewarning and took active steps to retain the children. However, his random sample of lone fathers (drawn from official records) contained two equally well represented and contrasting patterns of responses to the situation of lone fatherhood which he labels as 'patriarchs' and 'pioneers'. The patriarchs resisted being mother and father to their children. They desperately maintained their role as breadwinner, calling in female relatives to care for their children or expecting the oldest daughter to step into a mother role. The 'pioneers' became child-centred themselves and reorganized their lives around their children. Some were already unemployed, others gave up work to be with their children. These fathers were actively trying to be mother and father to their children and some came to see themselves as something of a pioneer. However, they got little support from other men and were generally rather isolated.

Graeme Russell (1983), in an Australian study, consciously sought out fathers who were highly involved with their children. Again he finds fathers whose style of fathering was not planned or the result of 'new man' convictions but who nevertheless feel they have gained as a result. (He identified a group of 71 'shared care giving' fathers who had sole responsibility for their children for fifteen or more hours a week and compared them with a group of 145 'conventional fathers' with lower involvement with their children. Shared-care-giving fathers and mothers spent about the same amount of time with their children, while in conventional households fathers spend considerably less time with children than do mothers). Many fathers explained their high levels of child caring as a response to the exigencies of their own and their partner's career. In other words the sharing was negotiated by couples in which women were more committed to their jobs or had better employment, career or earning prospects than men. The shared care givers were not typical of the fathers as a whole but rather were a highly educated group, with fewer and older children. Russell also notes that their devotion to fathering got little support from relatives and involved negative reactions from other men.

Can the fact that the men in these studies allowed circumstances to nudge them into involved fatherhood, despite lack of support, be taken to mean a growing willingness to abandon conventional divisions between 'men's work' and 'women's work' and to seek greater paternal intimacy with children? Certainly some British commentators have remained optimistic that more parent-friendly working conditions (shorter working hours, better and gender-neutral provision of parental leave, and better child-care provision) would lead to shared parenting and more intimate fathering (New and David, 1985; O'Brien, 1992). However, commentators on Scandinavian countries which have taken such policies further than Europe or North America, cannot yet agree on the effects. There is a suggestion in the Scandinavian research that more men are seeking deeper levels of knowing and understanding their children but without taking up a more equal share of the work and responsibility of their practical care (Bjornberg, 1995; Jensen, 1995). What studies such as Russell's prove is that fathers can have responsible, practical relationships with their children which include all the dimensions of intimacy characteristic of mothering. However, the whole body of research shows that fathers who are not very involved with their children remain common. The numbers of fathers who choose to be as involved as mothers with their children are as yet relatively small.

Parenting: Trends in Intimacy and Democracy?

For conservative moral entrepreneurs of the twentieth century a mythical patriarchal family is the touchstone against which parents are judged; parents such as working mothers, absconded fathers, 'soft' parents and the like cause social disorder by diverging from such a family. Social historians and historical sociologists have debunked rosy images of past family life as predominantly intact happy families in contrast to the present. At the beginning of the century, death was still a significant cause of the loss of a parent. For example, in the USA in 1900, one in four children under the age of fifteen had lost a parent; one in 62 had lost both (Uhlenberg, 1980). By the end of the century, divorce has replaced death as the cause of loss of a parent from the family home. The loss due to divorce now is no greater than that due to death in earlier times (but still in the modern period) (Anderson, 1980; Bane, 1976; Skolnick, 1991, 1992). While parent–child relationships are assumed to be the most durable of all personal relationships, they are not and never have been beyond breakdown and alienation. Voluntary withdrawal on either or both sides is documented throughout history (each historical period can yield documentation of wills which disinherit children, children who have run away from home and elderly parents refused homes by their children). The British sociologist Janet Finch (1989; Finch and Mason, 1993) has documented how the 'family obligations' of parents and children to each other remain and always were conditional on both the material circumstances and the quality of their relationship. For example, the social historian Michael Anderson traced how the development of state pensions actually enhanced rather than undermined the likelihood of elderly people being cared for at home by their children; until elderly people had an independent income many of their children were unable or unwilling to bear the financial burden of their upkeep. Finch would add that the quality of relationship between child and parent has always been a determining factor in whether support is given in old age. Similar factors shape the support teenagers and young adults can expect from their parents (Jones, 1995).

However, there are ever new waves of concern about the wellbeing of parent–child bonds. By the 1980s a number of sociologists were suggesting a general crisis in parenting. The parenting style of white middle-class Euro-North American parents, the group described by Talcott Parsons in the 1950s as at the forefront of the societally advantageous shift to emotionally intense child-centred parenting, is now under suspicion. For authors who share the pessimistic view of the late twentieth century, this is not a class-specific problem but the consequence of excessive individualism and/or consumerism which empties all relationships of authentic meaning.

Warning noises were made in studies carried out in Parsons' heyday, prior to middle-class married women's greatly increased participation in the labour market and the spectacular rise in divorce (the conventional culprits of conservative rhetoric). Sennett (1970) and Elder (1977) in their historical studies of middle-class families across generations, Sealey et al. (1956) in the Canadian study of Crestwood Heights and Deverson and Lindsay's (1975) study of English middle-class families are some of the many examples which portray a gulf between parents and their growing up children despite devoted child rearing. Moreover, something like the same malaise was identified in accounts of immigrant families (Sennett and Cobb, 1966) and in working-class families (Seabrook, 1982).

One version of the threat of emotional emptiness between parents and children sees the gulf becoming more acute because the speed-up in social change means that in each generation the children seek more individualism (making their own decisions earlier and going their own way more) than parents can cope with. Richard Sennett and his colleagues described in the 1960s how parents who felt they had made sacrifices for their children were often sorely disappointed because children took directions which did not fulfil parents' cherished ambitions (Sennett and Cobb, 1966). The theme of parents hurt by the individualism of their children has been recently supplanted by complaints on behalf of children hurt by the individualism of their parents, for example, Judith Wallerstein's conclusion, from her detailed research on divorce in the US, that parents are weakening their commitment to marriage and children with long-term ill effects on children's well-being.

Another version invokes a sliding scale of degeneracy into consumerism. For example, a rising standard of living across generations and ever more sophisticated media promotion of consumption heightens children's expectations of material well-being, regardless of parents' history or present circumstances. Parents brought up in less affluent times often experience this as children wanting too much or not appreciating what they have. Both parents and children are drawn into judgements of parental worth based on what parents provide for their children. Parents who feel children expect too much believe they are not being given enough credit for what their children have in contrast to their own childhood. Alternatively, parents who are bringing up children in less favourable circumstances than their own childhood may suffer an acute sense of failure. The British social commentator Jeremy Seabrook (1982) suggests that working-class parents and children judge the quality of their relationship by the flow of expensive consumer goods from parent to child. He suggests that working-class parents are both particularly vulnerable to being unable to deliver the goods and simultaneously cut off from ways of demonstrating alternative values to their children since working-class self-help networks characteristic of times of general poverty have all but disappeared. Bauman (see the previous chapter) takes this argument to its logical conclusion when he suggests that consumerism – making statements to each other through consumer goods – replaces social interaction. A related theme is that parents, with white middle-class parents in the lead, stopped teaching their children anything much beyond self-interested ambition. Deverson and Lindsay, speaking of London in the 1970s, say of middle-class parents: 'The expectations are extremely high. . . . Offspring were frequently described as "a bright child", "a musical child" or a "scientific child". . . . there were few references to such attributes as politeness, good behaviour, friendliness and warm-heartedness' (1975, p. 111). Again this suggests a tendency towards self-interested instrumentalism dominating all relationships, ultimately emptying out the intimacy of the parent–child relationship.

A commonly identified problem of late modernity in conservative political rhetoric is a loss of parental authority. Parents can no longer rely on traditional authority (you obey because I am your God-ordained parent) but rather have to bargain, justifying restrictions and demands, negotiating acceptance and respect from their children. The loss of traditional authority is an intrinsic aspect of the package of change from 'pre-modern' to 'modern' and a corollary of greater intimacy between parents and children. Talcott Parsons identified this greater intimacy as the new basis for parental control. In his ideal-typical family mothers manipulate their children rationally and emotionally with their power resting in threats of withdrawal of love, rather than appeals to traditional authority. The loss of traditional authority is not the loss of parental control; authority rests on an alternative basis. For Anthony Giddens, the authority of parents who are striving to be democratic rests on their ability to defend their control 'in a principled fashion' (1992, p. 109). Giddens argues as follows:

> Can a relationship between a parent and young child be democratic? It can, and should be, in exactly the same sense as is true of a

> democratic political order. It is a right of the child, in other words,
> to be treated as a putative equal of the adult. Actions which cannot
> be negotiated directly with the child, because he or she is too young
> to grasp what is entailed, should be capable of counterfactual just-
> ification. [Although parents and children are not equals, parents
> will offer principled justification of their acts as if they were.] The
> presumption is that agreement could be reached, and trust sust-
> ained, if the child were sufficiently autonomous to be able to de-
> ploy arguments on an equal basis to the adult. (1992, p. 192)

Contemporary parents may play down the power they have vis-à-
vis their children but parents are still undoubtedly more powerful
than young children. Parents are superior in their physical strength,
control of resources, knowledge etc. (although their right to do as
they will with their children is now legally curtailed in numerous
ways, in all Euro-North American jurisdictions, as children's rights
have been strengthened). These sources of power can be used to
legitimate authority over children but are not taken for granted as
entitling parents to demand that children be deferential and 'know-
their-place' (Jamieson and Toynbee, 1990). Sealey et al. were among
the first to claim that they were documenting a shift away from deferential parent–child relationships among middle-class Canadian
families of the 1950s: 'These children are not led to believe there are
certain adult privileges which children cannot share' (1956, p. 207,
see also p. 167). A number of authors have suggested that this process has gone far beyond parents using their greater closeness to
children to exercise more subtle and psychological parental control
as suggested by Parsons. Rather it is argued that parents have come
to feel at the mercy of their children. The British family sociologist
Christopher Harris presents such an account.

'The domain assumption of modern child rearing: parents are responsible for the characters of their children, itself effectively deprives
them of the degree of control over their children which they need if
they are to discharge their responsibility' (Harris, 1983, p. 241). Children perceive their power in the situation and behave badly without
fully understanding the effects of their action: 'To give the child the
power to determine the self and social esteem of its parents, particularly its mother, is rather like giving a 5-year-old a loaded revolver'
(Harris, 1983, p. 242). Harris suggests that parents', and particularly
mothers', sense of responsibility for the characters of their children
in itself exacerbates the ever present possibility of parents and
children doing each other psychological damage. Primary carers,

perceiving their children's characters as a judgement on their own competence, are paralysed by self-doubt.

Research has to be detailed and substantial if it is to support or cast doubt on these various fears for the future of parent–child relationships. Parent–child relationships are not, in any case, expected to be static in any one lifetime; the relationship inevitably changes as children get older, grow up and leave home. However, research is typically a snapshot at one stage of the life-course and many more snapshots than are currently available in the literature are needed to piece together a detailed picture. This section draws on a number of relevant pieces of research which suggest future directions, but it has to be said that conclusions are very tentative and further work is needed. Empirical work focusing on parents and young children lends only qualified and limited support to the disempowered parents and mutually destructive power struggle between mother and infant which Harris and others suggest. Mothers who have lost a sense of themselves and feel at the mercy of their children do indeed exist (there are fewer such accounts of fathers) but so also do mothers who have enhanced their self-worth through motherhood. Ellen Lewin's US study of single mothers found such women:

> The intentional single mother (whether she is lesbian or heterosexual) can achieve a central personal goal – the goodness that comes from putting the needs of a dependent being first. By becoming a mother through her own agency, she avoids the central paradox that motherhood represents to married women – a loss of autonomy and therefore of basic personhood in a culture that valorizes individualism and autonomy. (1993, p. 73)

Kathryn Backett's study of middle-class British parenting (1982) focused on married couples with children under five. This study is sufficiently detailed to use as an evidential test of a number of fears expressed in the literature including the extent to which parents feel disempowered, their attitude to individualism and consumerism as well as the extent of their search for intimacy. All of the couples had decided that the mother should withdraw from the labour force while the children were young. These parents accepted responsibility for developing the character of their children and were seeking relationships with their children in which they would understand and enjoy each other. Their sense of responsibility, which in practice fell much more heavily on mothers than fathers, never threatened to crush them.

They protected themselves from feeling entirely responsible for their children's character by a number of devices: they noticed and felt themselves to be responding to, not creating, differences between their children; very badly behaved children were accounted for by the notion that 'it's just a stage'. Whatever any child-rearing manuals they had read might have said, these parents had a confidence in their own expert knowledge of their children gained through trial-and-error. As parents they were actively working with and against individualism, on the one hand recognizing that each member of the family was different with unique needs and on the other adhering strongly to a notion of 'fairness' in family life. This meant even-handed treatment of family members. (Although sometimes, as with divisions of labour between the couple, a sense of fairness was maintained despite inequality.) Parents took for granted their authority to make judgements about what was and what was not fair. And while parents had no sense of their children as their actual equals they were manipulating notions of equality through their rules of fairness. Patricia Allatt and Susan Yeandle (1992) have documented how these rules are applied in families with teenage children. Fairness provides a basis for moderating demands for consumer goods from older children as anything one person might want has to be balanced against the wants of others. The in-depth picture built up through Backett's repeated interviews with parents finds nothing to substantiate the pessimistic accounts of parent–child relationships being emptied of intimacy. Backett's parents are, at least while their children are young, confident that they have a happy, fair and close family life in which they know and understand their children. While their social practices are complex and sometimes contradictory they are successfully producing a blend of intimacy and an appearance of democracy. Allatt and Yeandle (1992) similarly find middle-class parents of teenage children managing this balance.

There are a small number of detailed studies of how contemporary parents exercise control over young children and manage the balance between intimacy and authority in their relationship.[10] British educationalists Valerie Walkerdine and Helen Lucey focused on these issues in their analysis of interaction between white middle-class and working-class mothers and their four-year-old daughters. They concluded that working-class mothers were more likely to make their power over the young child explicit, without detracting from the intimacy of mother and child. If a child demanded attention when a mother was busy, working-class mothers were more likely simply to tell their children 'they cannot have what they want, when they want it' (1989, p. 115). Most middle-class mothers on the other hand tried to generate a sense of power-sharing with their young daughters and to create space for their daughters to challenge their authority. However, the authors concluded that the appearance of democracy in these middle-class interactions was just an illusion: either mothers were successfully operating covert forms of control of their daughters or they were in fact sacrificing their own autonomy. The busy middle-class mother was more likely to try to live up to the model of 'the sensitive mother', who makes her housework the basis for children's educational play. When conflict arose that could not be diverted, 'the mother takes the lead role in trying to diffuse the conflict by setting whatever is the particular bone of contention up as a 'problem' which must be reasoned out' (1989, pp. 111–12). However, reasoning does not always work and trying to intellectualize strong emotions can go seriously wrong. Middle-class mothers often experienced an escalation of their daughters' expressions of violence and had to resort to ignoring their daughters. Working-class mothers on the other hand did not expect children to always be reasonable and hence were more likely to develop ways of allowing the safe venting of these emotions in their young daughters.

Walkerdine and Lucey explain class differences in terms of different life experiences and conditions of mothering. This is much more than having different amounts of money, time and resources to spend on and with their children, although these factors are very relevant. For example, the middle-class use of reasoning and intellectualizing of conflict is telling the child about what it means to be middle-class and in control of your life. Working-class parents do not encourage their children to have fantasies of autonomy and control because, for them at least, life is not like that. The authors provide a powerful reminder that material and social circumstances can neutralize or render irrelevant the public story of 'the sensitive mother' for actual mothers. Their critique of the pathologizing of working-class mothers and the valorizing of the sensitive mother also casts doubt on the desirability of a trend towards sensitive mothering on the one hand and democratic parenting on the other. They are at pains to point out the sleights of hand involved in pseudo democracy and the failures of so-called sensitive mothering in dealing with violence as well as some of the strengths of so-called pathological non-sensitive mothering.

Christine Everingham's (1994) Australian study of mothers and young children in play groups brings a different vantage point as she has observed mothers in public settings rather than at home. She found mothers who sometimes felt judged and humiliated by their children. Some, for example, felt humiliation at not being able to stop a child crying in public, as the 'good mother' understands and can meet the needs of the child. Everingham identifies two patterns of mother–child interaction in her data which she describes in very negative terms. In one negative pattern mothers over-identify with the child to the extent that they almost totally organize their life around the demands of the child. This is closest to the dynamic which Harris (1983) identifies as so psychologically dangerous for mothers and children. Everingham contrasts this group with a third positive pattern. This group of mothers are characterized as follows:

> more clearly able to distinguish two perspectives [their own and the child's] and co-ordinate these through a process of understanding. The mother was prepared to inconvenience herself somewhat, but within certain limits that were arrived at through weighing up competing demands. Nevertheless, there were also absolute limits set by the child, which the mother had to come to recognize and accommodate if she was to demonstrate the appropriate maternal attitude [in front] of the group. (1994, p. 86)

These mothers and children then have a mutual understanding in which both make and receive concessions in order to successfully negotiate each other's good behaviour in public.[11]

The other negative pattern was exemplified by a particular mother, characterized as failing to reach an understanding of or empathy with the child's point of view. In this pattern there is limited intimacy between parent and child, no real negotiation, only self-interested demands and reactions and the parent has very limited control over the child. Her child's routine bad behaviour is seen as a matching non-empathetic response to the mother's denouncements, threats and smacking. The negative patterns which Everingham describes echo the more pessimistic accounts of trends in parenting. However, the majority pattern among the observed mothers is of self-possessed, successfully loving, caring and understanding mothers.

Jane Ribbens's small British study (including 24 mothers whose oldest child was seven, and who lived in middle-income households in the south-east of England), on the other hand, suggests that only a minority of mothers and children achieve a mutually constructed understanding of each other. She linked the stories mothers told of what it means to be a child to the way mothers interacted with their children. She noted that three typifications of children – 'natural innocents', 'little devils' and 'little people' – were each associated with a particular maternal response. Mothers believed that they had to do the changing and adapting if 'natural innocents' were to be provided with the right environment for their 'natural' development. 'Little devils', on the other hand require direction and guidance with mothers having to 'keep their cool' and remain in charge. On the other hand 'little people' are negotiated with, requiring some give and take on both the mother's and the child's side. Ribbens clearly regards the typification of children as 'little people' as least damaging to mothers and children.

> Children's expressed desires and demands are generally regarded as legitimate (but not necessarily given priority, as with the typifications of children as natural innocents), but so are mothers' own needs and preferences. However, neither is there a conception of a pre-existing social order that children must learn to fit into before they overthrow it to the detriment of all (as with the typification of children as little devils). Instead, the emphasis is on the needs and demands of household members as individuals, with a requirement to treat the younger person's point of view with respect. (Ribbens, 1995, p. 72)

Although some mothers drew on all three typifications, Ribbens suggests that the 'little people' typification is the least deployed.

A number of British studies (Allatt and Yeandle, 1992; Brannen et al., 1994; Hutson and Jenkins, 1989) document the complex negotiations between parents and teenage children as they try to weigh the emerging independence and right to privacy of the teenage child against an adjusted intimacy and sense of parental responsibility for their actions. These qualitative studies show that the type and degree of intimacy between teenage or young adult children and their parents is highly variable. Feeling emotionally close to mothers is far more usual than with fathers. There is some evidence that young people who have left home as teenagers through such conventional routes as 'going to university' or taking up a job elsewhere felt they could talk more easily with their parents once they no longer needed to negotiate their independence within their parents' household (Jones, 1995).

Julie Brannen and her colleagues (1994) document the complex negotiations between London-based parents and their fifteen- and sixteen-year-old children. While many fathers were rather shadowy figures in young men's and young women's lives, mothers typically continued to seek a good relationship with their children. Mothers wanted their children to know they continued to love and care for them; a 'good relationship' for many mothers also meant knowing and understanding each other. However, 'knowing' took on different connotations in many middle-class households because communication was also a means of keeping open the possibility of control and influence. Communicating as a means of keeping tabs on the young person was not routinely deployed in working-class and certain ethnic minority homes. Children were expected to be adults at an earlier age in working-class households and once they were acknowledged as adults they had a right to lead their own lives without investigation. There was similarly no need to question children whose freedom was restricted by strict cultural and religious norms, as, for example, in the case of certain ethnic minorities. For such parents, 'there ought not, therefore, to be private practices for the young person to disclose or confess to' (1994, p. 194). Parents who were constantly on the look-out for information that would warn them of possible trouble were necessarily working against their cherished desire to really *know* their child. Knowing as a means of control interfered with knowing as a dimension of disclosing intimacy.

Many parents in this study, particularly middle-class parents, believed that they were very close to their teenage child. They stressed empathy and understanding, being able to 'talk', having 'listened' and 'tried to understand'.

INTERVIEWER: How does your relationship with Emma compare with your relationship with your own mother?

MOTHER: I would think it is closer. I would hope so . . . it's a very close relationship and one where most things we can talk about. (Brannen, 1994, p. 62)

FATHER: Andrea is much better off . . . I think we do have a reasonable relationship . . . I have deliberately . . . listened to her and tried to understand . . . and given her that bedrock that I felt that I didn't have . . . of a dad you could talk to and maybe confide in . . . (Brannen, 1994, p. 63)

Brannen et al. spoke to teenage children as well as their parents. They found that what parents consider to be a 'confiding' relationship was experienced as one-sided pressure to make disclosures by the teenager. Mothers who were attempting to retain some control over their teenager while being like a friend and equal, could not conceal their precarious balancing act. Moreover, it is not clear that young people always wanted or expected to 'be pals' with their parents. For many their parents were taken-for-granted background support rather than foreground friends and confidantes.

This empirical work discussed here does not exhaust all relevant studies but is sufficient to illustrate that the pessimistic views of parent–child relationships in 'postmodernity' are over-simplistic. They also illustrate the complexities of intimacy between parents and children. The emphasis on achieving independence and autonomy in youth, which may be particularly acute in British–North American cultures makes negotiation increasingly delicate. 'Treating home like a cheap hotel' is a standing joke in many households reflecting the tension created by the young person's need for autonomy and independence combined with material barriers against young people establishing their own household. Parents or children who feel used or abused by the other or are indifferent to each other are not the norm. While there is considerable variation in the texture of the quality of parent–child relationships, the overall picture is not yet one of crisis. At the same time, the empirical evidence does not suggest that 'disclosing intimacy' is the dominant mode of parent–child interaction, (even when children are young adults) nor that it is the likely future. The data do not substantiate British sociologist Anthony Giddens's vision of parent–child relationships veering towards the pure relationship of friendships. The suspension of power relationship suggested in his image of democratic parenting is extraordinarily abstracted from the material inequalities between an actual adult and a young child. Empirical work suggests parents pursue divergent control strategies and have different degrees of interest in exploring democratic parenting (Brannen et al., 1994; Everingham, 1994, Walkerdine and Lucey, 1989). One of the most detailed studies of apparently democratic parenting suggests that it is (like many political democracies, perhaps) a sleight of hand covering the exercise of power (Walkerdine and Lucey, 1989). Nor do the broad-brush pictures of damage caused by rampant individualism and consumerism withstand detailed scrutiny through empirical work. Many working-class parents continue to tell their children without embarrassment that they cannot always get what they want, while middle-class parents strive to pseudo-democratically modify their children's demands through appeals to fairness.

Clearly there are parents and children who are trapped in negative, damaging dynamics. The absent intimacy and over-intimacy of Everingham's non-empathetic and over-empathetic mothers may be examples. The mother who over-identifies with her child and cannot distinguish her own and the child's needs can be seen as an inevitable occasional outcome of the story of 'the sensitive mother'. If the idealized image and the norm most people strive for is close parent–child relationships then over-identification, stifling a child's autonomy, is a likely form of excess – just as excessive exploitation of children for economic gain was a danger when children were generally regarded and valued as economic assets. Extreme cases of the psychological damage mothers could do to children by stifling intimacy were documented by the psychiatrist R. D. Laing before the label 'postmodern' became fashionable. While Laing documented the damage inflicted on children, the sociologist Christopher Harris focused on the damage done to mothers by over-identification with their children. Both seemed to suggest that the casualties were no longer the exception. Most empirical studies, however, suggest that parents and children locked in self-damaging intimacy are not the norm. Complaints of not being particularly close are more common in the literature on teenage children than feeling stifled. Parents and children have to negotiate the child's transition to independent adult. Young people's needs for autonomy and privacy conflict with disclosing intimacy. In the late twentieth century, expectations of achieving some measure of adult independence by the late teens and early twenties coincide with conditions prolonging young people's dependence on their parents. This often results in an extended period in which young people withdraw into the privacy of their own rooms, if they have them. A sense that co-residence is due to lack of alternatives does nothing to enhance the quality of the parent–child relationship. Tension and breakdown in parent–child relationships and subsequent youth homelessness are more likely in poorly resourced households in which parents feel compelled to make heavy demands on young people while offering them little space and autonomy in return (Jones, 1995).

CHAPTER 4

Are Good Friends All You Need?

This chapter is in two sections. It is possible to see kin and friends as similar types of relationships. They are personal relationships which connect people to others beyond their parents, partners, and immediate family household. Kin and friends together are seen as potentially constitutive of a 'community' of people bound by shared sentiments. However, it is also very common to pose them as different categories of relationship, the latter voluntary and achieved, the former obligatory and ascribed. The history of personal life implicit in some writing about kin and friendship speaks of a shift from 'community' to 'intimacy'. In keeping with this view, there is a tendency in sociological literature to juxtapose working-class kinship and community to middle-class friendship and intimacy. These views of the relationship between friendship, kinship, class and intimacy are scrutinized in the first section of the chapter by reviewing the relevant research. The second section deals with gender, heterosexuality and friendship. A common theme of the sociological research literature is that men are less intimate than women. Men are also sometimes depicted as disrupting intimacy between women. Again the relevant research literature is reviewed. Each of these areas of debate has considerable significance for the thesis that 'disclosing intimacy' is becoming a key dimension of personal life: gender and class differences should be diminishing and if 'intimacy' and 'community' are different principles, intimacy should prevail.

Friends, Kin and Intimacy

There are two main stories about the 'modern' juxtapositioning of friends and kin. One is that both friends and kin (other than the immediate family household) have become less important in adult personal life. The other is that friendship is increasingly valued and kin relationships only equal friendships when kin become friends.

One version of the fate of friendship in the shift from 'premodern' to 'modern' is that, as the family household founded by a heterosexual couple became a private, emotionally intense unit, then friendships and relationships with wider kin became relatively devalued in contrast to the partnership of the couple and the bonds of parenting. This version is consistent with the conventional view of the emergence of 'the modern family' discussed in chapter 2. In this account friends and kin are sited in a wider community which diminished in significance as individuals withdrew into the intimacy of their family home. This telling of history is consistent with an analysis of contemporary friendships as only having significance at exceptional transitional stages of personal life, such as when a partner has not yet been found or has been lost (Rawlins, 1992). In the 1950s and 60s Talcott Parsons claimed that peer friendships were particularly important in young people's lives as they provided psychological support in a transitional growing-up stage of the life cycle. He implied that the possibility of continuing to use peer friendships as a main source of psychological support is closed down as peers increasingly become absorbed in marriage arrangements.

More radical historians have also supported the thesis that the ascendancy of the intimate couple coincided with the diminishing of friendship as a social relationship of significance. It has been argued that the historical emergence of the loving heterosexual married couple as the key relationship in personal life coincided with the creation of a stigmatized category of homosexual person. Consequently, expressive, devoted and romantic friendships between adults were sexualized and, in the case of same-sex romantic friendships, pathologized in a way that was previously unknown.[1]

In direct opposition to the notion that adult friendship was (at least temporarily) devalued in the modern period, is the view that the intimacy of friendship was *heightened* along with the heightening in intimacy between couples, and parents and children. In this story, friendship relationships are not located as part of a wider community which is withering away, but rather are restructured into voluntaristic and altruistic bonds of 'disclosing intimacy'. This is the result of a heightened search for self-expression and disclosing intimacy in all personal relationships. For a number of contemporary authors this is a late twentieth-century phenomenon but the eighteenth-century philosophers of the Scottish Enlightenment saw intimate friendship as a 'modern' pattern emerging in their time (Silver, 1996). These eighteenth-century thinkers (David Hume, 1711–76, Adam Ferguson 1723–1816 and Adam Smith 1723–90) drew a sharp distinction between pre-modern friendship which was typically and necessarily bound up with self-interest and the modern friendship untainted by such concerns. The pre-modern friendship of necessity was always precarious and liable to fluctuate when fortunes and interests shifted. Hence maxims such as 'Live with your friend as with one who may become an enemy' (a maxim reflected on by Adam Ferguson, quoted in Silver) were once good advice. For Adam Smith such friendships were summed up by the Roman expression *necessitudo*: friendships imposed by the necessity of the situation (Smith, 1759).

Adam Smith believed that, prior to the development of the impersonal markets of commercial society and the impersonal administration of legal-rational bureaucracies, all friendships tended to have this character of necessity. It was only with the separation of commercial relations and personal life that friendship could become a matter of sympathy and affection devoid of calculation of interest. In Smith's view, the possibility of acting without self-interest, altruistically, towards friends, creates a form of moral integration and tolerance of others outside of the calculations of the world of commerce. When personal life had been relieved of the need for calculation, acts of kindness were seen as adding to the general civic good from which everyone benefited. 'No benevolent man ever lost the fruits of his benevolence. If he does not gather them from the persons from whom he ought to have gathered them, he seldom fails to gather them, and with a ten-fold increase, from other people' (Smith, 1759, p. 225, quoted in Silver, 1996). Not only was a new kind of friendship possible but also a new kind of stranger; to be not-a-friend was now to be a neutral and indifferent stranger rather than a dangerous individual who was potentially friend or enemy.

The contemporary sociologist Zygmunt Bauman offers a related but much less comforting description of modernity's positioning of friend–enemy–stranger (1990). Bauman, like the eighteenth-century Scottish philosophers, links the fate of friendship to the well-being of social integration and moral cohesion which is often summed up as 'community'. Following the turn-of-the-century theorist Georg Simmel (1858–1918), he sees the social process of friends uniting against enemies as a basic constituent of all societies. In this analysis, friends' sense of moral responsibility towards each other, reinforced by a shared lack of moral responsibility towards their enemies, is an integrative fabric of society. Friends hang together and maintain their moral responsibility because of the enemy. 'If not for the opposition between friend and enemy, none of this would be possible. Without the possibility of breaking the bond of responsibility, no responsibility would impress itself as a duty. If not for the enemies, there would be no friends' (Bauman, 1990, p. 145). In any social world, the stranger disturbs the classification of friends and enemies. However there are vast numbers of strangers in modern urban environments in contrast to the few and, therefore, more easily reclassified strangers encountered in pre-modern, small-scale communities. Unlike Smith, Bauman does not accept that the tendency to re-categorize strangers as friends or enemies has been abandoned in modern societies. He does not see any pre-modern or modern disjuncture between self-interested friendships of necessity and friendships of sympathy, affection, and altruism. For Bauman, moral responsibility and self-interest are both encapsulated within friendship and intrinsic to its maintenance: without a sense of mutual moral responsibility, co-operation and exchange could not be sustained, and co-operation and exchange are matters of mutual self-interest. Because Bauman continues to consider friends as constructing themselves in opposition to enemies, strangers remain disruptive until they have been re-categorized as friends or foes. He argues that all modern nation states adopt strategies to eradicate strangers and to force its remaining subjects to be as-if-they-were-friends. Strategies have ranged from state-endorsed genocide, murder and torture to subtle manipulation of the conditions of citizenship and the ideology of nationalism. Success is always only partial, however, with some proportion of people feeling no common cause with others of their nation-state. There is an implication that the more strenuous the efforts to mass manufacture friendship, the more empty everyday friendships may become. Like other pessimistic commentators on recent social change, Bauman sees intimacy as in constant danger of becoming 'emptied out' and all personal relationships devalued. Such commentators anticipate that friendships and partnerships are equally frail, superficial and demoralized.

Some more optimistic commentators on recent social change, see friendship as expressing a form of intimacy which supplants the social integrative work of 'community'. In the late twentieth century, the idea that 'good friends are all you need' has had a number of advocates. However, not all have seen friendship as a different principle to that of the creation of community. The North American and European women's movement of the 1970s called on women to lead more friendship-centred and women-centred personal lives. As feminist analysis increasingly exposed male dominance and gender inequalities in heterosexual coupledom, for women to direct emotional time and energy into a heterosexual couple was declared less desirable than women-centred friendships. Friendship was not idealized as a dyadic and individualistic enterprise but rather as 'sisterhood' emerging from women working co-operatively against aspects of male oppression. For those who were involved in the struggles of that movement, something like 'sisterhood' was sometimes achieved and sometimes illusive in practice. By the 1990s, due to combinations of success, more sophisticated analysis, and the more complex and conservative political climates, the women's movement and the concept of 'sisterhood' are no longer aspects of the political scene, although feminism is a permanent feature. The ideals of sisterhood were a very different form of friendship from that discussed by optimistic commentators of the late twentieth century, including the analysis of intimacy of Anthony Giddens. Giddens's account suggests that people seek to maintain happiness and stability through discrete, one-to-one, good relationships rather than integration into a cohesive interconnected moral and social world. Friendship is the model of the good relationship ('the pure relationship') and ideal parent–child and partner relationships are characterized as being like friendships. As in the vision of the women's movement, for Giddens, this coincides with less channelling of women into marriage and heterosexuality, which are losing their dominance as the ideal way of organizing intimacy. Women and men are freer to choose when and how to have intimate relationships.

The key issues raised in these different versions of social change are examined further in this chapter. Some are partly theoretical issues but many can only be clarified by looking at the empirical evidence offered by studies of friendship. Was it correct to characterize friendships as part of a withering community or did a new form of friendship blossom with modernity? To what extent are contemporary friendships bonds strengthened by a sense of the enemy? What, in modern societies, is the balance between self-interested friendships of necessity and relationships entered into only for the relationships' sake? Where now lies the balance of key intimate relationships in people's adult lives, in the family-household, in wider kin or in friendship? Is there still a strong contrast between the significance of same-sex friends in childhood and their attenuated significance in adulthood? What are the current gender differences in friendship and are they (still) implicated in gender inequalities? Is it possible to speak of convergence in style of intimacy between friendship, coupledom and parenthood?

Withering community or flourishing friendship?

Sociological and social historical interest in community studies is long-standing. The nineteenth-century intellectual founders of sociology, Karl Marx, 1818–83, Emile Durkheim, 1858–1917, Georg Simmel, 1858–1918 and Max Weber, 1864–1920, were all concerned with the ways in which the development of industrial capitalist societies transformed the basis of social relationships. While the theories they offered were never as simple as 'modernity destroys community', for a brief period of the history of sociology, in the 1950s and 1960s, this death of community thesis became something of an orthodoxy, although there were always dissenting voices. In this orthodoxy, a sense of belonging to, and being one with, the people of a particular locality, united by ties of neighbourliness, kinship and friendship, was an experience of a relatively homogeneous, premodern or traditional society, which was incompatible with complex modern society, except in remote rural or highly traditional backwaters. The demands of geographic and social mobility combined with the preference for private family-based personal life were considered to be incompatible with strong community ties. The death of community thesis became part of a conservative rhetoric which contrasted a rosy past in which everybody helped and was friendly to everybody with an unpleasant selfish present. Few scholars subscribe to this simple 'bad present' versus 'good past' view of the world but some nevertheless accept a 'death of community' has occurred. As Graham Crow and Graham Allan put it 'Intimacy implies a degree of intensity and uniqueness which it would not be possible to sustain with all members of a community, because intimacy and community imply different principles' (1995a, p. 10).

Careful historical scholarship in North America and Europe has unpicked components of this story of progressive community decline, finding threads woven from false premises.[2] Part of the mistake of the 'modernity destroys community' version of social change is due to a distorted picture of the communities of the past. For example it has been demonstrated that geographical mobility was a feature of pre-industrial life. Hence, the disruption of communities through work migration is not a uniquely modern phenomenon. Maintaining ties over distance was not absent from former times, even although modern forms of transport and communication make this much easier now. Also it is now clear that there has never been an idyllic time in which extended families and friendly neighbours typically looked after each other and overflowed with mutual kindness. Brutalized, uncaring, suspicious and indifferent relationships were a feature of the past as well as the present and circumstances of necessity sometimes worked against looking after others. For example, the old were not more likely to be cared for by kin in the past. In the nineteenth century many elderly people spent their last days in institutions (Anderson, 1980). Finch (1989) demonstrates that a sense of obligation to others has always been contingent on economic circumstances and quality of relationships.

Many of the community studies of the 1950s and 1960s focused on homogeneous working-class communities, assuming that they represented a long-standing way of life. These communities were often centred around particular heavy industries in localities where local employers hired a relatively undifferentiated (in terms of pay and conditions) male workforce long enough to support a stable population of locally housed workers and their families over two or more generations. Images of 'traditional' working-class communities have contributed to the legend of a past in which people were more willing to help each other. The detailed documentation of community studies reveals a less rosy and more complicated picture. The co-operation and trust people showed each other often stemmed from undesirable social conditions; sharing the same insecurities and the same lack of alternatives, all equally isolated from help or resources outside the locality (Bulmer, 1986, pp. 92–3; Keller, 1968, p. 116). Trust and co-operation could often break down. There are always limits to the extent to which people will help others (Finch, 1989). Even in such 'traditional' working-class communities there were (as there still are) people who fell or were pushed through the close-knit net (Ross, 1983; Stack, 1975). Moreover, people routinely maintained some social distance and privacy. While very elderly people have been able to say of their childhood home that 'the door was always open' further questioning typically reveals quite definite protocols concerning who was able to walk in and when (Jamieson, 1983). Studies also indicate concern to keep some distance from neighbours, for fear of gossip and nosiness.

Close-knit stable communities in which people can trace their roots for several generations and in which kin, friends, neighbours and workmates overlap do still exist, although they are not where most people live now, nor is this how most people lived in the past. Factors which structure opportunities for mobility, such as labour markets, housing markets, state housing policies, state income support, education and welfare provisions and racial discrimination, can operate to create populations tied to a particular locality. Claude Fischer, writing of the USA in the late twentieth century, suggests that some conditions conducive to tying populations to particular localities are more favourable than at the beginning of the century: geographic mobility has declined as home ownership has increased, and neighbourhoods have become more homogeneous in terms of the characteristics of their residents. Yet, at the same time, other factors make many people spend less time locally, as commuting distances have increased, and women, as well as men, leave family-households for employment, encouraging work-based rather than community-based friendships (Fischer, 1991).

Contemporary studies of particular places continue to find people for whom being a local is an important self-defining characteristic, involving some sense of moral responsibility for or common cause with other locals (Albrow et al., 1994; Wallman, 1986; Wight, 1993b). Such people feel part of a clearly delimited community. Their communality with other 'insiders' is often sharpened by the 'outsider'. (In Bauman's terminology they are friends defined by their enemies.) Nevertheless, this same research does not clearly confirm the view that 'community' and 'intimacy' are contradictory principles. People's sense of community does not necessarily override the valuing of intimacy. For example, the type of relationships which are most valued by 'locals' who feel part of a community are not necessarily markedly different from those who feel no such sense of community. For the majority of people, wherever they live, including 'the community local', their main sociability is with an inner circle of friends and kin. The 'local' does not share his or herself equally with all other self-defined locals. Their general sense of moral responsibility to the community may be rarely put to the test and their community spirit may involve little daily effort beyond friendly exchanges of pleasantries and a carefulness not to offend others who may remain neighbours for life. The many people who do not live in such close-knit situations where most people know each other, nevertheless typically have considerable contact with their own personal set of friends and kin. 'Urbanism may engender public estrangement but not private estrangement' (Fischer, 1982, p. 260). It is not clear that the friendships of urbanites are constructed on any different principle to those of rural or small-town locals. There is no evidence that the rise of intimate friendships is contingent on the demise of community because in this century at least, in some localities the two can and do coexist.

The overstated isolation of the nuclear family?

The view that kinship, neighbouring and friendship relations withered as the emotionally intense family-household became the key site of intimacy in adult lives was subjected to considerable critical modification in the 1960s. Within sociology, the most attacked version of this theory was that of Talcott Parsons. As soon as Talcott Parsons defined the nuclear family-household as having become relatively isolated from wider kin and community relations, so there developed an industry of researchers demonstrating the continued significance of kin, friends and neighbours in modern society. However, these critics were generally working within the same assumptions as Talcott Parsons. They accepted that the family-household was an adult's first and main source of emotional solace and that the encapsulation of emotional life in the family-household was a prerequisite for healthy individuals and an efficient society. However, they argued that two adults were not enough for each other and that, particularly in times of rapid social change, even smoothly functioning family-households needed occasional back-up and social support from the outside. Kin, neighbours and friends were found to be of continuing importance in people's lives and were theorized as supplements to close family relationships (Litwak and Szelenyi, 1969).

The question of whether friends and non-immediate kin are relationships secondary to those of immediate family is folded into a debate about who will voluntarily do what for whom and the nature of altruism. Researchers in the 1960s and 70s tried to map out the circumstances in which each category – kin, friends or neighbours – was utilized. It was found that kin were often the first line of help when major assistance was needed. Neighbours were more likely to be used for relatively minor types of help and immediate assistance. It was as if more could be asked of friends and kin than neighbours. It was also assumed that friends were substituted for kin and hence more likely to play the key role in the case of those who were distanced from kin by geographic or social mobility. Studies also showed that women often did more of the work of maintaining kinship and neighbouring relationships than men and this was seen as an extension of their responsibility for the emotional well-being of the household. The implicit ranking in significance of neighbours, friends and kin was partly supported by studies of who did what for whom, but it also emerged from the theoretical frameworks of functionalism and exchange theory dominant in this period. The main guiding question of a functionalist analysis was 'what are kin and friends doing which helps the functioning of society or some sub-system (like the family) of the society?' The guiding question of exchange theory was 'what do people gain from each other?' as all personal relationships were viewed as a process of bargaining and more or less consciously self-interested calculation. For exchange theorists, social life was structured by what Alvin Gouldner (1960) called a general norm of reciprocity: if somebody is good to you then you should be good to them. The perceived differences between what is asked of neighbours, friends and kin was theoretically understood in terms of different permissible degrees of licence with the norms of reciprocity. Giving without any direct return was explained as 'diffuse' or 'indirect' reciprocity (Sahlins, 1965), that is giving (like Adam Smith's benevolent man) in the knowledge that some good will come back indirectly or in the future. From this perspective, kin relationships were regarded as the most able to survive departures from direct reciprocity because of strong social support; there are cultural expectations that kinships are lifelong relationships in which people should help each other, just as there are social sanctions, such as ostracism and disinheritance, if the norms are not followed.

The eighteenth century Scottish Enlightenment authors saw altruistic relationships ('diffuse reciprocity') as a new and general feature of their society which was not restricted to kinship or to the activities of women. Studies of the late twentieth century demonstrate that altruistic relationships are a feature of a wider variety of social context than women's kinship relationships. Detailed ethnographic studies of friendship often reveal non-reciprocal relationships. Dorothy Jerrome's study of the friendships of the elderly provides documentation of continued friendship when ill health and the onset of death render reciprocity impossible.

> The fact is that periods of ill-health come and go, just as friendships wax and wane; that the balance of reciprocity is disturbed but the relationships survive; that friendship networks are often active and extensive until extreme old age, reduced finally by death rather than escalating demands for support which friends feel unable to meet . . . when the very old are near death and cannot reciprocate, friendship is bestowed as a gift. Its acceptance by the dying partner is highly gratifying to the remaining one. The rules of friendship, indeed, require that the frail person accepts help and advice when it is offered, even when this involves an imbalance. Friendship requires the demonstration of concern through the giving of advice and support, particularly in times of need when the possibilities of reciprocation are limited. (Jerrome, 1992, p. 109)

Jerrome studied elderly women and men in an English seaside town. In a very different context, that of a cafeteria on the edge of a rundown black neighbourhood of Chicago, Mitchell Duneier documented the development of consistent, unsolicited and unreciprocated assistance given by working-class black men, the regular customers of the cafeteria, not only to each other but also to an older friendless single white man (1992). Such studies suggest that the primacy of the nuclear family-household has indeed been overstated and the possibilities of altruism beyond the family and kinship have been understated.

The balance of friends and kin, exclusivity and 'community' in social networks

The theoretical traditions of functionalism and exchange theory no longer influence researchers to the same degree. Moreover, researchers now prefer the term 'social network' to 'community' (Bulmer, 1987; Crow and Allan, 1994; Fischer, 1982). The concept of 'social network' allows recognition that important personal relationships may not be gathered together in one place while recognizing that the significance and meaning of any type of intimate relationship, such as friendships, can best be understood by looking at the totality of people's intimate relationships (Allan, 1979, 1989). There is no assumption that those who make up a person's social network will be interconnected in the way that social groups are; they may never meet or even know of each other's existence. One of the largest recent comparative studies of patterns of social networks in contemporary industrial societies was conducted in the USA and based on interviews with over a thousand adults in fifty sampled localities (Fischer, 1982). This study confirms that US citizens as a whole remain embedded in networks of supportive relationships, but the balance between friends and kin varies between urban and non-urban areas. While urban and less urban respondents listed roughly the same number of social ties and had similar quality of relationships, the composition of their networks varied markedly. 'Small-town respondents tended to be more involved with relatives, city respondents with non-kin,' (Fischer, 1982, p. 258). Urbanism seemed to similarly discourage involvement with neighbours. Fischer argues that the population concentration of urbanism allows choice so that 'just friends' predominate. This is so whether or not people have kin nearby because urban life provides alternatives to relatives and neighbours. The greater selectivity in urban areas also results in greater specialization in relationships. In rural settings, relationships are more likely to carry a range of ways in which people do things for each other and spend time together. British community studies have used the label 'multiplex' to describe this aspect of rural relationships (Bell and Newby, 1976). Urban settings provide more possibilities for creating social networks made up from separate and unconnected social worlds.

Could Fischer's study suggest a contrast between the urban and rural area not only in the balance between kinship and friendship but also in the dominance of the principle of community versus intimacy? Rural residents are not typically strangers to each other. They know something of each other's history and business and cannot avoid awareness of both past and possible future connections between themselves and others that they meet. Graham Allan and Graham Crow suggest that the sense of general connection to others, community or communion, which inevitably develops in such a setting, inhibits forming exclusive private intimate relationships. Fischer suggests that this is not so, but rather that such private, intimate relationships are largely limited to kin because kin make up a large proportion of the immediate social world. While it is true that sometimes exclusive friendships work against more general friendliness, a phenomenon documented in English 'friendship clubs' for the elderly (Jerrome, 1992), rural dwellers maintain both private exclusive intimacy and general 'community' friendliness. Urban residents, on the other hand, are less likely to participate in any general 'community' friendliness. Rather than having a sense of a single 'community', most move between unconnected social worlds. While membership of an urban small club or activity group might have something of the feel of being known characteristic of a rural community, it is qualitatively different as it can never be as all-encompassing. Many urban social worlds lack even this quality, as they have no clear boundaries or membership. It is possible to read Fischer as turning the conventional story of social change on its head. It is not that friends have been substituted for kin as people left their kin behind, but rather the lack of alternatives makes kin a substitute for friends in rural settings. If you have to make do when choosing your intimates then nearby kin are an obvious pool from which to choose; the fact of kinship provides additional reason for doing your best to get on with them. This fits with Janet Finch's (1989) observation that kinship ties themselves have always contained an element of selectivity. In other words, it is not the case that once upon a time people gave unqualified automatic loyalty to kin and that this has been eroded by late modernity; relationships with kin were always qualified by personal preference.

An opposition between friendship and community has also been suggested by the way in which modern friendship is characterized in some recent writing. Theorists such as Giddens portray the essence of modern friendship as a private, dyadic and idiosyncratic intimacy, terms which suggest something very different from the socially integrative qualities implied by the concept of 'community'. It has already been noted that the integrative qualities suggested by the notion of community may be overstated: belonging to a 'community' is more a state of mind than a different way of organizing personal life and this belonging can co-exist with private exclusive intimate relationships. The 'something clicking' (Willmott, 1987) of friendship, the valuing of the other person for whatever is perceived as their unique and pleasing qualities, has been identified as a key defining characteristic of the strength of friendship (Wright, 1978). For some authors, friendship is raised above all other relationships as the essence of modern personal life. Alan Silver expounds this position.

In modern culture, the 'essence' of the personal is found, not in formal roles and obligations, but in subjective definitions of the situation. Not normatively constituted by public roles and obligations – indeed often constituted in distinction from them – friendship is, in formal terms, the 'purest' and most widely available instance of personal relations in this sense. Spouses, lovers, kin, and colleagues are friends to the extent that they treat the objective conditions of their bond as collateral or inessential. Friendship, as a continuous creation of personal will and choice, is ungoverned by the structural definitions that bear on family and kinship. . . . It is an ideal arena for that individualized conception of personal agency central to modern notions of personal freedom. Normatively, friendship is grounded in the unique and irreplaceable qualities of partners, defined and valued independently of their place in public systems of kinship, power, utility and esteem, and of any publicly defined status. (Silver, 1996)

Research into friendship confirms that this version of friendship is a widely held ideal, but some research shows that in practice there is not a sharp distinction between friendship and other types of kin and community relationship. Actual friendships are often closer to stereotypes of kin and community relationships (for example, based on mutual obligation, kept within careful predefined boundaries) than to the ideal of friendship.

A research focus on people's ideals and expectations may have exaggerated the degree of mutual self-disclosure, 'disclosing intimacy' in contemporary friendships. All research into what friends mean to people stresses the voluntary rather than the obligatory character of friendship (Allan, 1989; Lazarsfeld and Merton, 1954; O'Connor, 1992) The content of that relationship is often described as expressive and diffuse rather than instrumental and specific. However, studies also reveal a more complicated picture in how people behave towards each other as friends. Some people define friendship very narrowly. For example, in his study of couples living in London, Peter Wilmott encountered a few men who defined a friend simply as 'someone you can meet for a drink' (1987, p. 98). In general, however, his respondents talked of a range of characteristics some of which demonstrate a search for intimacy and enjoyment of the other's unique qualities, and some suggesting a more instrumental concern with what friends can do for you. 'The respondents in our survey saw the key characteristics of friends as their reliability as sources of help, their trustworthiness, their respect for privacy and readiness to act as confidantes, and the pleasure they gave as companions' (Willmott, 1987, p. 94). This mix of attributes might equally well be applied to good kin or neighbours. Studies which look more closely at how friends interact suggest a reluctance to put ideals of friendship to the test. For example, Pat O'Connor interviewed women in London who talked of friends with whom they could discuss anything but with whom they rarely spoke (O'Connor, 1992). This is not to diminish the symbolic significance of these friendships in women's lives. Such friends continue to provide each other with a sense of security despite little contact. Janet Finch's and Jennifer Mason's (Finch and Mason 1993; Finch, 1989) research on kinship in Britain indicates that believing kin will rally round in a crisis similarly gives people a sense of security despite the fact that the same people make very selective use of their kinship network, often going to considerable lengths to avoid asking for help. Much of the literature on friendships concentrates on dyads. However, larger friendship groups are typically self-conscious of their collective identity and see themselves as sharing common interests and responsibility to each other akin to the stereotype of community relationships. Mitchell Duneier's description of the sense of mutual responsibility demonstrated by the working-class black men who gather around 'Slim's table' in the Valois Cafeteria is an example (1992). Dorothy Jerrome's discussion of a group of eleven women friends is another example (Jerrome, 1984). Friendships at the end of the century are a much more mixed bag in practice than the ideal of the 'pure relationship', despite the pervasiveness of that ideal.

Working-class friendships of necessity versus middle-class pure intimacy?

The defining characteristics of friendship articulated by Willmott's respondents included friends' willingness to give assistance as well as disclosing intimacy. The fact that respondents emphasized both the moral obligations friends have to help each other and the importance of intimacy suggests these are seen as complementary rather than contradictory principles. When people speak hypothetically about how friendship should be, 'true', 'good' or 'best' friends are not 'fair weather friends' who disappear when you need help, but, at the same time, the relationship is assumed to have more to its history than mutual necessity. Nevertheless, studies of the practice of friendship indicate that help and advice play a bigger part in some working-class friendships, suggesting people with fewer resources may be drawn into relationships of necessity.

Oversimplifying somewhat, studies of the 1950s, 1960s and 1970s suggested that working-class lives were more dominated by kin than were average middle-class lives. While clearly it is not always the case that kin relationships are relationships of necessity and friend-ship relationships are relationships of choice and intimacy, this crudely fits urban patterns of gendered class difference in this period. Among married couples, working-class women's and men's social networks were more segregated than middle-class women's and men's, with working-class women's lives more dominated by kin than men's. Basically, working-class women's main sources of support were female kin while men's main sources of support were male friends.[3] This was a corollary of the traditional division of la-bour between husbands and wives and the gender-segregated worlds inhabited by men and women. In British working-class commu-nities like cockney London, assistance from her mother and some-times also her mother-in-law provided the core relationship in a young married working-class woman's social network (Ross, 1983). In poor black neighbourhoods of the USA the core focus is a cluster of co-operating female adults who are either kin or who speak of themselves as if they were sisters (Stack, 1975). In both examples, woman-to-woman relationships were closer and more co-operative than that of the woman and her male partner (if she had one). At the same time these close relationships between women were relation-ships of necessity. Young and Willmott talked of women forming a 'trade union' (1973). Ross (1983) has used the more appropriate term of 'self help networks.' For these women, a friendship of 'disclosing intimacy' was a luxury which never flourished or was squeezed out by the responsibilities of wife and mother. 'I don't see my best friend much. She's married too, and she's always round her Mum's like I'm always round mine.' 'Since we've had the children I've got no more friends – outside the family I mean' (Young and Willmott, 1957).

Friendships of necessity have to manage the tension created by the necessity. The more dependent that people are on each other, through trying to survive, the fewer resources available to them to be shared around, the higher the tension and fear of being let down. Stack (1975), documenting the relationships of poor black people in 'the Flats' of a midwestern US town, talks of the distrust suffusing interpersonal relationships. In the white 'traditional' working-class communities in which men were employed in the same demanding jobs, co-operation and friendship of workmates were important to survival and men's networks were dominated by workmates. Men's friendships were conducted outside the house in the male-dominated public space of bar, pub or club. (Dennis et al., 1969; Kerr, 1958). Unfortunately, studies are not generally sufficiently detailed to document stresses and strains in these relationships.

According to British studies of the 1960s and early 70s, when working-class households were geographically mobile, both men and women became separated from these same-sex networks and hence the focus on their relationship to each other increased (Goldthorpe et al., 1969; Young and Willmott, 1973). This was the period in which sociologists talked of the 'privatized' life of the workers and hypothesized their absorption into the middle-class (Devine, 1992). Middle-class families who were geographically mobile (Willmott and Young, 1976) and people from working-class backgrounds who moved geographically (Young and Willmott, 1973) or socially (Bell, 1968) were depicted as either shifting their focus from kin to friends or becoming socially isolated.

> The common pattern it seems, is to belong to a small, intimate network of 'friends', mostly coming from the surrounding 20 or 30 houses, though some people, particularly in professional or managerial jobs, also have friends living further afield. The size of this local network varies – sometimes it is just a pair, sometimes three or four, sometimes 10 or 12, sometimes an even larger group. . . . This system, largely organised by the women, is the analogue to the 'extended family' of the East End. (Willmott and Young, 1976)

However, the new relationships were not obviously relationships of necessity like the female kin networks of the East End of London. Friends were not necessarily locked into networks of reciprocal assistance. And although kin were now far away they might still be called upon first for certain sorts of help. This certainly continued to be the case for geographically mobile middle-class families. Colin Bell (1968) showed that financial assistance for middle-class households frequently came from kin, primarily from father and father-in-law to son and son-in-law. In a more recent study in London, Peter Willmott confirms that most practical support for families comes from relatives – not friends – for both working-class and middle-class men and women: 'friends are more likely sources of companionship or emotional support' (Willmott, 1987, p. 102).

Graham Allan's 1970s British study documented differences in behaviour between working-class and middle-class couples despite the fact that they generally shared the same ideal of a 'true' or 'real' friend. However, it was not the case that working-class friendships were predominantly or exclusively relationships of necessity. The study demonstrated a pervasive ideal of a 'true' or 'real' friend for life who would always have some particular magic to share. However, working-class people were far less likely than middle-class couples to claim that they had true friends. Their pattern of seeing friends was also very different. Allan describes working-class friendships as 'context specific', that is, friendships are contained in one setting (the pub, the club, the mother-and-toddlers group, or wherever they meet each other) and do not typically enter the home. Entertainment at home is generally reserved for close kin. Middle-class couples on the other hand used entertainment at home to transcend the particular setting in which friends were first made and to further develop the relationship. This does not necessarily mean working-class friends were less intimate, however. While public places can be used to keep people at a distance this is not necessarily the case, just as taking people home does not always signify the greater intimacy of allowing them backstage, since home may also be carefully stage-managed. In a more recent study, Willmott (1987) found that middle-class Londoners have more friends but working-class people tend to see their fewer friends more often. Pat O'Connor (1992) suggests that studies should pay more attention to what people say to each other than where they meet or how many friends they have; the range of topics they cover and the depth of feeling expressed are more indicative of intimacy than the setting or number. On the basis of a rather small study, Karen Walker (1994) characterizes middle-class men as only having occasional intimate conversations with long-time friends, perhaps precipitated by crisis, in contrast with working-class men who see friends more frequently and are more in touch with each other's troubles. She argues that the more gender-segregated social lives of working-class people allow more opportunity for intimate conversation than a pattern of couple-dominated sociability. Despite such conclusions, class differences have generally been read as indicating that middle-class people have more intimate friendships than working-class people.

In his more recent text, Allan sees class differences primarily in terms of the time, energy and resources that people have to give to friendship, as a consequence of their position in the division of labour and the material and economic circumstances that go with this (1989, pp. 35–8). There is no clear evidence that working-class friendships remain more dominated by necessity or instrumental concerns. The phrase 'the old boy network' captures the use middle-class or upper-class men make of their friends to further their career or business interests, but such middle-class instrumental uses of friendship are under-studied. Friends are not typically the main source of material assistance for either class, as kin, and particularly parent–child relationships, continue to be a front-line source of practical, material and financial assistance. Nor is there clear evidence that middle-class friendships are more intimate. Gender-segregated, context-specific friendships can lack intimacy. For example, the expression 'locker-room talk' suggests a restricted and impoverished dialogue in some men's relationships. However, same-sex, context-specific relationships are not necessarily in this mould and can provide opportunities for intimacy. It may be that different types of intimacy are sustained by a more frequent interaction with a smaller number of friends, characteristic of working-class men and women, than an occasional soul baring which may be more typical of some middle-class friendships. These latter events may be classifiable as instances of 'disclosing intimacy' but their infrequency makes it questionable to suggest that these are intense relationships founded on disclosing intimacy. Working-class and middle-class adults share the same ideals of friendship but this may mean little in both cases. The reality of their relationships rarely matches the romantic story of 'true', 'real' and 'close' friends and it may be that the greater deprivations of their lives make working-class people more predisposed to acknowledge the gap.

Gender, Heterosexuality, Friendship and Intimacy

The second section of this chapter focuses on gender and friendship. If 'disclosing intimacy' or what Anthony Giddens calls 'the pure relationship' is increasingly sought in personal life, and if friendship is the relationship which is most likely to approximate to 'the pure relationship', then men as well as women should be seeking out such friendships. If gender differences are softening due to a 'transformation of intimacy' (Giddens, 1992) then differences between the types of friendships that men have and the types that women have should be eroding. Also the tendency for friendships to be restricted to same-sex friendships should similarly be diminishing. However the picture that emerges from the research literature provides no evidence of such trends. Rather it confirms that gender-segregated patterns of friendship are firmly established in childhood and presumptions around heterosexuality continue to render cross-gender friendships problematic.

Childhood, youth and friendship

Friendship is a major concern for children; they want to have friends and much of their interaction with their peers is focused on making and maintaining friendship (Medrich et al., 1982; Rizzo, 1989). Schooling sets children apart from adults in age-graded groups and in some conditions this shared context creates a sense of community. Children's classroom peers, like the workmates, kin or neighbours of adults, are both involuntarily bound up with each other and a source of chosen friends. Until recently, psychological research suggested that young children were more interested in playing with other children than in friendship as such. The psychologist Thomas Rizzo now suggests that concern with friendship, and the techniques of making and maintaining friends develop from a very early age. Elliot Medrich and his colleagues (1982) surveyed Californian children (sixth formers attending Oakland public elementary schools) and found that friendships were a virtually universal part of their lives. Solitary children were a tiny minority concentrated in the smaller ethnic groups set apart by language barriers and/or relatively extreme cultural differences. The average (median) number of close friends listed by children was three, with Afro-American children having a higher average than white children. One of the most striking features of children's friendships, which persists into adulthood, is the preponderance of same-sex friends over friends of the opposite sex. Friends are typically also from the same ethnic and class background. Even when children attend racially mixed schools where they share classrooms and playgrounds with children of different races and the opposite gender to themselves, close friendships with opposite-sexed children or children of a different ethnic or racial background to their own are rare (Hewitt, 1988; Schofield, 1981). It seems that children quickly learn to reproduce wider social divisions and inequalities.

Gender segregation in childhood friendships can be seen as more or less significant for adult patterns of intimacy. Some authors see childhood friendships as expressing a male or a female style of intimacy, building on psychological differences which are either genetic or socially shaped in the psychosexual development of early infancy.

Then childhood friendships, like parent–child relationships, are seen as laying a difficult-to-demolish foundation for styles of intimacy in adulthood. Psychological literature often suggests different styles of friendship among girls and boys: girls are more often found in small, intimate, communicative and co-operative groups or pairs and boys are found more often in large, hierarchical, activity-focused and competitive groups. Feminists typically interpret this work as describing learned rather than inherent differences. For example, the popular feminist writer Naomi Wolf denounces these differences as a cause of women's lesser power than men. 'Girls who do not play team sports learn that "alliance" is not teamwork, but closeness; that "leadership" is not skill but popularity. Girls do not learn from their societies what fairness or victory feel like. Instead, they learn what love feels like. The goal of their social organization is not trophy; it is inclusion' (Wolf, 1993, p. 289).

For some authors patterns of friendship in childhood are not the result of deep-seated psychological or psychoanalytic differences between men and women, but the conditions of gender inequality as they are experienced in childhood. Such an approach de-emphasizes inherent differences between men and women, boys and girls, but nevertheless paints a picture of cross-gender relations in childhood and youth which works against encouraging any form of mutual intimacy across the gender divide. It is argued that even for young children, many activities are marked as 'male' or 'female' and to be male is typically valued more than to be female. Growing up as a boy or a girl inevitably involves learning the opposition and antagonism between boys and girls. Barrie Thorne, in her detailed study of Californian nine-year-olds at play observed that while boys and girls often come together without reference to gender, the disruptive potential for regrouping as opposites is ever present (Thorne, 1993). Assumptions about the meaning of being a boy or being a girl can always potentially be called on to turn boys and girls into separate camps. Thorne noted that while girls can give as good as they get, 'in several notable ways, girls act from a one-down position' (1993, p. 84). Boys controlled as much as ten times more playing space than girls, they invaded girls' space more than girls invaded theirs and they treated girls, their activities and their space as contaminated by the inferior status of being a girl. Pervasive gender inequalities mean that boys can very early on get a sense of boys being better-than-girls. Being like-a-girl can be used as an insult to a boy. Not surprisingly then, at the beginning of their school career, girls are more likely to want to be friends with boys than boys with girls. In his ethnography of how children make friends in their first class (at a US midwestern school), Thomas Rizzo (1989) provides examples of girls making friendship bids to boys but not vice versa. Elliot Medrich and his colleagues found very few children claiming a member of the opposite sex among their friends but twice as many girls than boys did so (Medrich et al. 1982).

When gender differences in friendship patterns are seen as more of a consequence of gender inequality than a cause, it is often also claimed that gender differences have been exaggerated. For example, surveys of children and young people's activities confirm that boys play more team games than girls but from a young age boys are encouraged to make more use of public space than girls. Medrich and his colleagues concluded:

> To the extent that any of the activities . . . was collective, took place out of doors, and was active, boys were more likely to participate than girls. This is not to say that girls had no interest in physical activities. Quite clearly they did. Physical activities remained girls' most favoured activities when they were with friends, and most of the activities they engaged in were at least as strenuous as those of boys. . . . Furthermore, the physical activities they most commonly engaged in were either individual or two person activities or indoor activities, such as dancing. . . . Girls were less likely to play outdoors and with large groups of friends and more likely to play in and around the house. (1982, p. 68)

Barrie Thorne has criticized literature which tends to dichotomize girls' and boys' friendship patterns into girls' dyadic intimacy versus boys' activity groups. In her fieldwork, she observed both considerable overlap and considerable variation between boys and girls. For some boys, the pattern of their friendship was dyadic. She also found girls in large groups of the type which the literature often attributes to boys. Indeed girls who have best friends and do things as a pair may also play in larger groups because interaction varies by activities and context.

Research on youth also documents the part played by gender divisions and antagonism in shaping friendships. Heterosexual practices and gender inequalities result in young women being likely to subordinate their friendships to a heterosexual relationship, while young men are more likely to fit their heterosexual relationships around their friendships. Once again there is overlap in how young men and young women conduct their friendships as well as difference. The survey data from a British multi-site longitudinal study of 16–19-year-olds suggested a general transition in patterns of sociability, from the dominance of same-sex friendships, to a social life more organized around a partner, with an intervening period of spending more time in mixed-sex groups. Girls tend to make the transitions a couple of years ahead of boys. Interview data in the same study confirmed that most young people retain a number of social scenes often including a best friend, a group of same-sex friends and a mixed group of friends, even although the balance of whom they spend time with shifts more towards a partner (Banks et al., 1992).

The relationship between women's friendships and heterosexuality was explored in a number of British studies in the 1970s and 1980s aimed at redressing the previous emphasis on young men in the sociology of youth. In the 1970s Angela McRobbie found that, on approaching adolescence, the white girls she studied conceded public space, unintentionally, to young men by withdrawing into their own alternative 'bedroom culture' as a form of resistance to the demands of the adult world. The major preoccupations of bedroom culture played into the conventional gender hierarchy, fantasizing romance, idolizing pop stars and agonizing over their (heterosexual) attractiveness (clothes, make-up, hairstyles) (McRobbie, 1978). McRobbie argued that teen magazines fed conventional femininity, stressing heterosexual romance above all else, reducing female friends to allies or competitors in finding boyfriends (McRobbie, 1991). Christine Griffin's interview study of 16–18-year-old young women (recruited from schools in Birmingham) outlined how

> if a young woman started to go out with a fairly regular boyfriend, she gradually lost touch with her girlfriends, often at the young man's insistence. . . . There was no equivalent breakdown of male friendships if a young man began to 'go steady' with a girlfriend. 'The lads' continued to see their friends in the local pubs and at football matches. (Griffin, 1985, 62–3)

This process of losing female friends affected young white women more than young Asian and Afro-Caribbean women because of the greater emphasis among young white women on the importance of going out with a boyfriend and the lesser cultural value placed on ties between women. The young white English women had a name for the experience of being dropped by your best friend because she had acquired a boyfriend: they had been 'deffed-out'. Griffin argued that because young women were less able than young men to go out alone for fear of harassment and censure, the loss of a best friend to her boyfriend seriously restricted a young woman's mobility. She then was under greater pressure to have a boyfriend.

Sue Lees, discussing her and Celia Cowie's study of 15–16-year-old young women (recruited from three London schools in the early 1980s), argues that the double standard in sexual conduct (requiring sexual decorum from young women but not young men) undermines girls' relationships with each other: the importance placed on a girl's sexual reputation means that girls cannot confide in each other without risk and possible betrayal. 'The most risky confidences centre around sexual behaviour and feelings. One reason why so few girls talk even to their closest friends about sexual desire or actual sexual behaviour is through the fear that their friends might betray them and gossip – spread the rumour that they are a slag' (1986, p. 68, repeated 1993, p. 80). More recent British ethnographies of girls' friendships illustrate more of the subtleties of their dynamics and the influence of heterosexual pressures (Griffiths, 1995; Hey, 1997).

Claire Wallace describes the converse pressures for boys to those described for girls, in her study of a group of 16–17-year-olds (school pupils on the Isle of Sheppey, an area of England with high unemployment, and with a population of 33,000), some of whom she follows until the age of 21.

> In Sheppey, sexual identities for boys had to be aggressively asserted. . . . Honour could be won through grand Quixotic gestures of defiance against those in authority – such as employers, the school or the police. . . . Honour could also be won through predatory sexuality – by aggressive sexism and by 'pulling the birds' – and hence was inversely related to girls' sexual honour. This too had to be publicly displayed, leading boys to invent or exaggerate their conquests when they retold them afterwards. For boys, masculinity was lost, won, or redeemed through their status in the peer group. (Wallace, 1987, p. 88)

Similar accounts of the pressure to conform to predatory sexuality by working-class male peer groups are found in ethnographies of working-class black youth (Anderson, 1990). While young women may be unable to confide freely in friends because of their need to protect their reputation, young men may be even more constrained in their confidences by the need to live up to conventional masculinity. Wallace observes that those young men who refused to conform to the rigid rules of masculine behaviour were labelled as 'poofs', 'not because any of them were homosexual, but because homosexuality implied an ambiguous masculinity. Hence "masculinity" was often defined against an imaginary idea of homosexuality, not a consideration that ever arose for girls' (Wallace, 1987, p. 88).

Gender differences in adult friendships

In her review of the literature on gender and friendship, Pat O'Connor notes that over and over again researchers have indicated systematic differences between men's friendships with men and women's friendships with women (1992, p. 29). Disclosure and 'really knowing' each other is more characteristic of women's friendships, while doing things together is more characteristic of men's friendships. Graham Allan in his text on friendship summarizes the explanations typically offered in the literature:

> Although the evidence is by no means conclusive, it can be suggested that the distinct roles that men and women typically perform in society, with the different obligations, opportunities and identities they embody, have an impact on the manner in which friendship and other ties of sociability are constructed. In essence, the argument put forward by a number of writers, including Pleck (1976), Hess (1979) and Bell (1981), is that men's position within the social structure tends in the main to encourage the formation of sociable relationships with others, but, at the same time, to restrict the extent to which the self is revealed within them. . . . Men, in other words are likely to be involved in a set of relationships whose basis is sociability and enjoyment, often arranged around specific tasks and activities. However, the majority, though not all, of these relationships are likely to be relatively shallow in terms of the degree to which personal worries, anxieties and other matters of consequence to the self are discussed. To this extent, they differ from the 'strong' model of friendship that philosophers abstract, and as importantly also fit somewhat uneasily into the category of 'close friends' so frequently referred to in sociological surveys. In contrast, women's friendships tend to be less extensive and less concerned with sociability as such, but to involve greater self-revelation and empathy, in line with the gender differences in childhood and adolescent friendships . . . (Caldwell and Peplau, 1982; Fox, Gibbs and Auerbach, 1985; Rubin, 1986; Allan, 1989, pp. 71–2).

Texts on friendship, like Allan's and O'Connor's are generally careful to acknowledge variation among men and among women as well
as claims of overall differences between men and women. A number
of authors have argued that differences in the intimacy of men's and
women's friendships have been grossly overstated (Walker, 1994;
Wright, 1988). One aspect of this overstated difference is the tendency
to exaggerate the extent of disclosing intimacy in women's friendships. In fact, many studies have found adult women carefully subordinating their same-sex friendships to the needs of their
heterosexual relationship, placing careful limits on the time and/or
degree of disclosure they allowed with friends. Moreover, despite
the notion that women's friendships are more intimate than men's,
Tuula Gordon's work (1994) on single women found that they often
felt there was very little intimacy in their lives. Gordon interviewed
fifty women without partners based in London, San Francisco and
Helsinki.

> There was great variation in the extent of intimacy women in this
> study thought they wanted or needed, and in how much intimacy
> women experienced in their social relationships. But there was a
> prevalent sense of intimacy not being taken for granted. There were
> frequent expressions of having to 'work at' obtaining intimacy, and
> having to learn to receive intimacy. Many women thought that lov-
> ing intimacy was easier in the context of monogamous partnership,
> marriages and families. (Gordon, 1994, p. 107)

It has sometimes been argued that men show their care for each other
more instrumentally through the practical help of fixing, mending
and doing things together and, therefore, that neglecting such activities exaggerates differences in intimacy between men's friendships
and women's. Women who claim good friendships in terms of 'disclosing intimacy' can find themselves without the practical help they
need. For example, Ellen Lewin's (1993) work on single mothers
found that lesbian and heterosexual mothers often could not get the
practical support they needed from their women friends prior to
motherhood. New friendships with other new mothers was a common solution. In summary, research suggests there has been a tendency to exaggerate the degree of 'disclosing intimacy' in women's
friendships, and that the importance of other dimensions of intimacy
for both men and women may have been downplayed.

Adult same-sex friends versus sexual/domestic partners?

The literature of the working-class communities of the 1950s and 1960s documented a persistent tension between the ideal of intimate marriage and the men's and women's same-sex ties with kin or friends. Men and women were characterized as embedded in gender-segregated networks which pulled them away from each other (Bott, 1964). Gender-segregated social worlds were considered to be more typically working-class than middle-class. Extreme gender divisions are still features of many social worlds (Wight, 1993a) and are still considered to be more typically working-class. In a US study conducted in the 1970s Lillian Rubin found that working-class women restricted their contact with their friends after marriage and resented their men going out with their all-male friendship group, particularly if they felt trapped at home with children (1976, p. 76–80). But by the later years of their marriage most men have given up nights out with their friends, and women, although no longer trapped at home by children, never developed the practice. Rubin explains this absence of going out with friends in terms of their efforts to keep the disappointments and conflicts in their lives in check.

> Thus, over and over, both women and men disavowed the wish for some desired activity – whether to spend some time alone, to develop some personal interest, or to see more of same-sex friends – with the comment that they don't want to get into "bad habits". Speaking of their wish to go out with her friends once in a while, one twenty-eight-year-old woman reasons: "I think about it sometimes. It would be fun to go with my girlfriends sometimes – you know, not to do anything wrong, but to have some fun. But then I worry what would happen if I did? I might get to like it. Then I get afraid, and I think I don't know if I want to taste that life. You know, sometimes when you taste something like that, then you start requiring it. My life is really my husband and my children and my home. I wouldn't want to risk taking any chances of losing them." (Rubin, 1976, p. 195)

These working-class women did not go out to have fun with their friends nor did they rely on their women friends as confidantes to the same degree as is suggested in studies of middle-class women. Pat O'Connor's (1991) British study of mainly white working-class married women (about sixty women, aged 20–42, with dependent children found that only one third had a friend who was a close confidante. The majority of women (about 70 per cent) confided in their husband and those who did not were no more likely to confide in a friend. The high rate of confiding in husbands did not necessarily mean women felt satisfied with their partner relationship. O'Connor found some wives who confided in their husbands and yet felt that he was unsupportive and emotionally distant. Whether women had friends as confidantes or not did not depend on the quality of the marital relationship but the depth of friendship her circumstances (length of her connections to the locality, the financial security of the family-household) had permitted. Those working-class women who did have friends as confidantes described their friendships as close and supportive.

When married women have close women friends they typically complement rather than compete with relationships with partners. Both US (Gouldner and Strong, 1987; Oliker, 1989) and British (Jerrome, 1984; O'Connor, 1991) studies of women's friendships describe how women use female friends to manage the strains of their marriage and maintain their commitment to it. Rather than undermining the emotional tie of marriage, these women used friendships to compensate for the lack of emotional intimacy in their marriage and to encourage each other to stick with it despite the failings. Many women were very clear that there were things they could not talk to their male partner about but could discuss with female friends. Even women who considered their husband to be their best friend still said they felt the need for a good female friend for 'the little moans and groans, like why doesn't your husband pick up his stuff' (Gouldner and Strong, 1987, p. 62). Women used moaning to friends to relieve and normalize their frustrations. A general shared logic was that it was unwise to expect marriage to provide for everything. Speaking critically of their husbands through moaning did not mean friends were permitted to initiate critical or hostile comments about their husbands. Critical comments about partners were generally taboo. Indeed, there were quite definite limits on what could be talked about with and said to friends. These undiscussed rules of friendship restricted mutual exploration in ways which protected their marriages. Even between very close women friends, not everything was a possible topic of discussion. Nor was always speaking your mind possible. To break these rules caused serious rifts between friends.

Kath Weston (1991, p. 160) discusses the tension between friends and lovers for lesbians and gays. In her late 1980s San Francisco study she found lesbians and gay men using the language of kinship to

encompass both their non-sexual friendships and their sexual relationships. Gay men and women were constructing 'chosen families'
to affirm the validity of their relationships. Weston argues that the
construction of 'chosen families' helped manage the tension between
friends and lovers. The ideal of ongoing kinship was held out to
friends, lovers and ex-lovers. 'Gay (or chosen) families dispute the
old saying, "You can pick your friends, but you can't pick your relatives". Not only can these families embrace friends; they may
also encompass lovers, coparents, adopted children, children from
previous heterosexual relationships, and offspring conceived through
alternative insemination' (Weston, 1991, 2).

Intimacy with same-sex friends is not automatically a threat to intimacy with a partner in either homosexual or heterosexual relationships. Nor is a partner necessarily a threat to friendship although
clearly this is the case in some relationships. The young men who
insisted that their girlfriends gave up going out with their friends
were exercising social control and sexual possession rather than
stamping out competitors in intimacy. Dorothy Jerrome's (1981) work
on elderly people finds some who blossom through more active
friendships after the loss of their partner. However, there are also
others who never recover a sense of intimacy. Friendships characterized by disclosing intimacy often provide support for maintaining
and managing partner relationships. Heterosexual women's friendships sometimes compensate for limits in intimacy with their partners. However, different types of intimacy in different relationships
are not always complementary. Rubin's study suggests that working-class men's same-sex friendships may support a style of intimacy
which is not only different from but perhaps inimical to the disclosing intimacy sought by their wives. For example, speaking about the
fact that he is unable to give his wife the emotional support he feels
she wants, one of Rubin's respondents commented on the impossibility of discussing this with his friends. 'The guys I know, they don't
worry about things like that. . . . People don't talk about those things;
you just know where those guys are; you don't have to ask them.'
The fact that he 'just knows' is a claim to privileged insight into how
his friends think without discussion. This knowing is a form of intimacy with his friends and a statement of acceptance of the limits of
that intimacy, an acceptance he may wish was shared by his wife.

Friendship as a non-sexual relationship

While Freudians see friendships as drawing on displaced sexual energy, whatever else friendship means to people in a more everyday sense, it is generally regarded as a non-sexual relationship. Friends who have ventured a single sexual encounter, and then agree it was a mistake which must make no difference to their previous relationship, may fear they have put their friendship at risk. It is often assumed that sexual relationships have a different basis from friendship. Friends who become lovers are no longer 'just friends'. These assumptions have less resonance outside of conventional heterosexual relationships. Gay men are likely to have been consciously sexually attracted to their friends but yet do not typically see this as threatening their friendship (Nardi, 1992). Ex-lovers as friends are a common part of lesbian social networks or 'chosen families' (Becker, 1988; Clunis and Green, 1988; Weston, 1991). First experiences of lesbian relationships often develop within established friendships while gay men's first homosexual encounters are often of a purely sexual nature. (Gagnon and Simon, 1973; Weston, 1991).

A general cultural presumption that relationships between men and women are sexual makes cross-sex friendships more difficult to negotiate as non-sexual relationships. Indeed, as Graham Allan notes, 'the dominant models for sociable interaction between the genders are based upon a more or less overt sexuality' (1989, p. 82). Lesbians do not generally have an equivalent problem negotiating non-sexual same-sex friendships with other women because typically neither their early socialization nor their adult experiences have led them to see relationships between women as primarily sexual relationships. Literature on gay men implies the shift from sexual relationship to friendship or vice versa is not typically a problem (Nardi, 1992). People, heterosexual or homosexual, who successfully negotiate cross-gender friendships may have to deal with the presumption of others that their relationship is in fact a sexual relationship. For adult heterosexuals who are already in partnerships, friendships with members of the opposite sex are often regarded as taboo unless they are rendered asexual in some way such as by socializing with partners present. Same-sex friendships can also face censure if they are seen by others as sexual or potentially sexual relationships. Very devoted or demonstratively affectionate non-sexual relationships run the risk of being categorized and, in many contexts, stigmatized as lesbian or gay. Heterosexuals who have same-sex friendships with lesbians or gays are liable to be categorized as lesbian or gay. In general however, same-sex relationships are less likely to be presumed to be sexual relationships than cross-sex relationships.

Friendship is theoretically closer to 'the pure relationship' than marriage or parenthood. However, the constraints placed on the practices of friendship by the norms of heterosexuality, as well as the social divisions of gender, class and ethnicity, illustrate how far removed everyday friendships typically are from the 'pure relationship'. Friendship as the 'continuous creation of personal will and choice . . . ungoverned by the structural definitions that bear on family and kinship . . . grounded in the unique and irreplaceable qualities of partners, defined and valued independently of their place in public systems of kinship, power, utility and esteem, and of any publicly defined status' (Silver, 1996) is a philosophical ideal which has become a pervasive public story rather than an everyday lived reality. Exploring the distance between friendship, parenthood and partnership and between the ideal of 'the pure relationship' and the diverse realities of friendship also clarifies why most people's lives are far removed from a situation in which 'good friends are all you need'. Given that friendship is culturally defined as a non-sexual relationship, and a pervasive public story is that adults need a sex life, then friendship is not all you need. The ideal of the 'pure relationship' does not allow for messy and asymmetrical periods of needing practical help or feeling dependent or needy which are routine occurrences in parent–child relationships, partnerships and some friendships. The circumstances of many people's lives render 'pure' friendships both difficult and insufficient.

CHAPTER 5

Sex and Intimacy

Introduction

In the late twentieth century, seeking sexual pleasure can be celebrated as more than lust or a matter of reproduction but as an expression of love, whether or not marriage is involved. Moreover, moralists fear and radicals hope that the process of 'finding yourself', or 'being yourself', now incites a more varied sexual repertoire than conventional heterosexual sex. This is the shift which Anthony Giddens calls 'plastic sexuality' and associates with the ascendancy of greater equality and 'disclosing intimacy' between sexual partners. Chapter 2 has already sketched stories of the history of sex and social change. This chapter is concerned with comparing late twentieth-century academic and popular stories about sexual behaviour with the much more complex and messy picture which emerges from research on everyday sexual behaviour and sexuality.

Sex, love and intimacy are analytically separate but in social practices they are often linked, as the phrase 'making love' illustrates. If the way in which people learn to feel sexy (when and with whom they want to have sex) is structured by a popular story of 'falling-in-love', then sex is linked to love in the construction of their sexuality. If a person learns to feel sexy only when they feel close to somebody whom they know and love, then, for them, sex is linked to intimacy. The converse is a learned separation between sex and intimacy such that knowing and feeling close to somebody makes them sexually uninteresting. A question to ask of the research literature, then, is, 'Are there routinely produced linkages and separations between intimacy and sexual relationships or behaviours in people's everyday lives?' This is crucial to deciding whether sex is becoming more or less tied to intimacy, as are questions around gender difference. Are we witnessing the decline of macho-male masculinity with its predatory sexuality which ritually denies intimacy? Is there convergence in men's and women's relationships to sex and intimacy? There are also a number of subsidiary questions; for example, if there is a closer realignment of sex and intimacy, what of the continuance and in some cases increase in forms of sexual behaviour in which sex is totally separated from intimacy (prostitution, cottaging, erotica) or aligned instead with violence and abuse (rape, child-abuse, violent pornography)? And what of the fact that the mass media makes the publication and consumption of sexual stories all-pervasive? Is increased intimacy compatible with the increased exposure of people's sexual lives?

There are no easy answers to such questions. Different theoretical understandings of how and why people behave sexually lead to different views of sex and intimacy. As noted in chapter 1, there can be no one story and no neutral reading. The chapter begins by looking at the dominant themes and images of sex and intimacy in public stories, paying particular attention to popular culture, the official messages of the state, and the vocal lobby of the Moral Right. This part of the chapter ends with the current academic notion that the late twentieth century is qualitatively different. The remainder of the chapter turns from public stories told from 'on high' (that is the stories of moralists, experts and academics) to the research literature, the more grounded stories told by ordinary people to researchers.

Stories of 'Normal Sex' and Intimacy

A common message of experts on medical, mental and sexual health, that 'sex' is good for you, has become a taken for granted fact in much popular culture. This is not an unqualified message – it generally means conventional ways of being sexual with a conventional category of 'suitable' other and the conventions are rather different for men and women. However, celibacy, in the form of chosen sexual abstinence, is not recommended or spoken highly of in popular

culture. The stereotypes of people-who-do-not-have-sex often con-
jure up people who are social isolates either because of their preoccupations or their inadequacies. While not always portrayed
unsympathetically, the incompleteness of their life is what makes them
a topic.[1] Sally Cline has conducted one of the few studies of celibacy
and commends women's celibacy as enhancing their autonomy and
independence. Referring to the 'sacred cow of sexual consumerism'
(1993, p. 1) she notes that 'fifty years ago it took courage for a single
woman to admit that she was enjoying an active sexual life. Today it
takes courage for her to admit that she is not' (Cline, 1993, p. 3).

On the other hand, 'lovers' are typically portrayed as on a higher
plane of happiness than others who do not have the combination of
love and sex in one relationship. In popular culture there are many
characterizations of lovers as equals focused on 'disclosing intimacy'
but there are also many traditional characterizations of heterosexual
lovers as masterful men and admiring, grateful, seduced women.
Numerous films, novels and plays have portrayed lovers as experiencing an intensity of not just sexual discovery but also of a more
general, knowledge-gathering intimacy, such that other relationships
seem like shadows in comparison.[2] In the successful romance of this
genre, the couple are typically both sexually passionate and engaged
in intense efforts of mutual understanding. However, another char-
acterization of lovers draws on themes much closer to conventional
macho masculinity. The man is the hero and the woman is the one
whom he has chosen or otherwise happens to have his special protection.[3] His heroic deeds of care and protection are shown as winning or sustaining her love. Women's love is then akin to gratitude
or admiration rather than constructed through mutual discovery. Both
genres frequently present sex between lovers as the ultimate peak of
intimacy. In portrayals of the action hero, sex and love are often collapsed into each other as the only episodes of intimacy in contrast to
scenes of macho male violence. The lovers-as-equals who are focused
on disclosing intimacy are mutually absorbed in a relationship which
is more intense than anything else in their lives.

The linking of sex and intimacy in cultural constructions of 'lovers'
echoes popular and expert assumptions that couples who are celibate
or for whom sex is somehow unsuccessful have a problem which
threatens their viability as a couple. In late twentieth-century Euro-
North American societies, sexual success is generally defined in terms
of mutual orgasm (Clark, 1993). Mutual orgasm as proof of success
and intimacy in sexual relationships suggests a common and equal

standard of sexual pleasure for men and women. The dominant popular representations of lovers portray sex as mutually enjoyable. There are two common representations of mutually pleasurable heterosex in popular culture which match the two common types of 'lovers': that of the couple for whom sex is a further heightening of their intense concern with knowing, understanding and pleasing each other, and that of the masterful and lusty protective male hero and his relatively passive, indebted and worshipping woman who gives herself to him sexually and to whom he gives sexual pleasure.

For most of the twentieth century, men have also been portrayed as pursuing and being enhanced by sexual adventures which split sex from love and intimacy, while women are presented as degraded by such exploits. Respectability for women has depended on their sexuality being restricted to relationships in which they lose themselves in love and yet do not make the first sexual moves. But, in the late twentieth century, women taking the initiative in love and sex has become a more common cultural theme. Angela McRobbie (1991, 1994) describes this shift in British magazines for teenage girls.

> Most strikingly the girl is no longer the victim of romance. She is no longer a slave to love. She no longer waits miserably outside the cinema knowing that she has been 'stood up'. She no longer distrusts all girls including her best friend because they represent a threat and might steal her 'fella'. She no longer lives in absolute terror of being dumped. She is no longer terrified of being without a 'steady'. . . . There is love and there is sex and there are boys, but the conventionally coded meta-narratives of romance which . . . could only create a neurotically dependent female subject, have gone for good. . . . femininity does indeed emerge as an altogether less rigid category. It is still predicated round the pursuit of identity (in beauty), the achievement of success (through fashion consumption) and search for some form of harmony or stability (through happiness). There is more of the self in this new vocabulary of femininity, much more self-esteem, more autonomy, but still the pressure to adhere to the perfect body image as a prerequisite for the success in love which is equated with happiness. (McRobbie, 1994, 164–5)

The popular culture described by McRobbie links intimacy and sex in love; 'good sex' is the sex of lovers, success in love results in durable, intimate, sexual relationships, and love is conducted in a 'new more equal climate of sexual relations that girls are encouraged to enjoy' (McRobbie, 1994, p. 166).

Themes of greater gender equality in sex, love and intimacy co-exist with strong reassertions of traditional and patriarchal versions of how things are and should be. Wendy Hollway (1984) and Francesca Cancian (1987) have described how stories denying men's need for intimacy and portraying loving intimacy as women's business, construct women as dependent on men. Double standards in sexual conduct continue to divide women into 'the good' (who are not out looking for sex) and 'the bad' (who are asking for it). The 'sex drive' story continues to characterize men as needing sex in a way that women do not, justifying predatory and aggressive male heterosexuality of macho masculinity. Many popular narratives continue to present the approaches of men and women to sex as polarized and crudely stereotyped. In much of Euro-North American popular culture, the most feminine woman exhibits what Robert Connell (1987) has called 'exaggerated femininity'. Sex, for her, occurs in the context of being helplessly in love with (and dependent on) a man. The archetypical masculine man of popular culture exhibits an aggressive heterosexuality as if his sexuality were an aspect of general physical toughness. Sex is part of the hero's command over his action-packed life; the relative weakness of his sexual partner is made clear as the hero rescues or protects her and sex is part of her gratitude. This is the hegemonic masculinity endlessly celebrated in popular culture from John Wayne through Arnold Schwarzenegger and beyond. Norbert Elias's (1978) account of the 'civilising process' indicates that the actual incidence of male violence has waned as the modern state removed the legitimate use of violence from the everyday lives of men. Why then has the popularity of this type of hero persisted? One possible interpretation consistent with Elias's account is that such heroes are cathartic, allowing men to act along with male violence in fantasy, while living a more 'self controlled' life. However, the continued high incidence of domestic violence and rape indicates that many men have retained a sense of their right to enforce their domination of women by the exercise of male violence. Indeed, David Morgan (1990) finds no evidence of a decline in the ideal of a 'real man' who is capable of killing; violence continues to be an aspect of the most celebrated form of masculinity. The similarity in justifications given by perpetrators of sexual and domestic violence indicates the continued viability for unextraordinary men of a misogynist world view in which women are for their use and abuse (Kelly, 1988).

Predatory male sexuality and passive succumbing femininity are pervasive cultural themes powerfully portrayed not only in popular culture but also in a number of expert domains. The social construction of the 'fact' of men's stronger sex drive has sanctioned views such as, that men naturally do the chasing and that women like to be chased, that men cannot help but sometimes lose control, and that women who 'lead men on' are asking for trouble; views which form part of the mythology of rape (Smart and Smart, 1978) and isolate men's sexuality not only from intimacy but from any form of social context. Laqueur (1990) and others[4] have documented dominant ideological medical/scientific understandings of sexual arousal and pleasure in men and women, and their counter-currents. Decades after the physiology of women's orgasm had been conclusively documented by Masters and Johnson as resulting from clitoral stimulation (1966), experts continued to define women's sexual arousal as if it could only occur in the context of penetrative heterosexual intercourse, and as if women could only learn to like sex in the context of a relationship with and under the tutelage of a man.

Stories of the sexual prowess of men and seducibility of women are stock stories told by 'experts' in a number of other social contexts. For example, they are routinely drawn on by defence lawyers in rape trials. The standard defence in rape cases is that the woman consented, either by welcoming or giving in to the man's sexual advances.[5] This means a defence which presents whatever sexual events are acknowledged as taking place as being 'normal sex'. Skilled defence lawyers successfully present sex between casual acquaintances, in uncomfortable surroundings, followed by extreme distress on the part of the woman as normal or the normal gone slightly wrong. In the process a predatory male sexuality and a readily seducible female sexuality are typically presented. Nevertheless, the picture of 'normal sex' which emerges is frequently the grim coercive event diagnosed by feminists of the 1970s (Greer, 1971). Courtroom speeches both draw on and reinforce the more pervasive public stories about gender, sex and intimacy, as courtroom dialogue frequently re-enters the domain of public stories through media coverage.

The various arms of the twentieth-century state are powerful filters, amplifiers, and sometimes producers of public stories about sex, intimacy and gender. However, modern states are complex and state agents – legal, medical, religious, educational, welfare workers – may pursue contradictory, competing and uncoordinated policies. What is not in doubt is that the frequency of state, official and quasi-official pronouncements about personal sexual lives has increased.

The points of contact between the state and personal life have multiplied since the previous century. For example, medical intervention to facilitate or prevent sexual reproduction, interventions regarding sexually transmitted diseases, and psychosexual counselling are services which create new points of contact between experts and their clients, allowing the exercise of subtle controls. The HIV/AIDS crisis provoked many governments to invest money in preventative campaigns, and the content of these official messages is a measure of the balance of power between conservative and radical voices shaping public stories. Initially AIDS was used by moral entrepreneurs as an opportunity to denounce sexual freedom generally and/or homosexuality in particular (Altman, 1986; Patton, 1985; Watney, 1987). However, the preventative campaigns have not declared sexual abstinence or monogamous marriage as the sole solutions, although both abstinence and monogamy have been recommended. Nor, however, have they rigorously promoted safe sexual practices which are an alternative to penetrative intercourse (such as mutual masturbation). Above all, preventative programmes have advocated condom use. Commenting on British 'safe sex' campaigns, Janet Holland and her colleagues note continued reluctance to give official sanction to any form of sexual behaviour which is divorced from reproduction (1991, p. 4) or challenges a conventional male view of sex as beginning with penetration and ending in ejaculation.

Many sectors of society attempt to influence the content of state-endorsed messages. The USA in particular has a very vocal right-wing moral lobby which presents problems of social order (crime, riots, truancy) as the consequence of the twin evils of sexual permissiveness and the breakdown of the family (for them, exemplified by divorce, illegitimacy, and single parents). For more conservative religious groups 'sex before marriage' remains a key indicator of moral decay, despite the fact that it is experienced by the majority of young people, most of whom no longer consider it to be morally wrong. Experts and state policy which emphasize 'relationships' rather than 'marriages' are condemned by the Moral Right. For example, the extension of the legal rights of married couples to heterosexual or same-sex couples forming a domestic unit (a practice now widespread with reference to heterosexual cohabiting couples but rare and legislated against in the USA, through the *Defence of Marriage Act*, 1996, with respect to same-sex couples), and the lowering of the legal barriers to obtaining a divorce are regarded as policies which undermine marriage. The concern of the Moral Right extends to the decriminalization of homosexuality, availability of abortion, contraception for young unmarried people, sex education in schools, the relaxation of censorship and the growth of hard and soft pornography. All of these are seen as sexual freedoms inciting men and women to moral degeneracy.

While many of the themes of the Moral Right do not have popular support, some are simply a more exaggerated form of themes well represented in popular culture, such as the double standard in sexual conduct and the stigmatization of homosexuality. However, political analysts note that the successes of these right-wing moral movements are limited (Durham, 1991; Milligan, 1993; Somerville, 1992). In both Britain and the USA, legislation has not been passed clamping down on access to contraception or abortion, for example, although there have been some increases in censorship and moves against homosexual rights. For Britain, Martin Durham (1991) traced the disenchantment of the Moral Right with Mrs Thatcher's government, despite its stand against liberal sex education and the introduction of legislation making it an offence for a local authority 'to promote homosexuality or publish material for the promotion of homosexuality . . . promote the teaching in any maintained school of the acceptability of homosexuality as a pretended family relationship by the publication of such material or otherwise' (Clause 28 of the Local Government Bill, which became the law of Britain with only minor amendment in May 1988 (Jeffery-Poulter, 1991)). While for homosexual rights campaigners, it was frightening evidence of homophobia, for the Moral Right this was seen as a minor success amongst a general failure to turn back the tide. (Durham, 1991).

The Moral Right and some more radical organizations have been united in campaigns against pornography although for very different reasons. For the Moral Right, pornography can incite depraved sexualities, simultaneously undermining conventional sex within monogamous marriage. Feminists are concerned with the significance and consequences for women of representations of women as objects for men's use and abuse (Coward, 1982; Kappeler, 1986). Pornography is not the only source or main source of such representations of women. Images which sexualize people, predominantly women, as if they were consumable bodies or bits of bodies are widespread in advertising and popular culture as well as being the dominant theme of pornography. Cultural and structural layers of assumed and real power differences between men and women mean that men represented as objects cannot convey a notion that men are for women's use and abuse equivalent to the message conveyed by images objectifying women. Susanne Kappeler (1986) begins her discussion of pornography by referring to a photograph of a black man taken in Namibia in 1983 by racist white men who murdered him. He is photographed as if he were a trophy, an animal captured by game hunters. While this man was not portrayed in a sexualized way, the picture conveyed the white racists' sense of ownership, of rights to use and abuse, and their objectification of the person in the picture. Men, then, can be portrayed in ways which suggest they are disposable objects but only with reference to racism, classism or some other system which incites seeing men as representatives of a subordinate category. Pornographic pictures of women often exemplify a taken for granted male supremacy just as this picture exemplified the racist mentality of these whites. The persistence of a pervasive sexism means no additional category is required to present women as subordinated objects. A particularly contested issue is the relationship between pornography and male violence towards women. While feminists are absolutely united in their will to combat rapes and sexual assaults by men on women, not all agree that censoring pornography will mitigate the problem.[6] The view that pornography was the theory and rape was the practice led the North American feminists Andrea Dworkin and Catherine MacKinnon to draft legislation against pornography, an example followed by some feminists in Britain (Assiter and Avedon, 1993). Anti-censorship feminists generally argue that the problems of sexual violence need far more radical attention than censorship and, moreover, that censorship may be used for odious political reasons leading to unwelcome restrictions on personal freedom.

It has been suggested that new story tellers and new stories have emerged at the century's end, extending the repertoire beyond popular portrayals of the ultimate intimacy of sex between lovers, the older stories of sexually needy men and seducible women, and the various messages promoted by state-sanctioned experts and vocal moralists.

> Whatever changes occurred in the nineteenth century to establish preconditions of sexual story telling, a qualitative shift occurs in the mid-twentieth. Most analysts of sexuality agree that something dramatic happened to sexuality during the 1960s and 1970s. . . . More specifically, shifts have been detected in the swings towards a libertarianism where sex is 'viewed as a positive, beneficial, joy-

ous phenomenon' (Seidman, 1992, p. 5), towards a feminisation of sex (Ehrenreich, Hess and Jacobs, 1987); towards a recreational sex (D'Emillio and Freedman, 1988) and ultimately towards a demo-cratisation of intimacy (Giddens, 1992). There is no one reason for these changes. One factor is surely the growth and proliferation of communications. Not only have the major means of mass commun-ication been put into place so to be widely available to most (from mass paperbacking to records, TV, telephones, videos, etc.) but enough stories have been told publicly and circulated freely to reach a critical take-off point. (Plummer, 1995, p. 123)

Kenneth Plummer identifies three new sexual stories as having reached a 'critical take-off point'. They are the 'breaking the silence' stories of female survivors of rape and sexual abuse, the 'coming-out stories' of gay men and lesbians, and the recovery stories of people who present themselves as previously addicted to a pattern of relationship which was doing them harm. What these stories have in common is that they are told in the context of imagining others who share a similar experience and hence drawing on an imagined community of support. The stories have a conventional narrative structure in which suffering is overcome and a new sense of self and community found, but at the same time the stories can be seen as part of the process of creating community and making it possible for stories like theirs to be heard.

> Stories need communities to be heard, but communities themselves are also built through story telling. Stories gather people around them: they have to attract audiences, and these audiences may then start to build a common perception, a common language, a commonality. Typically, stories that are not involved in commun-ity-building do not become strong stories. (Plummer, 1995, p. 174).

Reaching the critical take-off point in the case of 'breaking the sil-ence' and 'coming-out stories' has followed sustained and persistent effort by the women's movement and the gay liberation movements to make personal stories political. The recovery stories, on the other hand, emerge from a therapeutic self-help culture which individ-ualizes rather than overtly politicizes problems but, nevertheless, private pains are transformed into public ones shared with an imagined community.

Each of the sexual stories which Plummer identifies as unique to the late twentieth century repudiates a scenario which involves the separation of sex and intimacy and implicitly lends support to 'disclosing intimacy' as the ideal. The stories of recovery from sexual/relationship addiction are a story of dawning self-knowledge and the replacement of self-loathing with self-love. Anthony Giddens argues that an increase in addiction to sex and damaging relationships is characteristic of the late twentieth century and stems from the same cause as the search for mutual relationships of disclosing intimacy: tradition has been more thoroughly swept away leaving people vulnerable to being overwhelmed by choice and having to work at sustaining a sense of a stable self. An addiction is a compulsive behaviour which has dispensed with choice. 'The idea of an addiction makes little sense in a traditional culture, where it is normal to do today what one did yesterday' (Giddens, 1992, p. 75). The general message of the addiction recovery story is that good sex and good relationships are only possible when you know and accept yourself; you must seek intimacy with yourself before seeking it elsewhere. Survivors who speak out about rape and abuse are adding voice not only to a general feminist attack on male violence but also to a denouncement of the predatory sexuality of macho male masculinity. What happened was violent, abusive and deeply harmful and a pole apart from the narrator's ideal/normal sexual relationship. In this sense the account by a survivor told on her own terms contrasts sharply with that of the stories of rape which are often constructed in courtrooms by way of defence. The coming-out story is about escaping the impasse of the impossibility of intimacy. It is a story of leaving behind the self-censorship, doubt and isolation of feeling gay but not telling the people that you love. It is as if a secret sexuality damaged the basis of intimacy with family and friends. While 'coming-out' often results in the further loss of family and friends it also represents a new beginning with the implied possibility of real intimacy.

However, the increase in radical stories from people shaping and reclaiming their own sexuality coincides with the persistence of consequential antidotes to their accounts. As rape victims speak out about the terrible harms they have survived, rape trials reproduce a masculinist view of pressured yet apparently consensual sex as a defence. As films like *Philadelphia* (USA, 1993) contribute to the normality of being gay, other arguments convince both the US and the British governments that the armed forces should retain the right to discriminate against homosexuals and the US passes the *Defence of Marriage Act* into federal law. Recovery stories about knowing and loving yourself blend with the barrage of stories about who and how you might and should be as a 'healthy', 'real' or 'normal' man or woman.

The Realities of Sexual Lives

Some aspects of sexuality and sexual behaviour have been more re-searched than others. In general, areas which have been defined as relevant to social problems such as teenage pregnancy have been subjected to the most scrutiny. In 1994 large-scale surveys of sexual behaviour were published in Britain (of about 18,900 adults aged 16–59; Wellings et al.), and the USA (of about 3,500 adults aged 18–59; Laumann et al.). Surveys are more suited to exploring what people do than why they do it or what their behaviour means to them, although it is also possible to explore attitudes through sur-veys. In-depth interview studies are more suited to exploring the relationship between sex and intimacy. Young people have been the subject of such studies to a greater extent than other sub-groups of the population.

Sex surveys

The findings of both the US and British surveys of sexual life were greeted as remarkable only in the extent of conventionality found. One of the more highly publicized findings was how small the minority reporting homosexuality was, somewhat below the 10% found earlier this century by Alfred Kinsey (1948, 1953) for men and below 5% for women. The high rates of monogamy and modest number of sexual partners over a lifetime for the majority were also highly publicized as evidence of continued convention. In the US 75% of married men and 85% of married women say they have never had sex with anyone other than their partner since marriage. In Britain only 4–5% of mar-ried men and 2% of married women reported two or more sexual part-ners in the previous year. However cohabiting men and women reported a higher incidence of more than one partner in the previous year (15% and 8% compared with 28% and 18% for single men and women). In the USA, the average (median) number of partners over a lifetime was two for women and six for men (although the number of partners was higher for those who were teenagers in the late 1960s and early 1970s). Figures for Britain were similar.

The surveys provided some evidence with which to assess claims such as that of convergence between men and women's sexuality, the blossoming of personalized and varied repertoires of sexual behaviour and the closer fusion of sex and intimacy. Both surveys confirmed a continued gap in sexual behaviour between men and women, with men reporting higher rates for all forms of sexual activity, (on average, more partners, more orgasms, more masturbation and thinking about sex (asked only in the USA), more homosexuality and more adultery and higher rates of sexual pleasure. The overwhelming majority of US men said they routinely experienced orgasms when having 'sex' but only 29% of women (asked only in the USA). The British survey asked respondents to agree or disagree with the statements 'Sex without orgasm, or climax, cannot be really satisfying for a man', 'Sex without orgasm, or climax, cannot be really satisfying for a woman'. Men were more likely to see an orgasm as essential to either gender's sexual satisfaction and women were more likely to see an orgasm as essential to men than to women. Both surveys investigated a long list of possible types of sexual behaviour. The British survey reported: 'After vaginal intercourse, non-penetrative sex was the most frequently reported activity. 75% of women and 82% of men had experience of genital stimulation which did not result in intercourse (non-penetrative sex) at some time, and one in four had experienced this in the last 7 days' (Wellings et al., 1994, p. 149). *Time* magazine made much of the popularity of oral sex revealed by the US survey. A minority of heterosexuals had also practised anal sex. Both surveys also asked one or more questions about sexual practices which clearly separate sex and intimacy. Paying for sex was found to be very much a minority phenomenon. In Britain about 7% of men said they had paid for sex with a woman at some time and the pattern across ages suggested a decline in men's use of prostitution. Coercive sex was investigated in the US survey; 22% of women reported having been forced to do sexual things they did not want to do by somebody they love, and 3% of US men admitted forcing themselves on women. The British survey asked whether people agreed or disagreed with the statements 'Companionship and affection are more important than sex in a marriage or relationship' and 'Sex is the most important part of any marriage relationship.' The pattern of answers for men and women was very similar with 67–8% agreeing with the former and 16–17% agreeing with the latter.

Clearly the relevant evidence is mixed. Nearly 70% of men and women state that they value aspects of intimacy in a relationship more than sex. However, there are clear warnings against assuming convergence between men and women concerning how sex should be conducted and what is valued in a sexual relationship. There are persistent behavioural differences and different expectations about sexual satisfaction. The most disturbing evidence suggesting the continuance of a predatory male sexuality is the significant minorities of women in the US who report being forced to do sexual things. There is little evidence about behaviour in either survey to suggest a quiet sexual revolution except perhaps a diversification in many people's sexual repertoire beyond genital penetrative sex. The surveys throw little light on the meaning of acts such as non-penetrative sex, oral and anal intercourse. The same acts can vary enormously in meaning to the participants. For example, Jacqui Halson's (1991) study of British schoolgirls suggests that girls give in to pressure to 'suck off' their boyfriends because they are unwilling to have conventional sexual intercourse. It is a strategy of damage limitation. Lillian Rubin (1990) found that in her US adult population both men and women viewed oral sex much more positively. There is, as yet, insufficient evidence to conclude the beginning of the end of the dominance of conventional genital sex as 'real sex' and the flowering of a more 'plastic sexuality'.

Learning about sex and intimacy

Childhood and youth are particularly studied because they are seen as key formative periods in determining adult patterns of behaviour through the formation of emotional and sexual identities. Influences in childhood are seen as more potent than influences in adulthood. It is the relative powerlessness of children and young people, which makes them necessarily susceptible to the moulding of cultural prompting and external constraints. Moreover paths taken in youth often close off other options in adulthood. However, it remains a debated issue whether everything learned in childhood can be re-learned in adulthood. Emotional responses such as feelings of guilt and shame about sex or the body or longing for particular types of relationship may be difficult to realign once established (Connell, 1987; Poster, 1978; Scheff, 1990).

Writing in the tradition of symbolic interactionism, John Gagnon and William Simon basically laid aside notions of deep-seated psychological predispositions and focused on the social process of learning about sex and constructing a sexual identity. They provided an early detailed account (1973) of how male and female children and adolescents learn a different relationship to sex and emotion. Their account was subsequently elaborated by the British feminist author Stevi Jackson (1982). This work suggests that sexuality is built on gender identity. Girls learn more inhibitions, shame and guilt about sex than boys because of aspects of their gender socialization. Cleanliness, decorum and separation from dirt are frequently emphasized in everyday ways more for girls than boys. Also in childhood girls learn more self-censorship of their bodies than boys, they must keep more of their bodies covered and avoid certain postures, like sitting with their legs apart (see also Bellotti, 1975; Sharpe, 1976). So when children commonly confuse sex with urination and defecation it already seems more repulsive to girls than boys because of the stronger taboos surrounding their body and dirt. Gagnon and Simon described learning about sex as learning about guilt for both boys and girls. The negative messages from parents about what is not to be touched or exposed, and the rude, bad words that are never to be spoken, are rarely countered by any positive messages about the potential the body offers for sexual pleasure. Parents who expect to have feminine daughters and masculine sons will make considerably more effort to put a stop to exposed bodies and rude words from girls than from boys.

Other conventional gender differences in childhood and youth have consequences for the interplay of sex and intimacy in emerging sexual identities. Aggression is tolerated more in boys than girls. When young people come to see themselves as sexual, many boys are doing so in the context of an aggressive and self-assertive masculine identity and many girls in the context of a modest, self-censoring and self-effacing feminine identity. Of course the biographies of many result in their escaping the stereotypes but boys are more steered away from pursuits designated as girlish than girls are from pursuits designated as boyish. Because of the ranking of conventional masculinity above that of conventional femininity, to be a tomboy is a lesser offence for a girl than to be a sissy is for a boy. A boy trying to be 'like girls' is always more likely to be discouraged by parents than girls being 'like boys'. In adolescence, the physiological changes experienced by girls are often responded to by parents and others in ways which feed into girls' self-censorship, fears and guilt. Menstruation is explained in terms of reproduction. The message which many parents want to communicate is one of heightened danger because of the possibility of pregnancy. Moreover, menstrual blood is to be hidden; it is treated like dirt as 'matter out of place'. Gagnon and Simon suggested that the adolescent boy's experiences of spontaneous erections and nocturnal emissions are much more readily related to sexual activity and physical pleasure. Moreover, they argued that boys collectively reinforce the focus on sex through sex-talk, valorization of the penis, comparisons of size, and masturbation competitions, while there was no equivalent acknowledgement and celebration of masturbation among girls.

The social constructionist account of sexuality takes for granted that it is possible to learn to be homosexual just as it is possible to learn to be heterosexual. Biographical events can lead people into relationships or sexual encounters with the same sex or to rejecting the dominant heterosexual pattern and redefining themselves as lesbian or gay. Nevertheless, people need not perceive their sexuality as learned or chosen. Those who define themselves as lesbian or gay offer a wide spectrum of explanations ranging from being born that way to making a deliberate political choice (Kitzinger, 1987). Gagnon and Simon (1973) suggested that because of their different gender socialization, gay men were more likely to come to see themselves as gay through experience of sex, while women were more likely to come to see themselves as lesbians through the experience of an intense, intimate relationship with a woman. In testimony to the strength of the heterosexual norms, very few people define themselves as bisexual, despite the fact that many gay and heterosexual men have sex with both men and women. Gay men have created social contexts where they can go for anonymized sex with no need for social niceties or payment. For Gagnon and Simon, the cult of casual sexual encounters in gay culture is the legacy of men's socialization into obsession with sex without the modifying influence of women seeking romantic relationships.

There is some evidence to suggest that Gagnon and Simon's, and Jackson's account of childhood and adolescent sexuality need to be updated and a great deal of evidence that confirms much has remained the same. Contemporary studies confirm the continuance of boys' more confident use of their bodies and of public space, with its implications for sexuality. Barrie Thorne, in her study of 6–9-year-old US schoolchildren in the playground, found that games sometimes label girls negatively as a group, in a way that boys as a group are never labelled. Already boys are able to express separation from girls and power over them by treating them as contaminating. 'These pollution rituals suggest that in contemporary US culture even young girls are treated as symbolically contaminating in a way that boys, as a group, are not' (Thorne, 1993, p. 75). Research on schoolchildren aged 12 and 13 shows that girls' menstruation is used sometimes by boys to treat girls as contaminated. While menstruation is not as taboo as it once was, a recent British study indicates that menstruating schoolgirls are in constant fear of becoming an object of ridicule (Prendergast, 1994). Among their fears are the possibility of boys getting sight of, drawing attention to or seizing their supply of tampons or sanitary towels in order to cause them extreme embarrassment.

Data suggest that self-knowledge obtained through masturbation is less exclusively a male experience than earlier this century, although large gender differences still exist. In a random sample of about 150 18–24-year-olds (Laumann et al., 1994), 41% of boys and 64% of girls said they had not masturbated in the last year. In her 1994 report Shere Hite declared a 'major change in how girls feel about masturbation today, as compared to the 1970s . . . 61% now as opposed to 29% in the 1970s, feel no shame but even a kind of pride in their skill and knowledge about their own bodies, especially by their teenage years' (Hite, 1994, p. 73). Hite found that the majority of women and girls masturbated but her self-selected sample cannot be treated as representative of any bigger population. Nevertheless, the numbers taking part in her study are large and she can compare the results with that of her earlier similar study (1976). Hite stressed that women often report their girlhood masturbation as a solitary, private, guilty secret separated from 'grown-up, adult' sex. While many men who completed questionnaires had masturbated as boys with other boys (60% of her sample), women had not typically taken part in group masturbation (only 9% of her sample). If childhood masturbation is less taboo for boys than girls, this is not always the case for older teenagers and young adults. Interviews with working-class British boys indicate that once these teenagers expect each other to be having sex with girls, then masturbation becomes a sign of childishness and failure at achieving manhood (Wight, 1994).

However, the ability to negotiate sexual pleasure or achieve the ideal in which sex is a peak of intimacy continues to elude most young women. Rachel Thomson and Sue Scott (Women, Risk and AIDS Project) interviewed 70 young women aged 16–21 in Manchester about how they learned about sex in the late 1980s. They found that sex education in school generally stuck to a biological/reproductive paradigm. Neither the emotional, relational, social aspects of sex nor the physiology of sexual pleasure were typically discussed. The authors comment that

> This style of sex education shapes young women's understandings of what is normal, acceptable and discussible and, while many of them resist and reject these constraints they are nevertheless materially affected by them. What is left out of school sex education is often more significant than the actual content, what is left unsaid can be more powerful than what is spoken. Diagrams which show the vagina but not the clitoris are a powerful example of the sexual disenfranchisement of young women. (1991, p. 13)

Family-based sex education was also very limited and experienced by young women as protective warnings. Michael Wyness's interviews with Scottish parents indicated that parents prefer to rely on the school for formal sex education. While parents and children were able to communicate informally through reactions to TV programmes and the behaviour of others known to the family, these exchanges were often also limited to parents imparting moral judgements or giving brief answers to children's questions (Wyness, 1992). Parents were not typically filling the silences left by formal sex education in school.

The researchers on the Women, Risk and AIDS Project also confirmed that in adolescence sexual pleasure is not a regular topic among young women. There is far more sharing of experience about periods than sex, and general ignorance about female sexuality among 16-year-olds. Girls who did know about orgasms had usually learned about them from the problem pages of magazines or from books. Girls who were sexually experienced were often too concerned about their reputation to discuss sex. Deborah Tolman (1994) similarly found in the US that girls in high school lack a vocabulary for sexual desire and believed that gaining pleasure through their bodies made them bad or unworthy. But despite their rejection of sex for the sake of sexual pleasure the majority of young women become sexually experienced by their late teenage years as a part of their search for, or development of, a relationship with a young man. Boys' sexual talk is largely boasting rather than any real exchange of information or disclosure of feelings. Teenage boys typically communicate about sex through exaggerated talk, jokes and sexual insults (Wight, 1994; Wood, 1984) which can heighten anxiety about sexuality and deter openness about ignorance.

The first occasion of heterosexual intercourse is typically a shock and disappointment to young women. Lillian Rubin's studies in the US found that first heterosexual intercourse was rarely pleasurable for either sex (1990). For young men anxiety about performance dominates. For young women ignorance (about the details of conventional sex and their own body) and the romantic image of sex as the ultimate intimate expression of love make disappointment very likely, particularly if the young man is simply concerned to 'get the thing done'. To quote one of the Women, Risk and Aids Project respondents 'You see all these love scenes on TV and they are all panting away and saying that's lovely. And you think "Oh!" But when it comes to the real thing it's a big disappointment. I think it's the mass media that I got my expectations from' (Thomson and Scott, 1991, p. 32). Describing how her teenage daughter viewed the *Top Gun* 'love scene' which she played to herself over and over again, a mother commented 'She sees it in a sort of romantic, loving way; she doesn't really see it as sex. She sees it as love, and at the moment that's how she views sex, to do with love.' (Rafanell, 1995, p. 69). Clearly the mother may have misjudged her daughter but her account is confirmed by how many young women themselves spoke of their expectations of sex. A minority of young woman interviewed for the Women, Risk and Aids Project had learned about sexual pleasure through experience, typically because they were in a relationship characterized by adequate time, space and intimacy to make this possible. Others had continued in pleasureless sexual encounters, anxiously worrying if they were 'doing it right' and often defining 'right' in terms of the man's sexual pleasure, not their own.

John Gagnon and William Simon emphasized that young women were more schooled in romance than sex. While this remains true, the Women, Risk and AIDS Project suggests it may reflect the depths of ignorance about sex more than the extent of immersion in romance. Angela McRobbie has questioned whether young women organize their lives around the pursuit of romance in the 1990s. Having argued in the 1970s that the focus of young working-class female British teenagers was 'bedroom culture' where girls schooled each other in romance, dress codes and attractiveness, she now suggests a shift away from this previous emphasis on getting and keeping a boyfriend. She takes the popularity of 'raves', huge all-night disco dancing events associated with use of the drug Esctasy, as exemplary of the trend, arguing raves are not about romance, finding a partner or sex, but the fun of 'pure physical abandon in the company of others'

(McRobbie, 1994, p. 168). However, other authors continue to speak in terms of young women obsessed with romance. Eisenhart and Holland (1983, Holland and Eisenhart, 1990) have argued that in US college culture young women are, above all, educated in romance, constructing their femininity in romantic relationships. They argue that friends and classmates are particularly powerful promoters of conventional masculinities and femininities (Holland and Eisenhart, 1990).

Studies of young people's rules of sexual conduct invariably illustrate the strength of the assumption that 'normal sex' is heterosexual. Daniel Wight sums this up with reference to his own research with young men:

> In the course of both ethnographic and formal research explicit references to homosexuality were rare. However, this did not indicate that sexual orientation was not important to young men's identities, rather it demonstrated how taken-for-granted compulsory heterosexuality is as the cultural norm . . . When boys touched on the subject in group discussion there was a predictable expression of homophobia, as found amongst the young in other parts of Britain. (Hendry, et al., 1993; Clift, et al. 1990; Wight, 1994, p. 720)

And Stevi Jackson sums up more generally in her review article: 'We all learn to be sexual within a society in which "real sex" is defined as a quintessentially heterosexual act, vaginal intercourse, and in which sexual activity is thought of in terms of an active subject and a passive object' (Jackson, 1994, p. 10). There are no question marks in the literature about the tendency of all-male groups of friends to promote conventional, unromantic, sexually obsessed masculinity among boys and young men. Miriam Johnston (1988) has argued that the male peer group is the key source of social pressure which turns young men away from intimacy. The power of the all-male peer group as a promoter of a sharp separation between sex and loving intimacy has been documented in a number of studies. Recent British examples include the study of Janet Holland and her colleagues of 16–21-year-old men in London and Daniel Wight's work with 14–16-year-old young men in Glasgow. The young men talked of the competitive pressure to perform sexually. While some could reject such pressures, many felt compelled to lose their virginity as quickly as possible. As one young man put it when asked if sex means something different for boys and girls: 'Yes, definitely, men just see it as something that has to be done, that's what I think, so your friends don't tease you. Women see it as something that really means something to them. We are using them to get something, I don't know, it's all ego when it comes down to it for men . . . it's like an achievement' (Holland et al., 1993, p. 14). Boys talk of sex as something that men do to women (Wight, 1994). A number of young men described how during their first experience of conventional sex they were thinking throughout 'I've got something to tell my mates now' (Holland et al., 1993, p. 22). At this stage in their lives, such young men have uncritically accepted a male model of sexuality which separates sex and intimacy and identifies male power as sexual conquest over women.

Janet Holland and her colleagues found young men pursuing different sexual careers after using a girl to dispose of their own virginity. Some then sought something more like a sexual relationship. Others made a sexual career out of pursuing women for sex and then immediately losing interest in them. Young men who chose this career as self-styled 'bastard' wanted to believe in themselves as star sexual performers: 'men then have to prove their prowess to women, as well as report it back to men' (Holland et al., 1993, p. 31). But the lack of communication and caring in their sexual performance meant the impossibility of knowing anything other than their own version of good sex. Some were aware of this paradox and had a conscious policy of never asking 'was it good for you?' for fear of shattering their faith in their sexual prowess. One young man maintained indifference to what girls thought or felt for him as a person while asking them what they liked in terms of sexual technique to 'keep them happy'. Like some others in the sample, he eventually abandoned his 'bastard' career. He described himself as having fallen in love and talked of the contrast between sex in his previous relationships and with his girlfriend: 'It feels totally different . . . because I love her and that, we can actually make love without actually having intercourse, just being nice to one another and that . . . it feels we are making love. But with other girlfriends sex had to be intercourse, so it was sex' (Holland et al., 1993, p. 26). Daniel Wight (1993a, 1994) also found divergences between the norms of masculine sexual conduct and young men's behaviour. While conventions of masculinity required sex without emotional attachment, some teenage men did want to know and did have feelings for young women. However, those who had revealed a more sensitive side to themselves in individual interviews, nevertheless objectified women and stuck to the norms of masculinity in group discussion, remaining publicly vague or silent about sexual details in their actual relationships.

Research on gay men continues to give qualified support to Gagnon and Simon's inferences about men's and women's socialization into a search for sex versus a search for romance. Studies find that the majority of gay men seek intimacy as well as sex; most want lasting intimate sexual relationships (Bell and Weinberg, 1978; Blumstein and Schwartz, 1983; Weston, 1991). However, their frequent ability to separate sex and intimacy means that visits to cruising areas and the like for casual sex are not necessarily considered a threat to a relationship with a partner. On the other hand, there are many gay men in stable partnerships who never visit the sex scenes. Research confirms that women's sexual relationships with other women are more typically based on friendships and mutual support than sex. For example, Lillian Faderman referring to her own US research (1991) and that of Philip Blumstein and Pepper Schwartz (1983) notes that the emphasis on sex of the 1960s and 1970s passed lesbians by:

> Because most lesbians had been socialized first and foremost as female, they were no more able than most heterosexual women in the past to form relationships primarily on the basis of sexual lust. And unlike heterosexual women in the 1970s, lesbians generally did not have partners who would prod them on to greater sexual looseness. . . . Not only were lesbians outside of committed relationships far less sexual than gay male and heterosexual singles, but even within long-term relationships they tended to be much less sexual. (Faderman, 1991, p. 247)

Kath Weston (1991) is critical of the notion that sharing the same gender results in an intensification of gendered characteristics, but notes that because this is a commonly held belief among gays and lesbians, it impinges on the way 'both lesbians and gay men configured eroticism and commitment' (1991, p. 143). For example, some men considered their relationships as particularly susceptible to breaking down because they believe men do not learn to 'nurture' while many lesbians worry that their relationships are over-nurturing, causing excessive dependency (Weston, 1991). In the 1990s some lesbians are actively reacting to the notion that lesbian identities are about relationships not sex by advocating a more aggressively erotic sexuality.

Adult sexualities and social change

Psychoanalysis teaches that many of our early emotional reactions become lost to conscious scrutiny, yet they are consequential for the patterning of our subsequent emotional life. Robert Connell suggests that one of the most valuable insights of psychoanalysis is the fact that it does not conceive of the self as a simple homogeneous core identity but rather anticipates people building psychological tension and conflict within themselves and then acting in ignorance of their self-constructed contradictions. Connell attempts to build some of the insights of psychoanalysis into the social construction paradigm of how sexuality is acquired.

In his recent text on masculinity (1995) Robert Connell provides detailed accounts of the biographies of men who have chosen a route other than conventional macho masculinity, with its associated separation of sex and intimacy, emphasis on male sexual performance and conquest of women. In interpreting the stories that men tell about their lives he is drawing on a psychoanalytic framework and its feminist variants, including the work of Nancy Chodorow and Dorothy Dinnerstein.[7] Connell is not searching for definitive causes of particular sexualities, since sexuality is not predetermined but produced through specific practices. Rather he is illustrating the unfolding of sexuality in an individual biography by reference back to the emotional attachments, resistance to attachments and rejections of early family life, as well as the backdrop of conventional stories of masculinity, femininity and heterosexuality. Among the groups of men Connell studied were a group of eight men who identified themselves as gay. Connell used the phrase 'very straight gays' to communicate their commitment to much of conventional macho masculinity despite their sexual orientation. They all grew up in households with conventional divisions of labour and power structures between their mother and father. All learned to embrace aspects of the project of male dominance. However, in childhood all identified closely not just with their father but also with their mother or sister thus allowing them to internalize the possibility of being more like their mother or sister than their father, although as boys they all conformed to masculine stereotypes. The realignment of their sexual identity typically followed on from a same-sex encounter. Realignment of sexual identity typically coincided with a new sense of self and ended a phase of rebellion or unhappiness. Another group studied were men contacted through the environmental movement. They were self-consciously 'new men' who had distanced themselves from macho masculinity, were sympathetic to feminism and wanted to treat women as equals. In examining the biographies of these men Connell shows the point at which they reversed their developing commitment to conventional masculinity and how realignment of their childhood feelings for their immediate family were part of what made this possible. For example in his story of Danny Taylor, the implication is that if circumstances had not resulted in Danny feeling excluded by the strong bond between his father and brother then he would probably have continued down the route his older brother already followed. By early adolescence, his brother had tutored him in two important aspects of masculinity, sex (celebrating sex for its own sake, objectifying women as sex objects) and football. If Danny had followed the conventional mould then in his adult relationships he would have pursued sex without intimacy perhaps until deciding to 'fall-in-love' and settle down in a relationship in which he played the dominant partner to a woman. Instead, however, he formed a strong bond with his mother in adolescence, reassessed conventional masculinity and now in his adult life seeks open and honest relationships with women.

Although analysing alternative sexualities to conventional macho masculinity, Connell's analysis suggests how robust gendered patterns of sex and intimacy are. Both gay men and 'new men' rework rather than abandon the conventional male mould. While Danny Taylor's biography demonstrates how a profound psychosexual reworking is possible it also suggests the strength of the contradiction in conventional masculinity between sex and mutually disclosing intimacy. Danny sought a relationship of openness, intimacy and greater equality but the woman he sexually desired and with whom he fell in love was not an equal in his eyes but a superior. He saw his partner as a strong woman whom he looked up to. Connell implies that Danny is unwittingly recreating the contradiction between sex and mutual intimacy in his own psyche and replacing the mother of his adolescence with a strong woman in adulthood. The gay men who Connell also interviewed were 'very straight gays' in that although they sought men as sexual partners they liked masculine men and had not themselves broken wholly with conventional masculinity. They all wanted long-term, mutually loving relationships with other men but most found they were making do with casual sexual encounters.

Lillian Rubin's interview study also found contradictions in how men and women talked about what they wanted from heterosexual relationships. Her analysis suggests that individual conflicts and contradictions reflect a process of social change. Rubin (1990) interviewed 300 heterosexual men and women aged 18–48 (from 'all over' the USA) from a range of ethnic and class backgrounds (as well as a sample of 75 younger people), some in couple relationships and some not. Many of her interviewees, particularly those outside of coupledom, conveyed a sense of unsettled heterosexual relationships. Men stated both that they were seeking strong independent women who would be their equal and yet that they also wanted women who would be soft and submissive, in other words their subordinate. Or they admitted that when they found the spirited women that they sought, they then got nervous and were not sexually interested. Some women also wanted possibly contradictory characteristics in men – successful and ambitious as well as sensitive and feeling. Some men were very angry at their perception of the impossibility of living up to what women wanted: 'The women are always talking about how they want a man who's different, you know, one who's not just an aggressive prick. Then when a guy tries to be like that, what happens? They call him a wimp' (1990, p. 154). On the double standard in sexual conduct Lillian Rubin concluded that 'Men still hold the power to define the acceptable; women still conceal their sexual behaviour. But it's no small change that many, if not most, men now question the legitimacy of their own thoughts and feelings and that most women are now angry about such sexual inequalities' (1990, p. 120). Similar findings led the British sociologists Jean Duncombe and Dennis Marsden to conclude that 'traditional role and behaviour have been disturbed to the extent that men as well as women now experience an uncertainty and ambiguity in the most intimate areas of emotional and sexual behaviour' (1995, p. 11). Some men in Rubin's study had, nevertheless, opted for the separation of sex from intimacy characteristic of conventional macho male sexuality. A fifth of men had visited a prostitute in the previous year, a considerably higher proportion than the averages reported by Laumann et al. in their survey of sexual behaviour.

While Rubin found that the overwhelming majority of women and many men valued intimacy more than sex, those who had embarked on new relationships typically started having sex before they felt they really knew the other person. Even those respondents who strongly believed that it is better to delay sex until you get to know somebody in other ways found it impossible to do this. Elisabeth Badinter has suggested that sexual passion and consuming desire have faded from human experience as the price paid for greater sexual equality and freedom (Badinter, 1981). While not accepting Badinter's romanticized view of the passionate past, it is clear that building intense passion through years of sexually desiring someone would be an unusual pattern of behaviour in the late twentieth century. Public stories of the naturalness of sex if you are in love, portraying sex as the ultimate form of intimacy, and promoting sexual consumerism, sex as a good in itself, help set the scene for quickly progressing to sexual acts. The desire to 'know the other' combined with sexual desire almost inevitably leads to sex if there are no clear proscriptions against it and when the wider culture makes sex the obvious next stage. Other agendas for developing intimacy, loving and caring, knowing and understanding, are not necessarily subverted in the process, but studies of couple relationships indicate that this can and does happen. In so far as women pursue something like 'disclosing intimacy' more typically than men, then women are more likely to be dissatisfied if intimacy is reduced to sex. This is confirmed by a number of studies, although exceptions to the rule are also found.

While surveys suggest that both men and women value intimacy, in-depth studies find that reducing intimacy to the physical intimacy of sex and seeing sex as all the intimacy you need remains more common among men than women. The following typical example of what many women and men feel about this is taken from Lillian Rubin's North American study of working-class families. A woman said, 'If we have a fight, I want to talk about it so we could maybe understand it. I don't want to jump in bed and just pretend it didn't happen'. Her male partner said, 'I want to make love to her and she says she wants to talk. How's talking going to convince her I'm loving her?' (Rubin, 1976, p. 146–7). Many women find sex increasingly burdensome without the flush of romance or any effort from their partner to make them feel loved and special. In the following example, a woman explains that sex has got worse not because her partner is doing things differently but because there is no romance to make it tolerable. 'He didn't really bother with foreplay. But somehow I was so into him that it didn't matter, and I never said anything' (interviewee quoted in Duncombe and Marsden, 1996a, p. 226). Pat O'Connor (1995) found that for most of the working-class women she interviewed (57 predominantly white married women living in London) good sex and high intimacy typically went together. However, a small minority of women rated sex as pleasurable and a time of closeness but yet did not rate their relationship highly on other measures of closeness. They had very segregated marital relationships with little disclosure or sharing of activities. For them, sex was evidence of love, and all the evidence they had. An earlier study of British middle-class marriages similarly identified unusual couples in which sex was the only time when the woman felt close to her partner. For example, a couple who were collusively drawing on both the public story of sex as the most intimate expression of love, and macho masculine notions of sex as something-men-do-to-women, said,

> 'At least, while we're having sex, I how that Brian is with me. I have his attention and his mind is completely on the job and he's not thinking of anything else.' . . . 'I can't talk to my wife, but I can throw her on the bed and then talk to her. I do feel I communicate in bed. It's obviously an intense awareness of each other, and afterwards, that's it, I change the subject mentally and physically.' (Deverson and Lindsay, 1975, p. 153)

A recent British study of long-term heterosexual couples found men complaining about lack of sex and women complaining about lack of intimacy, illustrating persistent gender differences and inequalities. Jean Duncombe and Dennis Marsden found that of the 40 long-term married couples they interviewed, the happier couples felt close and had maintained a sexual agenda of mutual orgasm but in many couples at least one partner was unhappy with their emotional or their sexual lives. Most had experienced a diminishing of sexual activity and some were currently celibate. Women's main sources of dissatisfaction were inequality in providing 'emotional reassurance and comfort' (1993, 1995b, p. 13). Cuddling, kissing, saying 'I love you' and other such emotional reassurances were wanted by women but rarely initiated by men. The complaints that men made to the interviewers were of women who 'don't try' or were 'not interested' in sex. The paucity of men's 'emotion work' influenced how women felt about sex. These themes were found to be already present among recently married couples (Mansfield and Collard, 1988). The newly wed wives reported that after marriage, men were less likely to express love when having sex, that they found it difficult to say no to sex because they did not want their husbands to feel rejected and that they tolerated sex they found less than pleasurable. Duncombe and Marsden suggest that women as new wives felt obliged to do more 'sex work' on behalf of their husbands, but men as husbands felt that 'security of possession' in marriage meant they could expend less effort on sex. Women were doing more 'sex work' to please men while men were doing less to please women. In conventional heterosexual activity men take the initiative and the lead throughout the action and are responsible for it being 'good sex' for their partner as well as themselves. What is being suggested is that, after marriage, men want to carry less of this burden. Given that most men regard their orgasm, unlike women's, as a more or less inevitable outcome of conventional sex, this means resentment at carrying the work of 'giving her one'. The consequence for women is both less satisfactory sex and feeling less loved, a loss of intimacy which feeds back into less satisfactory sex.

When men regarded women 'letting them' have sex as a part of the marriage contract, then their resentment at women's reluctance to have sex became righteous perhaps justifying coercive behaviour: 'It would be no skin off her nose . . . Sometimes I just want her to let me put it in and do it . . . She's broken the contract. Sex is part of marriage, and I can't see that anything's changed enough to alter that' (Duncombe and Marsden, 1996, p. 12). 'Pete used to say, like, he didn't mind . . . [when she did not feel like sex after the birth of their child]. But every now and then, you know, 'the erection in your back' . . . I used to feel it was my duty . . . and sex was horrible, I used to cry afterwards' (Duncombe and Marsden, 1996a, p. 229). The nature of intimacy between these couples did not lead to them talking about dissatisfaction with their sexual lives, despite a cultural backdrop of public talk about sex.

Stories, Practices and Social Change

Neither public stories nor what is known about everyday practices indicate a clear trend in sexual relationships towards equality, disclosing intimacy, and mutually negotiated do-as-we-enjoy sex. Public stories about sex offer a variety of contradictory messages which sustain both a strong narrative of predatory male sexuality separated from intimacy and a romantic fusion of sex and intimacy. The dominant narrative of official 'expert' stories emphasizes the fusion of sex and intimacy, although expert supporters of 'male sex drive' stories can still be found. The emphasis in expert stories on 'relationships' rather than roles, responsibilities and obligations has seriously displeased sections of the Moral Right. It is impossible to definitively judge the balance of narratives of popular culture, films, advertising, television soaps, novels and the like, but predatory male sexuality remains a celebrated theme and a commercially successful formula. While feminist and homosexual stories can be heard in public discourse, the dominance of heterosexual conventional sex certainly remains ensconced. New sexual stories are being told but assertions that they are the leading edge of social transformation remain a radical political desire and a conservative nightmare rather than an established trend. Stories which speak of equality, disclosing intimacy, and mutually negotiated do-as-we-enjoy sexual relationships are popular but easily matched by more conventional tales predicated on gender inequality and conventional heterosexual practices. In these stories men are propelled by sex drives and women are perpetually seducible. Although contradictory, both stories are inevitably consequential for everyday life.

Recent empirical work suggests that most adult men and women, heterosexual or homosexual, share the ideal of a fusion of sex and intimacy. It also suggests some diversification in heterosexual repertoires beyond conventional sexual intercourse. However, research also reveals a fairly bleak picture of sexual relationships between young men and women. It is a picture which incites sympathy with the more damning feminist accounts of heterosexuality (MacKinnon, 1982, 1987; Rich, 1980). It shows that young men and young women often share a phallocentric view of 'normal sex': it begins with penetration of the vagina by the penis and ends in male ejaculation. Young women lack a vocabulary for sexual desire; early sexual experiences are often devoid of pleasure and many young women continue to fake orgasm in order to please their male partner. John Gagnon's and William Simon's description of heterosexuality over twenty years ago continues to capture how many men and women begin their heterosexual careers: 'males – committed to sexuality and less trained in the rhetoric of romantic love – interact with females who are committed to romantic love and relatively untrained in sexuality' (1973, p. 74).

The image of young women cut off from their own bodies and denied sexual pleasure in their first heterosexual relationships sits uneasily with the recent findings of Shere Hite. A similarly upbeat analysis of changes in women's sexuality is to be found in the work of Barbara Ehrenreich and her colleagues who wrote in the 1980s of the quiet revolution of an historical shift in women's power to demand and receive sexual pleasure. The evidence they cited included the earlier Hite reports and figures for the increased sales of vibrators. Ehrenreich and her colleagues were concerned with the experiences of adult women rather than young women entering sexual relationships. The evidence of women in long-term couple relationships provides very limited support for this optimism. Indeed, it is impossible to wholly reconcile these optimistic views with the grimmer picture painted by other researchers. Perhaps they serve as an important reminder that many more women live in circumstances which allow them to explore the possibilities their bodies offer for pleasure than earlier in the 'modern' period. Women's expectations of sex and intimacy are higher than ever before and so perhaps it is not surprising that disappointment is common. The public stories which talk of passionate sex and intense intimacy constantly flag the possibility of negotiating mutually satisfying sex. Even when men and women come together in conditions and with ideas which work against a fusion of sex and intimacy, they both have some notion of a possibility which they are not inhabiting, even if they consider it 'not for them'. The celebration of separating sex from intimacy in conventional masculinity does not cancel out nor is it cancelled by the stories of the loving, disclosing, mutual intimacy. Each remains a consequential representation of a possible way of being in the world.

CHAPTER 6

The Couple: Intimate and Equal?

While for some academics, friendship is regarded as the quintessentially intimate relationship of the late twentieth century, the couple is the more popular choice. Friendship has the theoretical edge over domestic and sexual partners as a likely candidate for 'the pure relationship', a relationship based solely on mutual appreciation of each other's qualities. However, the couple is often treated as the more significant and central personal relationship in both public stories and in everyday practices. The historical shift from 'the family' to 'the good relationship' as *the* site of intimacy (see chapter 2) is the story of a growing emphasis on the couple relationship. By mid-century, the marriage relationship was hailed as the core of personal life, but by the late twentieth century the language is of partners rather than spouses. In the late twentieth century the term 'couple' is typically used to mean people committed to maintaining a sexual and domestic partnership, people who may well call each other 'partner'. Of course, it is also possible to qualify the term couple by talking of couples who live separately or couples who are celibate.

Those who are alarmed by the shift from spouses to 'partners' see high rates of divorce and single parenting as indicative of an associated demise of responsibility for children and of familial and moral obligations. More optimistic analysts see the softening in the monopoly of conventional marriage over personal life as allowing a healthy proliferation of ways of being a couple. For Anthony Giddens, a leading proponent of the optimistic position, greater instability in couple relationships is a corollary of the shift towards mutually disclosing intimacy and 'the pure relationship' of equals. Giddens refers to this instability as the structural contradiction of the pure relationship:

> To generate commitment and develop a shared history, an individual must give of herself to the other. That is, she must provide, in word and deed, some kind of guarantees to the other that the relationship can be sustained for an indefinite period. Yet a present-day relationship is not, as marriage once was, a 'natural condition' whose durability can be taken for granted short of certain extreme circumstances. It is a feature of the pure relationship that it can be terminated, more or less at will, by either partner at any particular point. For a relationship to stand a chance of lasting, commitment is necessary; yet anyone who commits herself without reservations risks great hurt in the future, should the relationship become dissolved. (1992, p. 137)

This chapter uses empirical research on the details of couples' lives to examine the extent to which couples are striving for equal relationships constructed through disclosing intimacy as they live together and as they part. Are the practical arrangements necessitated by living together enhancing or detracting from the quality of the relationship? The data are examined for evidence of how important equality is to couples and how being intimate emerges and evaporates in couples' lives. Research on different types of couples, married couples, cohabiting heterosexual couples, cohabiting same-sex couples, is scrutinized for the similarities and differences predicted by the optimistic visions of change. If couples are increasingly premised on 'the pure relationship' then they should desist from seeking external validation or falling back on traditional ways of being a couple in favour of sustaining their relationship solely through intense interaction with each other. Cohabiting couples and same-sex couples are then immediately at an additional 'advantage' over married couples since they have not gone through a formal legal procedure which demands public recognition for their relationship. Homosexual couples are arguably also at an 'advantage' as temptations or pressures to adopt traditional male and female roles may not be so salient to them.

The Heterosexual Couple: Still She the Housewife, He the Earner?

Much of the research on married couples has been concerned to assess how far men and women have moved from traditional relationships in which women serve men as the accepted head of the
household to a partnership of equals. Commentators of the 1960s
and early 1970s talked of marriage becoming more symmetrical.
Michael Young and Peter Willmott argued this symmetry could be
seen in divisions of labour in the home, with the old distinction between men's and women's jobs becoming increasingly blurred, a shift
to joint decision making, and increasingly shared social life (Young
and Willmott, 1973). Greater intimacy was an implied effect of greater
equality; Giele talked of men and women being better able to 'identify with each other' (Giele, 1974). However, even in the last decades
of the twentieth century many studies have found only a modest
moderation in inequalities, despite the fact that many married women
are paid employees as well as wives and mothers. The most studied
measures of equality are how domestic work in couples' households
is divided up and how their total income is distributed. A number of
authors have argued that these dimensions of personal life can have
a considerable bearing on the intimacy between couples, on how they
perceive themselves as caring and cared for, loving and loved. Exceptional couples do exist and stand out, but heterosexual coupledom
remains surprisingly organized around man-as-the-main-earner and
woman-as-domestic-worker/carer despite the prevalence of dual-
earner households. As cohabiting increases and becomes a subject of
study, a pattern of gender inequality has been documented among
cohabiting couples which is similar to marriage in many respects.
Again there are exceptional couples. Clearly radical change is possible and actually happening for a minority, however, the overall picture is one of persistent inequalities. This has led some feminist
authors to suggest that men's conservatism, their unwillingness to
give up privileges and meet the changes that women have made in
their own lives, is the cause of instability in marriage.

A number of studies of dual-worker couples in Australia, Britain,
New Zealand and North America have documented a shift, albeit
modest, towards redistributing domestic work between husbands
and wives. Ellen Rosen (1987) interviewed 233 US working-class
married women from a number of ethnic groups who were all in

blue-collar jobs or had recently become unemployed. When wives were working their husbands did more domestic work; 72% of working women had husbands who shared at least one 'inside' task as opposed to 35% of non-working women's husbands (Rosen, 1987, p. 106). This is a finding repeated in a number of studies (Pahl, 1984) including large surveys (Nickols and Metzen, 1982, and see the figures for routine domestic work and shopping in Gershuny, Godwin and Jones, 1994). However, the extra work done by men was relatively insignificant in comparison with the extra hours women added to their overall work time by entering paid employment. This is so even despite the fact that employed women cut the number of hours they spent on housework. Wives' employment has a more dramatic effect on the (reduced) hours women spend on housework than on the (increased) hours their husbands spend on housework (Geerken and Gove, 1983). Nevertheless, women have been unable to give up anything like an equivalent number of hours of housework to the hours they have taken on in paid work (Gershuny and Robinson, 1988). Studies suggest that women working part-time, fitting paid employment around young children, typically had a heavier 'double burden' of housework and employment since their husbands were far less likely to increase their contribution to domestic work than husbands of women working full-time. In general, men only routinely take up domestic chores previously done by women when women are unavailable to do them. Men are more likely to supplement the work normally done by women than to substitute themselves as the person who does the work (Berk, 1985). Using detailed 'time-budget' surveys in which people keep diaries of what they do in a day, Canadian analysts were among the first to argue on the basis of statistics that inequality between married men and women was increasing not decreasing (Meissner et al., 1975). Jonathan Gershuny and his colleagues (1994) have more recently taken issue with this analysis and used longitudinal data to argue that men are slowly increasing their share of housework, particularly in households in which women are in employment. They agree, however, that the shifts are not marked.

Historically, women carrying the main responsibility for housework has been regarded as the complement of the position of men as the main earner/provider for their wife and children. A man's position as the provider for the family was, and for some still is, a keystone of his sense of masculinity and power (Morris, 1987; Wilcock and Franke, 1963; Wight, 1993b). Men's authority in the family household has been bound up with their position as main earner. In terms of the dynamics of husband and wife relationships, this does not necessarily mean that men have in everyday ways always used money to control and dominate their wives. Oral history shows that many working-class men have routinely handed over their entire wage packet to their wives and current research indicates that this remains the system in some low-waged households.[1] However, while it may be possible for a division of labour between he-the-earner and she-the-housewife to be lived as equal teamwork, male earners' claims to special privileges and deference from the rest of the household have long had social and cultural support. Husbands and wives have often operated on the assumption that the man's delivery of the wage entitled him to expect deference and domestic service from the woman. Couples who claim symmetry, complementarity or equality for a conventional division of labour often also take for granted ways in which men have more privileges (more leisure time, more spending money, more decision-making power, more freedom to come and go).

Extensive research on household incomes, systems of money management and who controls the money, demonstrate that patterns of management and control of money between couples have changed and are changing. In Britain, for example, there has been a clear shift towards joint bank accounts and formal pooling of income away from systems in which men give women an allowance or hand over the entire wage (Pahl, 1989; Morris, 1990; Vogler, 1994). However, despite the fact that about half of couples now pool their money, in many of these cases (estimates vary between about a third (Buck et al. 1994) and three-quarters (Vogler, 1994) one person, typically the man, exercises more control. Men and women keeping entirely independent finances with each managing his or her own money is highly unusual, slightly more common among high earners and cohabiting couples.[2]

The notion of man-as-the-main-earner persists among many heterosexual couples, despite the fact that many women are working as well as men. This is partly a reflection of the different work and promotion opportunities for men and women which result in men typically earning more. But it is also the result of associated persistent assumptions about gendered responsibilities. For example, it is still often assumed that child care is primarily mother's work and therefore that women must bear the brunt of the difficulties in combining employment and bringing up children, resulting also in child care costs being mentally deducted from women's earnings rather than the combined pool. It is similarly still often assumed that men's work or career is crucial to being a man while women's employment is not bound up with being a woman, and that a wage is a man's appropriate contribution to the family-household. While in some cultures earning money has been a taken for granted aspect of being a wife, in many Euro-North American cultures women in paid employment have been viewed as either an unfortunate necessity because men cannot earn enough to fulfill their role as the main earner or as a choice made by women (unlike men who have to work to be the provider) for their own gratification.[3] For example, a North American study (Weiss 1985) found that occupationally successful husbands view their jobs as a family responsibility and their wives' jobs as a personal indulgence. The view of women choosing to work for personal satisfaction rather than for the benefit of the family persists despite the fact that most women in dual-earner households spend a higher proportion of their income on the family-household and a lesser proportion on themselves than their husbands (Pahl, 1989).

The tenacity of the conventional division of labour between couples is shown by the relatively small proportion of couples who institute radical reorganizations when a conventional arrangement is upset by male unemployment (Morris, 1990; Wheelock, 1990; Habgood, 1992). Men at home do not typically take on an equivalent burden of housework to that carried by most full-time housewives (Haas, 1982; Hunt, 1980; Russell, 1983), although this does happen in some households. In a study of men suffering unemployment in middle-age (in the North East of England), Jane Wheelock estimated that substantial changes were made in 20 per cent of cases. Several studies of households in which women are the main earners confirm that women do not translate their consequent financial power into the privileges conventionally assumed by male earners (Stamp, 1985; Morris, 1990).

Studies of cohabiting couples also demonstrate the strength of the woman-main-houseworker man-main-earner pattern, although as with married couples, there are a minority who break the rule. The similarities of cohabiting and married couples is remarkable given that:

> those who live together outside of marriage as a matter of conscious choice frequently portray their decision to do so as a means of avoiding what they regard as the stereotyped roles and conventional scripts

attached to being married. They regard their relationship as an essentially private matter which might be undermined by pressure to conform to the expectations of others. (Burgoyne, 1991, p. 247)

Despite eschewing marriage,

> as they described the details of their housekeeping arrangements, the way they divided their domestic tasks, the balance of work, home and leisure in their weekly timetables, frequent comments were made about being 'just like a married couple really'. (Burgoyne, 1991, p. 251)

In a more detailed British study Susan McRae (1993) found no significant difference between long-term cohabitees and married couples in money management, financial decision making and domestic divisions of labour. However, childless cohabitees were found to have slightly more egalitarian divisions of labour than childless married couples, although sharing tasks equally is a minority pattern among both groups (34% and 24% respectively) (Kiernan and Estaugh, 1993).

Consequential disruption and resentment?

Has women's entry into paid employment without a matching take-up by men of women's work disrupted the ease with which heterosexual couples can sustain a sense of equality, symmetry or complementarity despite inequalities? Women working potentially disrupts the conventional gendered exchange of wages and housework. If couples have typically overlooked everyday differences in power and privilege when visualizing their relationship in terms of complementary gifts – the man's wage as his expression of care for her, and the woman's matching gift of housework which expressed tender loving care for her man (Cheal, 1988) – then, when the woman also brings home a wage, her new gift requires a balancing response. However, couples can minimize the disruption to their conventional picture by talking down the woman's gifts and talking up the man's gifts, seeing, for example, women's employment as a minor supplement and praising men's occasional help with housework. Visualizing their relationship in this way centres on an intimacy which is somewhat removed from the 'pure relationship'. Love and care as expressed by material gifts is at the crux of their relationship, not a process of mutually discovering and enjoying each other.

Since the 1970s, research on the practices of couples has documented both a new sensitivity to inequality and the new ways of papering over inequalities and containing resentment and disruption, such as 'talking up' and 'talking down' each other's contributions. Lillian Rubin's study of US working-class couples (detailed separate interviews with both partners in fifty white working-class marriages) found that many women complained about the 'double shift' or 'double burden'. While they had previously accepted full responsibility for housework, entering paid employment caused some reflection on the arrangements. 'When I'm not working, I think it's perfectly natural and right that I should do everything. Even now, I still feel it's my job; but it would be nice if he could help a little when I'm gone at work so much' (Rubin, 1976, p. 104). Nevertheless, these women did not generally seek to renegotiate the division of labour although tensions were visible between many couples.

> On the surface, working-class women generally seem to accept and grant legitimacy to their husbands' authority, largely because they understand his need for it. If not at home, where is a man who works on an assembly line, in a warehouse, or a refinery to experience himself as a person whose words have weight, who is 'worth' listening to? But just below the surface, there lies a well of ambivalence; for the cost of her compliance is high. In muting her own needs to be responsive to his, she is left dissatisfied – a dissatisfaction that makes her so uncomfortable she often has difficulty articulating it even to herself. (Rubin, 1976, p. 113)

Hochschild's study of working couples with young children led her to speak of a 'stalled revolution' in which women's entry into paid work had not been matched by changes in men's behaviour (1990). The term 'stalled' also refers to the fact that many women had expected more, that they had come to believe that marriage should be a relationship of equals and now were having to manage a gap between the beliefs and the practice. Her work provides documentation of how women kept disappointment and resentment at bay by drawing on traditional beliefs about manhood and womanhood to make sense of the inequality. (People need not believe in natural gender differences to accept them as intractable; for some, it is sufficient to acknowledge that 'it is how he was brought up'.) The examples Hochschild gives sometimes echo the strategies adopted by the middle-class British couples studied by Backett (1982) to maintain their sense of a fair relationship despite actual inequality. One woman, for

example, 'confined and miniaturized her ideas of equality successfully enough to do two things she badly wanted to do: feel like a
feminist, and live at peace with a man who was not [a feminist]'
(Hochschild, 1990, p. 57). She created an I-do-the-upstairs-he-does-
the-downstairs myth of an equal division of labour. The upstairs was
the house and the downstairs, the basement and the garage. Unwillingness to threaten their marriage also inhibited women from making more demands on their men: 'If women's work outside the home
increases their need for help inside it, two facts – that women earn
less and that marriages have become less stable – inhibit many women
from pressing men to help more.' (Hochschild, 1990, p. 249). But at
the same time Hochschild perceives men's lack of help as actually
destabilizing the marriage because women experienced it as a lack
of gratitude and care.

Like Rubin's earlier work, Hochschild's analysis projects contradictory images, both a sense of crisis and the inevitability of change,
on the one hand, and a sense of containment and business as usual,
on the other. The crisis view indicates that either men shape up and
do more at home or ultimately marriage-like relationships between
men and women will not be sustained. However, Hochschild shows
that many women work at suppressing their discontent in order to
sustain their marriage. A number of British studies stress acceptance
of inequality and very muted discontent rather than crisis. A study
of dual-earner couples who were also coping with a new baby (a
longitudinal study of 243 London-based women who returned to
employment after maternity leave) found most of the women continuing to carry the responsibility for housework as well as the new
responsibility for child care. But few expressed dissatisfaction with
their partner (Brannen and Moss, 1991). Conventional views of a division of labour between 'the good mother' as carer and 'the good
father' as provider were invoked to lower women's expectations of
their husbands, mute their criticisms of their partners' lack of contributions and encourage voluble praise for the help that their men did
give (Brannen and Moss, 1991). Penny Mansfield and Jean Collard's
study of 65 British couples who were newly married in 1979 found
that despite the fact that they were both working and had only been
married a matter of months the majority had settled into a pattern of
the women doing more chores than the man. Only about a fifth of
couples had an equal division of labour. While a minority (more wives
than husbands) expressed egalitarian views, the dominant view of
the division of labour in marriage was that the wife had the main

responsibility for housework with the right to regular help from her husband. Although two-thirds of the wives were doing three-quarters of the chores, for most, their main dissatisfaction was not with their husbands but with themselves for not coping with being both an employee and a wife.

Some of these couples sought a sense of equality and disclosing intimacy and yet recreated conventional gender inequalities. As in a number of other studies, some couples claimed to have ignored gendered notions of men-as-earners and women-as-housewives but yet, nevertheless, reproduced this division of labour in their own lives. Such couples explain their apparent conventionality by self-deceiving diversionary cover stories of gender neutral accidents of fate: 'she happens to like cooking and I'm no good at it' (rather than 'I am choosing not to learn to cook'); 'I work nearer home than him and can get back earlier to cook the tea' (rather than 'I have to organize my work so that I can do domestic chores and he has not'). Many of the couples studied by Mansfield and Collard had barely discussed their arrangements; they just 'fell into place' and could be justified by referring to circumstances (like the first person who gets home cooks the dinner) competences (the person who's best at it does it), and preferences (the person who enjoys doing it does it). Each of these justifications concealed the recreation of domestic work as women's work. 'Circumstances' meant that women did more domestic work than men because more women had already organized their lives so that they were able to be at home for greater amounts of time to tackle domestic chores. Marriage had involved more women accommodating their working lives to their husbands than vice versa. Two-thirds of the women (twice as many wives as husbands) had changed jobs in the last twelve months. Many had taken less demanding jobs so that the couple could live near the husband's work. Similarly, 'competences' meant that women did more domestic work and men were responsible for cars and DIY work because previous experiences were often gendered. However, the invoking of 'competence' as a justification for division of labour involves implicit support for traditional roles, by showing a tacit unwillingness to learn new skills. Closer scrutiny of 'preferences' confirmed the earlier finding of Edgell (1980) and others that men and women do not have equal rights to exercise a preference with respect to domestic work which nobody claims as enjoyable work. For example, 'I would do the washing up normally. I mean she did that Wednesday morning because we were both very tired after a busy day on Tuesday' (husband quoted in Mansfield and Collard, 1988, p. 123).

Other studies have shown that men and women with unequivocal beliefs in gender equality can nevertheless sustain unequal gendered arrangements. An Australian study of couples at various stages of the life cycle found a pervasive discrepancy between people's egalitarian beliefs and their practices (Bittman and Lovejoy, 1993). Once again these couples talked in a neutral ungendered language about preferences and competences. They claimed mutual participation in tasks by inflating the significance of men's occasional participation, downplaying the fact that the burden of getting the task done rested with the woman by classifying it as a choice reflecting the wife's preference for a higher standard, her liking for the work or her competence at it. To take one striking example, 'Nick, who scored as very egalitarian on the attitude scale, claimed his partner Sharon "likes cooking, so she prefers to do it. I don't cook much at all, I'd rather eat food that doesn't have to be cooked. But Sharon likes cooked food, so she cooks it and I eat it"' (Bittman and Lovejoy, 1993, p. 315).

Studies of heterosexual couples suggest that imbalances in the degree of closeness each seeks from the other are common and gendered. After reviewing the North American research, Linda Thompson and Alexis Walker (1989) conclude 'Overall, women tend to be more expressive and affectionate than men in marriage, and this difference bothers many wives' (Thompson and Walker, 1989, p. 846). British studies, ranging from newly married couples (Mansfield and Collard, 1988) and long-term relationships (Duncombe and Marsden, 1993, 1995a) to marriage in trouble (Brannen and Collard, 1982), find women's main complaint is men's lack of emotional participation in their marriage. 'Overwhelmingly women reported that their male partners had seemed to "psychically desert" them by giving priority to work, becoming "workaholics" and working long hours or bringing work home. As some wives bitterly observed, "he wanted the picture" (wife, house and two children) rather than the emotional intimacy for which they had hoped' (Duncombe and Marsden, 1993, p. 226). Men, on the other hand, may not be aware of the problem: 'because men perceived themselves as working essentially on behalf of their partners and families, women's desire for emotional connectedness – coming at the end of a hard day when men felt drained by work – could too easily be seen as unreasonable 'demands' and disloyal 'whingeing' (1995b, p. 153).

Arlie Hochschild suggests that doing yet further emotional work is one of women's strategies for muting their disappointments in their relationships. 'Deep acting' (Hochschild, 1983) is the devotion of strenuous emotional effort to bringing actual feelings in line with the ideal of how a person ought to feel. Acting as if they were 'ever so happy really' while working to suppress or ignore the internal doubts closed the gap between the reality and the appropriate feeling. Duncombe and Marsden call this deep acting, to be 'ever so happy really', 'playing the couple game'. An alternative response among women in long-term relationships was to blame themselves for expecting too much and to slowly and reluctantly build an emotional life apart from their husbands, through children, part-time work and friendships with other women (1993, p. 276). Such women continue to 'play the couple game' in public but are 'shallow acting' rather than 'deep acting' (Duncombe and Marsden, 1995b; Hochschild, 1975), that is, they retain a sense of the gap between public image and private feelings. Both deep acting and shallow acting are far removed from mutually disclosing intimacy.

These studies together with that of Backett discussed in chapter 3, illustrate in some detail men's and women's skills in papering over disappointments and denying inequalities in their relationships. The stories told to researchers suggest both success and failure at protecting a sense of intimacy. Rubin speaks of a deep dissatisfaction and Hochschild of crisis. Their studies suggest that women see an imbalance in efforts made by themselves and their partners on behalf of the household, and in 'gifts' to each other, as a failure of mutual loving care. But at the same time a variety of devices are documented in these and other studies which serve to suppress discontent and rationalize inequality. Talking up men's gifts while talking down women's gifts is the device stressed by Hochschild and Brannen and Moss. Claiming who-does-what is the result of 'circumstances', 'competences', and 'preferences' is the strategy identified in studies by Mansfield and Collard and Bittman and Lovejoy. When a couple co-operatively produce justifications of conventional divisions of labour, this may signify a shared view of the world and a sense of knowing each other well. But studies also discuss strategies used to deal with failures of knowing each other. 'Deep acting' and 'surface acting' are identified by Hochschild and Duncombe and Marden as strategies used by women who felt thwarted in their desire to be close to their partner, to 'know' him and 'be known'.

Not all couples contain dissatisfaction successfully, however. About a fifth of the couples in Mansfield and Collard's study, were already sufficiently disappointed with their marriage to have doubts about the future. Many of the arguments cited as triggering doubts were women expressing dissatisfaction with the domestic division of labour and demanding that husbands do more. However, it seems that while divisions of labour triggered disputes, the crux of the discontent was the lack of emotional closeness that women felt. This fits with the analysis of Brannen and Moss (1991) who suggested that women are substantially helped in overlooking inequalities if they feel they are getting emotional support from their husbands. In combination, this work suggests that intimacy is multi-dimensional for many couples. A deficit in practical love and care can be balanced up by intimacy generated in other ways but women seem to particularly value 'feeling close', yet often experience men as emotionally absent.

Heterosexual couples who did things differently

Research also identifies another group. These are heterosexual couples who claim to work out their lives without gender stereotyping and succeed in escaping the conventional divisions of labour. Among recent studies, the Australian work of Jacqueline Goodnow and Jennifer Bowes is the most optimistic about progress towards not only a more equal division of labour among heterosexual couples but a more profound equality and deeper intimacy. This study set out to recruit a sample of couples who did things differently from the conventional gendered division of labour. They decided not to restrict the study to couples with a highly shared or equal division of labour, such as those interviewed in North American studies by Haas (1982) and Kimball (1983), and in Britain by VanEvery (1995) as these studies had tapped into politicized feminist networks and generated a sample of highly educated middle-class couples. Goodnow and Bowes wanted to recruit a less extraordinary and more varied population. Their study is far removed from a random sample, however.[4] The couples were recruited from a list generated by asking everybody they knew including their students to come up with names and addresses of couples who 'did things differently'. They recruited 50 couples among whom one or both partners took responsibility for an area of work not conventionally assigned to their gender. For 28 couples, their main style of organizing household jobs was to specialize, each with their own jobs, but men had taken responsibility for a job conventionally designated women's work vacuuming, cooking, shopping, cleaning bathrooms, washing clothes and ironing. The other couples had much more fluid arrangements for get-

ting the jobs done, switching responsibilities back and forth, sometimes doing jobs jointly, sometimes one or the other getting on with
it alone.

These divisions of labour had been negotiated, in the case of half
the couples after much talk and sometimes argument, often having
started off on a different footing. In other words, things had not 'just
fallen into place'. Discussion had sometimes taken couples back to
basic questions like: Does this job need to be done? Who should do it?
Where does the work come from and who gave rise to it? How much
pain or pleasure does the work cause each of us? (Goodnow and Bowes,
1994, p. 72). Other couples talked less but also appeared to view the
work as jobs that both of them had to get done rather than men's and
women's jobs. A list of principles and goals of fairness emerged as the
ideals underlying their allocations of tasks: if it's your mess then it's
your job; if it's to your benefit, and you could do it yourself, you should
do so; no one person should do it all; no one should get 'stuck' with all
the 'dull' jobs; if one person is not working, both should be not working; subservience and privilege should be avoided – I am a person,
not a servant; things should be kept equal; who does what should
involve choice rather than expected roles (Goodnow and Bowes, 1994,
p. 64, 104–15). These principles did not translate into rigid formulas
but offered rules of thumb that couples referred to when explaining
the fairness of their own arrangements or in negotiating adjustments
between themselves. The process of negotiating was often a painful
one. Women were more often the initiators of discussion and sometimes had to work very hard to get their partner to see the need to
talk. It was difficult to renegotiate divisions of labour without bringing awareness of power issues to the surface. One woman described
the difficulties she had in asking her partner to do things: 'I don't want
to beg, and Don doesn't like to feel he's taking orders' (Judy, quoted in
Goodnow and Bowes, 1994, p. 87).

The 'circumstances', 'competences' and 'preferences' other couples used to justify unequal divisions of labour were not, of course,
irrelevant to these Australian couples. Individuals' different approaches to and degrees of pleasure in ordering their domestic lives
were factors which influenced who specialized in what task, but specialization that involved the degree of inequality of the conventional
division of the 'inside' as women's work as and the 'outside' as men's
work was not acceptable. They wanted fairness that was more real
than apparent and hence when negotiating, 'somehow, they must
work their way through the use of "doesn't know how" or "doesn't

see" rather than [the less self-serving honesty of] "would rather not"' (Goodnow and Bowes 1994, p. 30). Goodnow and Bowes argue that their respondents saw doing things for each other as an expression of care for each other. Their ethos was one of give and take, not of constantly watching each other to see who was doing more and, for each of them, doing more some of the time was a gift to the other person. Unlike some couples, however, they openly acknowledged that to be a gift, the gift must be freely given and cannot be taken for granted. Therefore, it was never acceptable for the women to be the main givers and the men the main receivers. The couples generally avoided the 'coercive style' of insisting 'this is how I am and I cannot change', leaving the other with no choice but to do the work. The couples who did things differently are not necessarily distinguished from couples in other studies by the kinds of things they wanted and valued from each other. Other couples claimed to want both the openness and honesty of mutually disclosing intimacy and more practical forms of love and care. However, the couples who did things different ultimately made a more mutual effort to match their ideal and reality. The process was often initiated by women who opted for speaking out, rather than deep or surface acting, despite the conflict that was often the initial consequence.

Domestic Violence and Forced Intimacy

'Domestic violence', typically men being violent towards their female partners, provides a contrasting example of couples in which women dare not speak out. Couples in which men are violent may manage an appearance of intimacy but, as violence supplants negotiation by coercion, the possibility of mutually constructed intimacy is undermined. Violent partners rarely acknowledge their violence and may claim to be intensely intimate. Janet Askham (1984), in a study of the complexities and tensions of married life, interviewed a couple in which the husband was clearly controlling and dominating his wife through threatened if not actual violence.[5] Because this study was centrally concerned with intimacy it provided insight into the extent to which a relationship was being constituted as intimate while overshadowed by the threat of violence. The husband, Alan, said he knew his wife, Anne, inside out, but, by his own testimony, he did not talk much to her and, by his wife's testimony, he was not interested in listening to her. His main confidant was his workmate of many years standing. The couple had a conventional division of labour. He controlled the money. She did the housework. In addition, she was frightened of him.

> Alan: [speaking of his wife] I think I know her very well. I think I knew her before I got married. I can tell you anything what she thinks before she says it. I can tell you what she is thinking. . . . And as much as I know her I don't think she knows that much of me. I can tell when she's going to say anything, do anything. (Askham, 1984, p. 33)

> Anne: [speaking of her husband] There's a lot of things that I can't talk to him about. A lot of things that I would like to say. I'm a bit frightened of him at times, you know. . . . I think that I would get to know him better if he maybe did tell me a little more. . . . He doesn't want to hear when he comes home from work he doesn't like to hear what's happened during the day. Things like that. He likes to think more about working to a budget and what he's going to buy, things like that. (Askham, 1984, p. 51)

The interviewer asks Anne whether her husband likes to think of himself as, and whether he is, master of the house.

> I think that he is, but it makes me angry as well that he is – a bit angry that he won't listen to some things that I say. . . . If I ask him to do something, if he doesn't feel like doing it he just won't do it, but if there's something that he wants done, sometimes I'm so frightened of him I just go and run and do it. And then I get so annoyed that he *can* do that and I come running. (Askham, 1984, p. 102)

Anne has tried to be open and Alan has responded by a variety of controlling tactics, including deliberately withholding himself and acting to generate her fear. Alan claims intimacy when he speaks of how well he knows his wife. However, this is certainly not mutually disclosing intimacy, nor is it intimacy based on a taciturn shared understanding. What is going on is an attempted imposition of his view of how the marriage will be conducted and how his wife will behave and speak, if not think. Alan is partially successful in that his wife is frightened to say what he does not want to hear and runs to do what he wants done. However, he is not entirely successful because his wife recognizes withholding and controlling behaviour and builds this into her picture of Alan. In time, she may decide that he is not a person that she can continue to love or live with. The dynamic between them of controlling and trying to survive being controlled is a stunted form of intimacy which involves one person wilfully not knowing another and disregarding their well-being while typically refusing to acknowledge that this is what they are doing. Domestic and sexual violence often has this character (Dobash and Dobash, 1979, 1992; Kelly, 1988; Gordon, 1988; Scutt, 1983). Men who have been convicted of violence to their wives typically refuse to discuss their violent behaviour with their wives. Moreover they use a variety of strategies to reinterpret and minimize the seriousness of their violence, just as men convicted of rape often refuse to acknowledge that it was rape and minimize and rationalize their behaviour (Scully, 1990).

The fact that 'domestic violence' remains prevalent demonstrates the gap between the lives of a significant minority of heterosexual couples and the ideal of 'the pure relationship'. While there is no way of being certain, the various estimates of incidence suggest that heterosexual couples in which men intimidate women are probably more common than those who negotiate exceptional equality. A large survey of US marriages estimated that a violent assault would occur between husbands and wives in the course of over a quarter of US marriages (28 per cent, Straus, Gelles and Steinmetz, 1980), and that attacks by husbands on wives are both more common and more dangerous to life and limb than attacks by wives on husbands. The problem of estimating the incidence and trends in domestic and sexual violence are considerable and fiercely debated (Kelly, 1988 includes a critique of Strauss et al.; Kelly, Burton and Regan, 1996). However, the evidence of widespread prevalence of male domestic and sexual violence is unequivocal. Men's use of their body as a tool and weapon is one source of men's power as men, although only a minority of men routinely use violence or threats to dominate and control their partner. Those who are optimistic about the future of intimacy and gender equality categorize such men as remnants of desparate traditionalism trying to hang on to private patriarchal power, while 'couples who do things differently' are in the forefront of social change. However, male violence seems to retain much wider roots than this analysis would suggest.

Same-sex Couples

An obvious difference between heterosexual and homosexual couples is that assumptions about differences between male and female may not play the same role in their relationship. Ideas about the gendered appropriateness of being a 'provider' or a 'housewife', notions about outside jobs as 'men's work' and inside jobs as 'women's work' cannot be unthinkingly applied to allocate tasks within a same-sex couple. However, Lawrence Kurdek puts the case rather too simply 'gay and lesbian couples . . . cannot use gender to assign roles in their relationships for the obvious reason that both partners are the same gender' (1993, p. 127). Kurdek forgets that femininities and masculinities can be constructed without regard to the biological sex of the physical body. From the 1940s to the 1960s a working-class form of lesbian subculture emerged in the USA in which women were 'butch' or 'fem', with styles of dress and patterns of interaction which looked like male and female roles (Faderman, 1991, 167–74). Kath Weston has explored the use of gender, divisions of labour and equality in gay and lesbian relationships (1991, 146–53). She found that lesbian and gay men valued equality in their relationships, although there was a considerable range of views concerning what constituted equality. A commitment to equality did not prevent some lesbians and many gay men from using gender categories. Some lesbians were strongly against any revival of butch/fem roles because they believed that contrasting roles recreated the inequalities of conventional heterosexual relationships. Others strongly denied this charge (Nestle, 1984). Most gay men use the categories 'queen' and 'butch' to place other gay men along a gendered continuum but 'the majority agreed that within an erotic relationship they were inclined to seek congruence rather than complementarity, with a preference for the butch end of the spectrum' (Weston, 1991, p. 146).

When same-sex couples use gender categories, they are not typically translated into a conventional main-earner-main-houseworker pattern. Many studies have found that same-sex couples typically have more equal divisions of labour than heterosexual couples.[6] Most of these studies indicate that women in couples typically adopt an equal division of labour regardless of who earns what. However, Ruth Habgood states that in same-sex couples the more employment-oriented partner has the greater ability to distance her or himself from domestic commitments (Habgood, 1992 p. 175). Philip Blumstein and Pepper Schwartz (1983) found that gay male couples tended to adopt practices in which higher income translated into greater power, including exemption from domestic work, although divisions of labour were not typically as extreme as a traditional husband and wife relationship. Gay and lesbian relationships that are very unequal create a heightened possibility of violence, just as violence is more common in heterosexual relationships in which men see themselves as akin to lord and master. However, violence is particularly uncommon in lesbian relationships not only because they are less frequently unequal but also because women are generally less skilled in techniques of violence and bodily intimidation than men.[7]

While studies do not always provide sufficiently detailed accounts to clarify the dimensions of intimacy in gay and lesbian relationships, literature suggests that emotional closeness through the knowing of mutual disclosure and through practical caring are characteristic of lesbian relationships. Indeed, as Kath Weston notes, lesbians sometimes report concern that their relationships are too intense while gay men are more likely to feel they have trouble in sustaining intimacy (1991). The combinations of equality, mutuality and knowing-each-other reported in literature on lesbians has led Anthony Giddens to argue that this is the group that currently most typically achieves 'the pure relationship'. However, a relatively small body of research is not a good basis for such strong generalization.

Intimacy and Relationship Breakdown

Giddens's analysis of the fragility of the pure relationship (Giddens, 1992, p. 136–40) was outlined in the opening paragraphs of this chapter. By way of supporting his case, he notes that lesbian relationships, which he identifies as exemplars of 'the pure relationship' do not typically last as long as marriage or heterosexual cohabitation. Whether or not lesbian relationships approximate to 'the pure relationship', North American authors lend support to the view that relationships founded only on mutual pleasure in an intense knowing-each-other are inevitably fragile. Lillian Rubin's years of empirical research on heterosexuals has convinced her that if intimacy is sought purely as a realization of the self through another then it is inherently contradictory (self and other can never be totally one) and bound to fail (Rubin, 1990 quoted in Duncombe and Marsden, 1995b). Some psychoanalytic authors have also been at pains to stress that disappointment in close relationships is an inevitable consequence of the contradictory desires sedimented in the human psyche (Craib, 1994). The conclusion seems to be that if there is, indeed, a trend towards pursuing disclosing intimacy, then the pain and suffering of breakdown in a couple relationship is doomed to be a recurrent feature with all the unfortunate consequences for the children and other members of the couple's previously joint social networks.[8]

Some authors suggest that if a pattern of fragile serial relationships of intense disclosing intimacy is becoming the typical pattern, then such relationships must not be the core of a personal life if damage is to be minimized. A number of studies suggest that many of those who are held up as exemplars of 'the pure relationship' by Giddens – that is, lesbians do not seek intimacy through couple relationships alone but rather through their 'family' of friends and ex-lovers. However the public stories about the couple and the practical circumstances of men and women work against more general adoption of this pattern by the heterosexual majority.

> Yet the power of this image of heterosexual intimacy is an obstacle to the pursuit of other options more transient heterosexual 'monogamy', lesbian relationships or celibacy particularly while women remain economically and legally disadvantaged. Alternatively, women might retain the goal of some kind of commitment in a longer-term relationship with a man, but recognise the ideology of permanent *emotional* intimacy is flawed and too demanding. Perhaps, intimacy cannot survive familiarity and habituation, and must inevitably decay albeit with a compensatory residue of companionship. (Duncombe and Marsden, 1995)

Are those relationships which are theoretically more likely to be constituted as 'pure relationships' – cohabiting relationships and same-sex relationships – unequivocally so? Is it possible that, even if cohabiting and same-sex relationships are more fragile than married relationships, then this is for reasons that have nothing to do with 'disclosing intimacy'? The evidence on the fragility and quality of same-sex relationships is limited. Recent British work (Dunne, 1997, and the work in progress of Jeffrey Weeks and colleagues at the University of the South Bank, London) reaffirms that same-sex couples themselves often believe their relationships are more intimate, more equal and less possessive than heterosexual relationships. However it is not clear whether the quality of intimacy in their relationships is different from that of heterosexual couples who 'do things differently'. Many studies which have considered this issue have been small and the most commonly studied population is in the San Francisco Bay area of California.[9] A number of studies have found a range of ways of having relationships rather than one pattern. Moreover, it is worth reiterating that instability in couple relationships does not necessarily mean constant radical change in personal social networks as ex-lovers can remain friends. There is a growing body of evidence that cohabiting relationships are somewhat less long-lived than marriage relationships. The British Household Panel Study suggests that cohabitation is substantially less stable than marriage (Buck et al. 1994; McRae, 1993). In Britain and North America about half of those cohabiting are planning to marry at some stage. The British Household Panel Survey notes that twice as many cohabitations end in marriage than separation but there is some evidence of a trend away from marriage to separation (reported by Clarke and Burghes, 1995). One possible interpretation is that more cohabitees are founding their relationship on mutually disclosing intimacy alone than married couples are, and that Giddens is correct in noting that such relationships are inherently unstable. However, the data reviewed in this chapter suggest that the majority of couples, married and cohabitees, conventional and couples-who-did-things-differently, do not found their relationships on disclosing intimacy alone. Cohabiting relationships may be less stable than marriage because they have low levels of social support from others and few binding economic and material ties. These are factors which Giddens associates with a 'pure relationship' founded on 'disclosing intimacy' but they can occur for other, more contingent, reasons in any relationship which is not a conventional marriage.

Even those cohabiting couples who are eschewing the social recognition of marriage are less different from married couples than they might appear at first sight. Interview studies suggest that cohabitees typically treated as unwelcome any assumptions that they were 'unattached' individuals who were therefore possibly romantically available. Most desired recognition as a committed couple without being reduced to an adjunct of their partner (Burgoyne, 1991; VanEvery, 1995). Moreover, cohabiting couples are not a homogeneous category. Some are trying to be more actively different than others. A small minority may pursue more open relationships. Surveys suggest the minority of people with two partners is higher among cohabiting couples than married couples.[10] However, it cannot be concluded that cohabiting relationships that are closest to a conventional marriage are least likely to break down. For example, in Burgoyne's study the most unstable couples were those in which one wanted to marry and one did not. In this study a minority of the men and women who had chose cohabitation in preference to marriage (rather than those who were planning to marry eventually anyway) now wanted to marry because they felt their relationship was insecure. The women who wanted to marry typically did not have access to permanent jobs and wanted to have children. When their partners resisted both the idea of children and marriage they set a 'spiral of uncertainty and insecurity' in train (1991, p. 253). Several men who felt in the shadow of their partner and her career were similarly advocating marriage and a family, with their insecurity in the relationship increasing when met by their partner's resistance.

However, there is another possible direction to pursue in trying to understand the fragility of relationships and their likely future. Much of the evidence of this chapter suggests that 'disclosing intimacy' is not the dominant type of intimacy in most couple relationships. One story about heterosexual couples is that men are not willing to make the same effort as women in sustaining the intimacy of their relationship and that women are increasingly dissatisfied. Some authors suggest the failing is men's lack of emotional openness, their unwillingness to participate in disclosing intimacy. Duncombe and Marsden's solution to relationship breakdown is that 'people *men* as well as women should learn that the sustaining of relationships demands emotion work from *both* partners' (1995, p. 164). However, much of the evidence is also about men's underparticipation in more practical loving and caring. Here too many men are not matching the efforts put in by women to their household. This also affects the quality of the couple relationship. For most couples, intimacy was intertwined with and expressed through practical arrangements of who did which household chores, who spent what money and the like. Men and women did not bracket off these aspects of their relationship in how they viewed each other but saw them as part of how they loved or did not love each other. Arguably, it is the persistence, not the demise of, the notion of man-main-earner and woman-main-houseworker/carer which is destabilizing, at the century's end. Failure to fully set such notions aside perverts men's and women's efforts to find a balance in practical caring and emotional work, a balance which does not simply paper over a gap between ideal and real, glued down with lurking resentment.

CHAPTER 7

Conclusion

An overarching task of this book is to assess the claim that a particular form of intimacy, 'disclosing intimacy' – a process of two or more people mutually sustaining deep knowing and understanding, through talking and listening, sharing thoughts, showing feelings – is increasingly sought in personal life. This claim goes further to suggest that a shift to 'disclosing intimacy' has affected or will affect all the significant relationships in personal life with consequences for the wider social fabric. Assessment of such a vision of the near future requires that we distinguish public stories about social change from the everyday private practices. Is there a sense in which the alleged shift to 'disclosing intimacy' is just a story or are actual lives being lived differently? One possible reading of this book is that widespread stories about personal life have changed much more dramatically than private practices. In other words, 'disclosing intimacy' is not becoming the crux of personal life as it is lived, despite a much greater emphasis on this type of intimacy in public stories about personal life. However, the distinction between public story and personal life needs immediate qualification.

The main and often only way of finding out about everyday practice is through the stories people tell about themselves. In telling their own stories, people often draw on public stories to reinterpret and make sense of their own lives. But, as noted in chapter 1, the very process of drawing on public stories can be consequential for how people think about themselves and can affect the way they conduct their lives. If private lives are affected by public stories, then so also are public stories dependent on being heard and retold in everyday lives. Practices, private stories and public stories are not neatly separate but interconnected and mutually creating. The interconnections then must limit the possibilities for disassociation between public stories and private practice. At the same time, some divergence between public stories and private lives is not unexpected, as public stories are necessarily schematic and partial, offering stereotypes and ideals rather than the details and contradictory complexity of real lives. However, given the interconnections, it would be very surprising if shifts in public stories over time do not, however imperfectly, indicate something of the direction of change in private lives. It is impossible that a new emphasis on 'disclosing intimacy' in public stories does not have some resonance with the everyday ways in which people live their lives. Nevertheless, this book suggests that the story of a shift to 'disclosing intimacy' is too selective a story to be anything other than a very partial picture of an emerging future.

One of many reasons why the story of disclosing intimacy is not more fully resonant with private lives is because it is not the only current story of how lives should be lived. There are other often repeated and pervasive refrains. If the connectedness of public stories and private lives is taken seriously, then the gap between any particular public story and everyday realities can be partly explained by the existence of alternative and competing public stories. New public stories have not drowned out previously dominant stories of how personal life should be lived, despite marked shifts over the duration of the twentieth century. As was noted in chapter 2, in the second half of the century stories of 'the family' speak less of the good of the family itself, as an institution, as a domestic, economic and social unit, and more of good family 'relationships'. By the closing decades of the century, the story of 'a good relationship' holds up one dimension of intimacy above all others, the knowing and understanding of 'disclosing intimacy'. Stories often celebrate disclosing intimacy by depicting the damage done to the self and others by those who do not participate in this way of being intimate. The message is that the unfortunate character has lost or never found the path of being in touch with his or herself and others. But at the same time as disclosing intimacy is so eulogized, the Moral Right remain particularly vocal advocates of a family life in which parents and children, husbands and wives have relationships marked by appropriate social distance, respect and obligation. The story of the

conventional family of husband/father/provider and wife/mother/
carer and domestic worker continues to influence parenting and
couple relationships. But the Moral Right have no monopoly over an
even older and more persistent story of sexual relationships, that of
sexually driven men and seducible women, and of heterosexual sex
as the natural mastery of men over women. A version of this story is
also told by pornographers, by rapists, by many popular films and
ordinary people, and like many versions of the story of the conventional family, it contradicts the ideal of equality between men and
women required by heterosexuality founded on 'disclosing intimacy'.
In both heterosexual and homosexual relationships stories of gender
differences between men and women continue to help shape how
people go about having sexual encounters and relationships.

Another way of assessing the claim that 'disclosing intimacy' is
increasingly sought in personal life is to ask questions about the
nature of intimacy. It was suggested in chapter 1 that there are other
ways of being intimate and several possible dimensions of intimacy
which can be distinguished from 'knowing and understanding'.
Hence, it is possible to conceive of social change such that relationships are felt to be more intimate without this necessarily being based
on 'disclosing intimacy'. Might the thesis that 'disclosing intimacy'
is increasingly sought in the personal life of the 'postmodern' or late
modern period, overdramatize a selected aspect of the variety of ways
in which people create intimacy? Research suggests that there is a
greater emphasis on 'knowing' and 'understanding' than in early
decades, but that 'knowing' and 'understanding' are not necessarily
becoming the key or central focus of personal life. Love, practical
caring and sharing remain as or more important in many types of
personal relationships. When people are asked about their ideal
mother, father, friend, lover, or partner, then 'someone who you can
talk to' or 'someone who understands me' are not uncommon responses, but unconditional love, support, help, and care are often
also mentioned, and in many relationships these aspects of intimacy
remain more important than the dynamic of disclosing intimacy.
When people share living arrangements, as domestic partners, or as
parents and children typically do, they necessarily have to negotiate
practical activities and the use and care of resources. In such situations, what people do for and with each other necessarily affects
how they feel about each other. Sometimes actions do speak louder
than words. Moreover, disclosure is not automatically associated with
intimacy, as viewers of the Oprah Winfrey genre of talk show will

know. Research also throws up examples in which disclosure, telling and knowing, between partners and family members is not cor-related with close and loving relationships. There are also empirical examples of people who feel really close to others with whom they rarely speak. Moreover, some who say that they 'really know' and are 'really close' have their view contradicted by the person whom they 'really know'. Intimacy remains a great deal more complicated than most claims to mutual knowing and understanding.

It has been suggested that parent–child relationships, friendships, sexual and couple relationships are all converging towards 'the pure relationships' founded on equality and disclosing intimacy and sus-tained only by the mutual satisfaction of parties to the relationship. This means that aspects of the parent–child and couple relationships which historically have not matched the defining characteristics of friendship are becoming less significant. Hence, it is suggested that the obligatory, rather than voluntary, and hierarchical, rather than equal, character of the parent–child and husband–wife bond has dis-solved. It is quite possible to demonstrate a greater emphasis on be-ing-like-friends, being 'pals', as the ideal for parents, lovers and partners in both the stories of experts and popular culture. In public stories, the good mother is not only, or even primarily, providing practical care and a secure sense of being loved but she knows, un-derstands and responds to her children's inner selves. In some re-cent public stories about fatherhood, neither the disciplinarian patriarchal father nor a more indulgent father-provider has done enough to qualify as a new sensitive father with a deep knowledge and understanding of his children. These public stories support the view that parents and spouses are or will be like friends to each other, having broken with the past of each-in-their-place, playing out a fam-ily role. However, it is not so clear that this picture of change sums up how people are behaving towards each other in practice.

The suggested shift to voluntary, equal, relationships of disclosing intimacy is particularly difficult to sustain with respect to parent–child relationships. It is true that mother–child and father–child re-lationships are voluntary in the sense that they are relationships which can be broken. Fathers and mothers do abandon children and re-cently there have been cases of children using new children's rights to divorce from their parents. The analysis of Janet Finch suggests that a lifelong 'good relationship' between parents and children is a negotiated affair sustained by mutual appreciation. Historically, this voluntarism in practice has coincided with the public teaching that the parent–child bond is a natural and God-given bond of sacred obligations. While public teaching is now more the domain of psychological than religious experts, the emphasis on the sacred nature of the parent–child bond has hardly lessened, although love is stressed without reference to God-given duties. There is no empirical evidence to suggest that once people have become socially recognized as parents, then parent–child relationships are seen as more profoundly voluntary now than earlier this century. Despite media attention to 'home alone' cases, there is no evidence that mothers are now more likely to see mothering as an activity that can be abandoned, if it does not bring pleasure, than they were in the past. While there are always examples of relationships which have broken down, the dominant picture is of mothers working hard, and typically harder than fathers, to keep 'good relationships' with their children. What a good relationship means continues to vary by class and ethnicity, despite the cultural dominance of a particular notion of 'the good mother'. The frequency with which fathers abandon children following divorce indicates that being a father is practised as a more voluntary activity than mothering. This gender difference certainly cannot be attributed to a shift in father–child relationships towards 'disclosing intimacy'. In the minority of cases in which previously very involved fathers desert their children following divorce, the difficulty of trying to sustain an intense emotional relationship without everyday routine contact may be a factor, but most fathers who absent themselves were already relatively uninvolved with their children. The persistence of a limited view of fatherhood as father-as-provider and father as mother's helper is more implicated than a shift to 'disclosing intimacy'.

Parent–child relationships differ from the ideal-typical friendships in another more important respect. Parents cannot start as equals to their children, and no matter how democratic they try to be it will necessarily remain a relationship between superordinate and subordinate for many years. In chapter 3 I suggested that the notion that parenting could be as-if-parents-and-children-were-equals was implausible as a feat of everyday parenting. Parents have proudly told researchers about how they talk to and listen to their children in a way that their parents did not talk to or listen to them, and such parents recognize that they do not demand the deference and distance that their own parents expected. However, this does not necessarily mean that parents seek either equality or all the other aspects of 'disclosing intimacy'. Parenting is necessarily embroiled in practical, financial and domestic arrangements which typically give parents power over children in addition to the power of any greater knowledge, social skill or wisdom parents may have as a result of their older years. Parenting is not a homogeneous experience, as parents work with very different financial and other resources. Class, ethnic and gender differences in styles of parenting persist, despite the consensus among experts about how to be a good parent. Research suggests that white middle-class parents are more interested in disguising their power but that this need not lead to either less conflict with children or a closer relationship. For example, those who hope to surreptitiously exercise influence by knowing the details of their older children's lives often undermine their project of maintaining a 'good relationship'.

The overwhelming majority of parents do not treat their children as-if-they-were-equal but protect their children from their own thoughts and feelings. Even child experts who advocate attentive, listening, responsive parenting do not advocate a mutual disclosing intimacy between parents and children, because children are to be protected from adult worries and burdens. Parents are enjoined not to use non-adult children as confidantes and support systems. Expert advice about what to tell children when there is a divorce for example, focuses on how to help the child: 'this is not your fault' and 'we still love you' are the key messages. Advice concerning avoidance of burdening children with worries may stem from seeing children as vulnerable and in need of protection and hence as dependents. But it also incites parents to recognise a divergence between their own needs and the needs of their children which encourages seeing them as independent. As children get older, negotiating a more equal relationship is part of successful parenting and successful growing up. For some people, this means parents and children having less to say to each other, respecting each other's right to get on with their lives.

The suggestion that couple relationships have become more like a friendship based on 'disclosing intimacy' is only marginally easier to defend. When sociologists of the 1950s and 1960s talked of a shift in marriage from 'institution' to 'relationship' they were already proclaiming the tendency for marriage to come closer to the characteristics of a friendship. There are theoretical reasons why not only marriage but other forms of sexual/domestic partnerships typically bind people by more than friendship. A domestic partnership may involve a different level of economic security and material comfort than could be assured outside of the relationship. Moreover, unlike friendship, coupledom is expected to be and to remain a sexual relationship, which adds another complicating dimension. If a couple embarks on the project of having children, then this necessarily means they are no longer a dyad whose focus is simply each other. Sexual/domestic partners often stand to gain or lose much more than the enjoyment or otherwise of their relationship if they split up. The thesis that couples are increasingly centred on disclosing intimacy suggests that it is theoretically possible for a couple to bracket off the material, economic and social aspects of their relationship; whether this is theoretically possible or not, there is no clear evidence that it is happening in practice. It has been argued that if such a shift were occurring then more fragile relationships would be a consequence. The current high rate of marriage breakdown, cannot be explained primarily in this way, however. Complaints of partners who do not talk or listen or understand are powerfully expressed in the literature but they are typically alongside other complaints of imbalances in loving and caring which seem to carry equal weight. Research suggests that many couples believe they express love and care for each other through gifts, tokens and practical activities, including putting effort into their household through bringing home a wage and housework. Loving, caring and sharing remain as important as knowing and understanding. Stress in heterosexual couple relationships often originates from conflict over who does the housework as expressing an imbalance of love and care as much as failures of knowing and understanding.

For any particular couple, what makes for a good relationship, what is in and out of balance when generating intimacy through talking, 'knowing and understanding' versus the doing of more practical loving, caring and sharing, is complicated and difficult to untangle. If, for example, a heterosexual couple have agreed that the best practical arrangement is that the woman stays at home to care for their child, despite their belief in equal parenting, then it may be important to their relationship that they continue to explore feelings of compromise and sacrifice (about foregoing employment, associated with career, financial independence and status or foregoing full-time parenting) involved in this choice. However, actions at the weekends or evenings which affirm the man's commitment to parenting might be equally important to sustaining a sense of mutual respect and a shared project. Backett's research demonstrated couples successfully maintaining intimacy despite inequality, without very direct or open acknowledgement of the gap between their ideals and reality. These couples made light of the mother's much greater involvement with their children, saying it was just a stage or phase. They boosted their sense of the father's participation through talking about what children and mother had been doing and by giving symbolic significance to small or occasional acts of fathering as proof that the father could and did participate. Their balance between 'knowing and understanding' and practical loving and caring involved a degree of conspiracy in self-deception rather than deep exploration of each other's feelings. A more traditional couple, who have no sense of mothering and fathering as similar activities but, rather, are comfortable with the view that the man's role is that of earner/provider and the woman's main role is that of mother/carer, need neither self-deception nor compensatory work.

Friendship relationships have been characterized as the purest example of relationships based on 'disclosing intimacy' uncomplicated by legal, financial and material ties, but the empirical research again shows a more complicated picture. Although it may be the ineffable 'something that clicked' which makes for good friends, good friends are expected to help each other and sometimes do. Friends are often contrasted to kin as voluntary versus obligatory relationships. However, in practice friends and kin do not look very different. Relationships between parents and children often carry higher expectations of mutual help than relationships with other kin and friends. In practice many parents and children sustain lifelong flows of assistance, but in all kin and friendship relationships, assistance is unlikely to be sustained without mutual liking and intimacy. In the case of both friends and kin, several different styles of intimacy can be found in practice, and there is no clear evidence that disclosing intimacy is the dominant or ascendant type of friendship. Indeed, very few friendships fulfill the ideals of friendship. More middle-class people claim to have 'true' or 'real' friends for life who are 'always on your wavelength' and always 'there for you'. This is partly an artefact of inequalities in resources of time, health and wealth, but it may also be because more dispersed middle-class social networks make it easier for them to romanticize friendships with people they rarely see. As an ideal, 'pure friendship' may have significance for other types of relationships, but when many people actually settle for much more modest forms of intimacy in their actual friendships this may moderate the potency of the ideal.

Perhaps the main reason for doubting a shift towards disclosing intimacy is the relatively modest change in gender inequalities. This is highlighted particularly in heterosexual behaviour and couple relationships. But it is also shown in the differences in conduct between gay men and lesbians and in the differences in commitment to and participation in parenting by men and women. Many people continue to make sense of gender inequalities by drawing on older stories about how personal life should be led; stories in which men are earner/providers and masters of the house and stories in which men need sex and women need someone to love.

Gender differences in parenting persist. Some men, perhaps a minority, continue to play the part of a patriarchal father. When they dish out treats or stern words, they act as the benevolent ultimate authority, drawing on a masculinity which celebrates men's power as men. Many men continue to see fatherhood as having much less involvement with children than motherhood. Many children continue to feel that their fathers are more shadowy figures in their lives than their mothers. Even those men who believe that being a father and being a mother should be very similar tasks often fail to implement this in practice. There are exceptionally involved fathers who are involved in the full range of loving, caring, sharing and understanding their children. They demonstrate that change is possible but yet remain not only a small minority but unsupported by approval from their fellow men. The hoped-for pay-offs of more equal parenting, for men, women and children, outlined in chapter 3, remain elusive. If parent–child relationships do set the scene for subsequent emotional life then most children still begin their life feeling much closer to a mother than a father, experiencing at close hand a division not only of domestic labour but of 'emotion work'. What if, as Scandinavian commentators hint, a pattern of the future is for men to seek to know and understand their children more without taking on additional practical caring and sharing? Such a separation in parent–child relationships seems unlikely. It is difficult to spend time with young children and not be engaged in practical caring, and knowing and understanding take time.

Friendship patterns also remain gendered and much research continues to suggest that women's friendships involve more mutual disclosure and sharing of thoughts and feelings than men's (see chapter 4). Some research demonstrates that gender differences in how girls and boys play, make and be friends are exaggerated and that there is considerable overlap in how boys and girls do things. However, in childhood friendships, girls and boys typically learn gender division and antagonism, with boys taking more command of public space collectively as boys, and learning to treat girls to a greater or lesser degree as the second sex. Inequalities of class, gender, race and ethnicity continue to structure friendship patterns. Better resourced and higher status groups are unlikely to make friendship bids to those who are less privileged and friendships which do cross boundaries often have to pay penalties of social discomfort. Men and their friends make more use of public leisure facilities than women do. Working-class friendships are more context-specific and gender-segregated. The preference for same-sex friends, and the different activities of boys and girls, are explicable by analyses of gender and power. Dominant views of masculinity and femininity and the associated gendered conventions of heterosexuality, continue to play an important part in shaping adolescent friendships. As yet there is little sign of boys and girls, young men and young women being able, in significant numbers, to transcend these limiting conventions.

In the area of sexual life, gender differences prevail and diverge from the public story of good sex as mutual loving sex (see chapter 5). Those who speak of a transformation of intimacy predict a world in which sexual encounters are about mutual sexual pleasure and sexual relationships heighten the intimacy achieved by non-physical knowing and understanding. Hence, the ideal couple are friends and lovers immersed in disclosing intimacy of mind and body. Stories of teenage and young adult sexual relationships throw up the starkest contrast between what happens in practice and what would happen if personal life were focused on disclosing intimacy. Conventional stories about the sexual prowess of real men and the need to 'do it' or 'have it' with a woman continue to be powerful stories in many young men's lives. There are recurrent and pervasive reports of unpleasurable first sex, with young men talking of use of another's body and young women of disappointment at lack of love and romance. There are few stories of early heterosexual experiences which suggest any recognizable form of intimacy. Moreover, what is considered to be sex remains a scripted conventional ordering of events and arrangements of organs and orifices rather than a mutual exploratory discovering of what each other enjoys. Women's stories of sex in long-term heterosexual relationships also provide examples of complaints about unpleasurable pre-scripted sex devoid of intimacy. The ideal of 'making love' as the climax of intimacy and sexual pleasure is not how many experience sex in their lives. Research continues to find more men than women whose interest in sexual acts stems from preoccupation with the potential for sexual pleasure and more women than men who see sex as an expression of intimacy and, therefore, as unenjoyable if they do not feel close to and loved by their partner. The different emphasis on sex in gay and lesbian relationships continues to be used as evidence that men learn to want sex and women learn to want intimacy. There are counter-examples in the literature, men whose willingness to pursue sex without intimacy was transformed by 'falling in love' and women who enjoy sex in relationships which otherwise lack intimacy. However, these counter-examples do not suggest a radical transformation is under way.

The research on young people's sexual relationships is not very encouraging. It clearly documents continued pressures on boys towards the conventional emotional hardening of macho masculinity and on girls towards less confident and more relational femininity. The fact that some young people successfully resist, overcome or rework these pressures is not new and it is difficult to know whether more do so now than in previous decades. At least there are alternative and shifting versions of masculinity, femininity, love and sex offered in public stories. However, the process of learning about sex and intimacy typically remains different for boys and girls. For some theorists, the strong emotional attachments, wrenching distancing and deep ambivalence felt for gendered members of the immediate family in early childhood sets the scene. For others, the significant factors are gender training which shapes the sense of self, including training in bodily decorum, physical confidence, guilt about sex and dirt, interest in romance, and 'emotion work'. Both are probably important in shaping predispositions for or against working at certain types of intimacy. While some authors see more equal parenting between men and women as a necessary condition for a radical realignment of gender, sex and intimacy, Robert Connell (1995) shows that some realignments are possible and do occur in conventional family households with full-time mothers and employed fathers. If more women than men are looking for caring, loving sex and more men than women for erotic pleasure without any investment in a social relationship, these are not alternatives which characterize the natural path of women versus men. Rather they are outcomes for some men and some women of complex social processes shaping identities and bodily feelings and, as yet, not fully understood.

Gender differences also persist in how men and women contribute to couple relationships (see chapter 6). Research on how heterosexual couples share housework and money has provided insight into how people manage caring and sharing. Some of this work also illustrates 'knowing and understanding' as couples describe their negotiations and their own and each other's feelings. Many couples see both wages and housework as gifts that each brings to their relationship and therefore do not automatically consider a conventional division of labour, in which the man brings home the wage and the woman does the housework, as unequal. However, because women are often both earners and the main domestic worker, the balance between his and her gifts has often become a source of tension. The weight of empirical evidence suggests that change in the distribution of housework is painfully slow. Large-scale studies show men taking up more domestic work at a snail's pace. The way that money is distributed in heterosexual relationships has changed somewhat faster, as women and men with independent incomes increasingly abandon arrangements whereby men blatantly control the money. Meanwhile, there are still significant numbers of couples trapped in deeply unequal relationships in which intimacy is at best the forced intimacy of a coercive and controlling dominant figure. Many men fail not only to resist translating their greater earning power into domination but they also use the physical power of their bodies to dominate their partner. The couples who 'do things differently', by not only articulating ideals of fairness but also striving to match their ideals in practice, are proof of the possibility of radical change rather than an indication of rapid progress in that direction.

At the same time the research evidence shows skill and diversity in excusing lack of equality and covering over the gulfs between heterosexual couples' egalitarian ideals and women's greater input into maintaining their domestic and personal life. What many couples hold as a fair arrangement is a modified conventional division of labour in which women continue to do most of the housework and men are the main earners, albeit that women supplement male earnings and men supplement female housework. When both men and women work full-time, as increasingly they do, then expectations of equality are often higher. But when the reality turns out to be very asymmetrical, in practice this is often papered over. It is particularly when women feel emotionally deserted and personally unsupported by their partner that dissatisfaction is acute. Men are far more frequently accused of not being there emotionally for their partner than women, and men's response is generally to deny or play down the problem. Duncombe and Marsden suggest that 'gender asymmetry in relation to intimacy and emotion work may be the last and most obstinate manifestation and frontier of gender inequality' (1995, p. 150).

A recent story about personal life at the century's end, alternative to that of the increase in 'disclosing intimacy', is that intimacy is ravaged by rampant self-interest and consumerism with potentially catastrophic consequences for personal and social life. In addition to marriage, two other sets of personal relationships are singled out as having allegedly gone into decline: the parent–child relationship, and friendship and kinship as expressions of the solidarity thought to have once made communities.

Extreme individualism has often been cited as a causal factor behind the increased fragility of marriage. For some right-wing commentators, feminism and women's desire for equality in relationships, are an example of a negative excessive individualism rather than a positive democratization of personal life. Research suggests that many marriages are unsettled by women's expectations and subsequent disappointment, although many studies also show women working very hard to maintain relationships which are far from their ideal. Failures of heterosexual intimacy are often confounded by or stem from failure to renegotiate the old bargain of he-the-wage-earner and she-the-housework. This failure results from men's conservatism not women's individualism (see chapter 6). After the breakdown of a marriage, men's remarriage rates remain higher than women's. However, this reflects continued gender inequalities in opportunities to start new relationships rather than women's loss of commitment to marriage-like partnerships. If women's willingness to abandon children were approximating to that of men's, then there would be stronger evidence of a new 'rampant individualism' among women. A slight increase in voluntary childlessness, a marked increase in cohabitation prior to marriage, and a slight increase in cohabitation as an alternative to marriage do not constitute a trend away from women seeking marriage-like arrangements both for long-term partners and as a basis for committed and lifelong mothering.

One version of troubled parent–child relationships is that rampant individualism and consumerism have undermined parental authority. Many authors observe that the ethos of respecting the rights of the individual is incompatible with traditional authority. Parents' desire to be close to their children and the demands of being a 'sensitive mother', and the later demands for 'sensitive fathers', have also been linked in the literature to the demise of parental authority. Some authors implicate consumerism by suggesting that parents feel they have to buy their way to children's affections. The research literature does not always directly address these concerns but there is no evidence to indicate that the more negative images of parent–child relationships are appropriate portrayals of the dominant picture. It is true that parents no longer typically claim a God-given right to rule their children. Nevertheless, most parents remain unembarrassedly confident that they know what is best for their child. Social distance between parents and children has reduced and parents generally acknowledge the ideal of 'being pals' or 'having a good relationship' with their children. It is not, however, possible to conclude that intense intimacy and democracy reign between parents and children in the majority of Euro-North American households. Styles of intimacy and the extent to which parents attempt to appear democratic vary. Research has found some parents, usually mothers, who in giving children the right to make decisions, sacrifice their own autonomy. But more often mothers are trying to remain in charge either openly or by exercising subtle control, for example moderating their children's demands through stress on the norm of fairness (including in some cases demands for consumer goods – 'even if we can afford what you want we cannot afford to get what everyone wants'). Parents typically remain confident judges of what is and is not fair. Despite pessimistic predictions to the contrary, the assumption that parents, and particularly mothers, are responsible for their children's psychological well-being is a crushing burden for only a minority. Most mothers have strategies for taking the role of 'sensitive mother' more lightly and making it more manageable. The oversensitive mother whose self-esteem is dependent on her child's good behaviour is neither the typical mother nor is her's the only troubled parent–child relationship. Mothers and, more commonly, fathers who lack any empathic relationship with their children form another troubled group. The fact that many men give up on their children after divorce (in contrast to non-custodial mothers) is more likely to reflect men's continued peripherality in relation to children than the spiralling of fathers into a new self-obsessed individualism.

Reproductive technology, with its potential for modifying biological parenthood, has also been implicated in an alleged shift in mindset to a destructive individualism. As noted in chapter 2, Marilyn Strathern has suggested that the new reproductive technologies disrupt the symbolic power of kinship. Kinship provided a metaphor of the relationships between individual and society, nature and culture, but now these categories collapse into each other, Strathern suggests, along with morality. I argue that this case is overstated even although the connections between social, biological and genetic parents can be severed or jumbled by techniques such as *in vitro* fertilization, egg donation, artificial insemination and surrogate motherhood. The dominant uses of reproductive technology do not take the possibilities of separating social, biological and genetic parents to their limits. Indeed, 'only those technologies that reinforce the value of having one's "own" child, one that is genetically related to oneself, are being developed' (Wajcman, 1991, p. 62). Even once a technology is developed, it is not necessarily generally available. Just as medically supervised contraceptives were once only available for married couples so medically supervised assistance in having babies remains restricted. However, Strathern's argument is about the symbolic significance of these technologies rather than their actual use. The fear that people no longer feel connected to either a natural or moral order has been a recurrent refrain among social commentators, and was prominent in the writing in the 1950s and 1960s on the death of community. However, research on personal life shows that most people remain firmly attached to a personal network of kin and friends. If the late twentieth century brings a heightened awareness of being unique individuals, this does not for the majority mean an absence of definitive social connections to others. People continue to sustain self-locating primary relationships with kin and friends, if not with communities.

Giddens's vision of 'the pure relationship' (see chapter 2) and Silver's discussion of 'pure friendship' (see chapter 4) assume a society in which people are able to come together for no other reason than an appreciation of each other's unique qualities. For the Moral Right, if personal life were reduced to such ties, then this is hyperindividualism as people are not bound by appropriate responsibilities and mutual obligations. Critics of contemporary society from all parts of the political spectrum often allude to a better world as some form of ideal-typical community in which each feels a moral responsibility for the other. Many different names are given to this world depending on the political persuasion of the speaker, 'true socialism', 'a stakeholder society', a 'Christian community', for example. It is sometimes assumed that individualism, with its emphasis on choice and voluntarism, is incompatible with this notion of community and that communities have only survived when their interrelationships are about necessity. However, as chapter 3 illustrated, the theoretical dichotomies between the principle of community versus the principle of intimacy, between friendship of necessity versus 'pure' friendship cannot be sustained as a description of practice. History is not as simple as the ascendancy of private intimacy resulting in the death of public community. In practice, relationships with some kin and some friends remain significant in late modernity, regardless of the well-being of community. There is often little to differentiate the quality of relationships between friends and kin. Close relationships with particular kin are, like friendships, typically sustained by choice, but kin and friends remain the people from whom assistance is sought in necessity. Whether in times of need or not, relationships with both kin and friends generally contain a mix of dimensions of intimacy, rather than simply disclosing intimacy and mutual appreciation of each other's unique qualities.

It may be useful to distinguish the principles of public community and private intimacy but they are not necessarily mutually cancelling principles. Even in the contexts where everybody knows everybody and shares some sense of common cause with them, it is also possible for people to maintain private intimate relationships. What communities lack is a preponderance of strangers; it is not that they necessarily lack private intimate relationships. In populations which are small and stable enough for something to be known about most people, the friends and neighbours of intimates are acquaintances who can be treated as if they were allies, friends in Bauman's sense. Allies are not intimates nor necessarily active helpers, rather they are people with whom an attitude of mutual benevolence can be taken for granted. In many small communities the main flows of generosity and assistance are not between the whole network of allies but restricted to inner circles of friends and selected kin with whom closer intimacy is maintained. An example of an urban parallel to the inner circles of a small town community resident is the 'chosen family' (Weston, 1991), created by members of San Francisco's gay community. The San Francisco 'gay community' is too amorphous and large for people to know each other even as acquaintances, but yet they affirm that they are potential allies when they turn out together on the ritual occasions devised to affirm gayness. The sense of community generated in the process is not, however, the sole or main source of social support in their lives. As in the small town, it is their inner circle of intimates who are the crux of personal life.

Pessimism about death of community is fuelled by a sense of contemporary urban societies as not only impersonal but populated by

dangerous strangers. While it is clear that the overwhelming majority of urban dwellers have a personal network of intimates, friends
and kin, it is less clear how many have a loose network of acquaintances who could be called allies or communities. A number of
theorists have looked to 'intermediate institutions'; institutions that
lie in between close friends and kin, on the one hand, and impersonal bureaucracies on the other – church groups, parent–teacher
organizations, self-help groups, trade unions, political groups, sports
and hobby clubs and the like – as sites for growth of such communities and as the building blocks of civil society. Such institutions are
typically found in greater density in areas of cities inhabited by socio-
economically privileged populations although, exceptionally, some
poor areas are also rich in community institutions. This distribution
of 'community', used in this sense, does not fit with the pessimistic
view of rampant individualism and destructive consumerism. Surely,
the most plausible candidates for falling victim to excessive individualism and consumerism are the more privileged sectors of
society. However, the most socially isolated people are not typically
or necessarily those with the means to selfishly pursue personal pleasure but more often those who are socially excluded and can take for
granted few if any allies, because of their extreme lack of means. The
least privileged are often excluded not only from consumerism but
from much of civil society by mutually sustaining poverty, social
stigma and dire personal circumstances.

The notion of 'a pure relationship' and the thesis that relationships
sustained by intense disclosing intimacy are becoming more common presumes a world in which the necessities of life are easily taken
care of. This unfortunately is not the world that many people live in.
In the eighteenth century, the philosophers of the Scottish Enlightenment believed that altruism, benevolence towards others, and appreciation of others simply for themselves, all became more possible
when relationships were not dominated by necessity. The majority
of people in Euro-North American societies have lives which are sufficiently privileged to seek 'good relationships' which are not dominated by necessity. However most personal relationships include a
mix of love, care, sharing, understanding and knowing, which involve a degree of relying on, needing or depending on the other, if
not desperate necessity. Few people sustain relationships, even friendships, which are based exclusively on disclosing intimacy separated
from mutually negotiated practical assistance. Nor is it clear that such
a separation is likely to offer a better future. In terms of radical changes

in relationships between men and women, the couples 'who do things differently' offer the most hope. These couples work hard at how they treat each other and what they do for each other in practical ways as well as learning about each other through knowing and understanding. It is through the negotiation of their divisions of labour and the resulting adjustments in their practical activities that they know each other better, sustain their relationship and effect social change. Arguably they have engaged in a process of negotiation similar to that of same-sex couples who talk of being different from and more equal and intimate than their image of heterosexual couples.

Nor is it the case that 'disclosing intimacy' or the more varied types of 'good relationships' that people have with each other are breaking down the pervasive divisions between socio-economic classes and ethnic groups. The empirical evidence suggests that in many Euro-North American societies social divisions are becoming more, not less, extreme.

Notes

Chapter 1 Introduction

1 The term 'primary group' was used at the beginning of this century by the American social psychologist Charles Cooley (1909) to describe co-operative, face-to-face associations in which participants sympathize and identify with each other as a 'we'. Since then the term 'primary relationship' has been used more commonly as a 'higher order construct' (Scanzoni, 1983, Scanzoni et al., 1989) which subsumes such relationships as family, friendship and sexual couple relationships.

2 The literature review is also restricted to texts available in English. I apologize for the awkwardness of the phrase Euro-North American and any offence caused by subsequently including Australia and New Zealand under this heading, but I consider this preferable to 'Western societies'. The notion of the West and the East is a social and historical construct that offered a very particular point of view on geographical realities and cultural dominance which no longer seems appropriate. But Australia, New Zealand, North America and Europe are not easily grouped together by any geographical label and Euro-North American points to both the geographical origins of Australia and New Zealand's colonial white populations and the more recent economic and cultural influence of the United States, without evoking the older cultural baggage of 'Western'. The term Euro-North American is a shorthand for the societies of Europe, North America, Australia and New Zealand. It is not meant to suggest that all of their inhabitants are of European origin. It refers to a group of societies, not their inhabitants.

3 *Verstehen* literally means understanding and was a key concept in Max Weber's sociology. Meads concept of the 'generalised other' refers to an internalized sense of the likely attitude of others to one's own actions (Mead, 1927, 154; Scott, 1995).

Chapter 2 From 'the family' to sex and intimacy

1 For histories of marriage in Britain, see Gillis, 1985, and Stone, 1979, 1993. For North America, see Coontz, 1988, Demos, 1986, Mintz and Kellog, 1988, Rothman, 1984. For Australia, see Gilding, 1991.

2 Authors discussing the uniqueness of the 1950s in North America include Coontz, 1992, Mintz and Kellog, 1988 and Skolnick, 1991. Britain, Australia and New Zealand are also discussed in these terms, for example by Finch and Summerfield, 1991, Gilding, 1991 and May 1992, respectively.

3 The term 'plastic' also has negative connotations since it is sometimes used pejoratively to mean cheap and artificial. Giddens does not acknowledge these negative connotations. This may be a tongue in cheek, provocative way of being upbeat about modernity, as if to say there is nothing wrong with plastic.

Chapter 3 Parenting and intimacy

1 The US historian John Demos suggests that fathers were as much the intimates of children, and particularly sons, as mothers prior to the nineteenth century (Demos, 1986). See Pleck (1987) for a rather different account of the history of US fatherhood.

2 Obvious examples include *Kramer versus Kramer*, (USA, 1979) *Mrs Doubtfire*, (USA, 1993) and *River Wild*, (USA, 1994).

3 For example, *Renaissance Man*, (USA, 1994) *The Man with No Face*, (USA, 1993). Drawing a clearer line between discipline and understanding, *The Dead Poets Society*, (USA, 1989) juxtaposes a sensitive teacher and a bullying patriarchal father who neither knew nor understood his child.

4 Social psychological experiments in which small groups were asked to perform tasks in laboratories also led Parsons to believe that every group needs an 'expressive leader' who keeps the group intact and sufficiently harmonious to function and an 'instrumental leader' who keeps a focus on making progress with the task in hand. For Parsons, the ideal family-household had a mother at home as the 'expressive leader' of the family and a father in employment as the 'instrumental leader' of the family.

5 Literature discussing these different experts includes: Busfield, 1987; Ehrenreich and English, 1979; Hardyment, 1983; Hays, 1993, 1996; Reiger, 1985; Ribbens, 1994; Richardson, 1993; Riley, 1983; Rutter, 1972; Toynbee, 1995; Marshall, 1991; Newson and Newson, 1976; Walkerdine and Lucey, 1989.

6 See for example: Davies (ed.), 1993; Dennis and Erdos, 1992; Morgan, 1995.

7 Examples include: Day and Mackey, 1986; Demos 1982, 1986; Pleck, 1987; LaRossa, 1989; LaRossa et al., 1991.

8 The following is a selection of relevant research monographs, review articles and collections: Backett, 1982; Brannen and Moss, 1991; Busfield, 1987; Coltrane, 1990; Evans, 1988; Gilbert, 1993; Gerson, 1985; Hertz, 1986; Hochschild, 1990; LaRossa and LaRossa, 1981; Lewis and O'Brien (eds), 1987; Lewis et al., 1992; McKee and O'Brien (eds), 1982; Rapoport and Rapoport, 1971; Rapoport et al., 1982; Ruble et al., 1988; Russell, 1983.

9 See: Brannen and Moss, 1991; Evans, 1988; Hertz, 1986; Hochschild, 1990; Lewis et al., 1992; Gilbert, 1993; Gerson, 1985; Rapoport and Rapoport, 1971, 1976, 1978.

10 Probably the most detailed substantial study of how parents control young children was conducted in Britain by the psychologists John and Elizabeth Newson in the 1960s (Newson and Newson, 1963, 1976).

11 Lars Denick (1989) has suggested that dual-earner parents pursuing a blend of intimacy and apparent democracy will be even more likely to make concessions to their children. They have a particular interest in avoiding conflict when their children express anger or behave badly because their time together as 'a family' is limited by parents' employment.

> Modern parents negotiate to reach an understanding with their children and tend to go out of their way to let the child have its way. . . . However this must not be taken to mean that there are not a great deal of situations in which the child is, as a matter of fact, obliged to adapt to strictly enforced, though abstract, requirements. Thus, for example, the child must go to bed at a particular time, so it will not be tired when the parents rush off to work; and it must learn to tear itself away from the parents without making a fuss, when they wave good-bye in the morning, and so on. (Denick, 1989)

Chapter 4 Are good friends all you need?

1 See for example, Cott, 1977; Faderman, 1981; McIntosh, 1968; Raymond, 1991; Smith-Rosenberg, 1979; Weeks, 1981.

2 See Crow and Allan, 1994; Anderson, 1980; Bulmer, 1987; Finch, 1989; Fischer, 1991.

3 The relevant studies include Bott, 1964; Dennis et al., 1969; Gans, 1962; Kerr, 1958; Komarovsky, 1962; Rainwater, 1970; Stack, 1975; Young and Wilmott, 1957.

Chapter 5 Sex and intimacy

1 To take one example from films on general release at the time of writing, the main character in *The Net* (USA, 1995) is a woman who spends all her time in front of a computer screen and is an acknowledged expert in the management of computer viruses. She is so socially isolated that when the villains wipe her identity from the national computers there is almost no living person who can testify that she is who she is. Her lifestyle has led to long periods without sex and the limited number of sexual partners who have presented themselves (her drug-addicted psychiatrist and the villain to whom she is attracted before realizing that he is trying to kill her) turn out to be highly unsatisfactory in terms of emotional support.

2 Compare the intense talking in the relationship of the lovers in *Bridges of*

Madison County (USA, 1995) with that of silent, much more low-key loving and caring between husband and wife.

3 The examples are many but one which remained popular at the time of writing is *Speed* (USA, 1994). Supporters of this film will deny that it reproduces conventional stereotypes by arguing that the main woman character plays a part like that of the male hero, showing courage through her actions and thus winning his love for her. Nevertheless, the male-saviour-of-helpless-woman formula is spectacularly invoked in the final sequence leading up to the closing scene of their romantic embrace.

4 For example, Bleier, 1991; Jackson, 1987, 1994; Koedt, 1991; Scully, 1973/4.

5 Discussions of defence tactics in rape trials include Adler, 1987; Brown, Burman and Jamieson, 1993; Chambers and Millar, 1986; Edwards, 1986; Estrich, 1987; Lees, 1989; Matoesian, 1993; Naffine, 1990; Temkin, 1987.

6 For example, Assiter and Avedon, 1993; Brown, 1992; Rubin, 1993; Segal, 1990; Segal and McIntosh (eds), 1992.

7 See chapter 3 for references and discussion pertaining to these authors.

Chapter 6 The couple: intimate and equal?

1 See, for example, Blumstein and Schwartz, 1983; Grey, 1979; Luxton, 1980; Morris, 1984, 1990; Pahl, 1980, 1983, 1989.

2 For example, see work by Edwards, 1981; Hertz, 1986; Jowell, Witherspoon and Brook, 1987; Pahl, 1989; VanEvery, 1995.

3 This is a finding replicated in a number of countries. See Brannen and Moss, 1991; May, 1992; Rosen, 1987; Weiss, 1985.

4 Statistically, large random samples are most likely to reproduce the characteristics of the population from which they are drawn, hence studies which wish to generalize to larger populations try to approximate to a random sample. In social science a random sample is often practically impossible as there is no appropriate list of the population from which to draw a random sample. (Also there are often good theoretical reasons for using some other kind of sample.) There are no lists of 'people who do things differently' or 'dual-earner households' for example. However, couples traced through official records, such as the women returning from maternity leave contacted by Brannen and Moss, or through large surveys, such as the couples contacted by Vogler, are more likely to be 'representative' than small-scale studies. Representativeness is not always the aim of research, however. Goodnow and Bowes are more interested in documenting the processes whereby couples succeed in being different than in a representative group.

5 Curiously, Askham does not directly address issues of gender or power in her otherwise insightful study of tensions between individual identity and the stability of the marriage.

6 For example, Blumstein and Schwartz, 1983; Kurdek, 1993; McWhirter and Mattison (eds), 1984; Peace, 1993; Peplau and Cochran, 1990; Weston, 1991.

7 For an anthology of women speaking out about violence suffered in lesbian relationships, see Lobel, 1986.

8 Finch and Mason, 1990; Furstenberg and Cherlin, 1991; Vaughan, 1987; Wallerstein and Blakeslee, 1989; Wallerstein and Kelly, 1980.
9 For example, Bell and Weinberg, 1978; Blumstein and Schwartz, 1983; Lewin, 1993; Weston, 1991.
10 See discussion of Laumann et al., 1994, and Wellings et al., 1994, in chapter 5.

Bibliography

Adkins, Lisa and Merchant, Vicki (eds), 1996. *Sexualizing the Social: Power and the Organizing of Sexuality*. Macmillan, London.

Adler, Zsuzsanna, 1987. *Rape on Trial*. Routledge and Kegan Paul, London.

Albrow, M., Eade, J., Fennell, G., O'Byrne, D., 1994. *Local/Global Relations in a London Borough: Shifting Boundaries and Localities*. Roehampton Local/Global Studies, Roehampton Institute of Higher Education.

Allan, Graham, 1979. *A Sociology of Friendship and Kinship*. Allen and Unwin, London.

Allan, Graham, 1989. *Friendship: Developing a Sociological Perspective*. Harvester Wheatsheaf, Hemel Hempstead.

Allatt, Patricia and Yeandle, Susan, 1992. *Youth, Unemployment and the Family: Voices from Disordered Times*. Routledge, London.

Altman, Dennis, 1986. *AIDS and the New Puritanism*. Pluto, Cambridge.

Anderson, Elijah, 1990. *Street Wise: Race, Class, and Change in an Urban Community*. University of Chicago Press, Chicago.

Anderson, Elijah, 1993. Sex codes and family life among poor inner-city youths. In Wilson, W.J. (ed.) *The Ghetto Underclass: Social Science Perspectives*. Sage, Newbury Park, pp. 76–95.

Anderson, Michael, 1980. The relevance of family history. In Anderson, M. (ed.) *The Sociology of the Family* (2nd ed). Penguin, Harmondsworth, 33–63.

Anderson, Michael, Bechhofer, Frank, Gershuny, Johnathan (eds), 1994. *The Social and Political Economy of the Household*. Oxford University Press, Oxford.

Argyle, Michael, 1991. *Cooperation: The Basis of Sociability*. Routledge, London.

Asher, Steven R. and Gottman, John M., 1981. *The Development of Children's Friendships*. Cambridge University Press, New York.

Askham, Janet, 1984. *Identity and Stability in Marriage*. Cambridge University Press, Cambridge.

Assiter, Alison and Avedon, Carol, 1993. *Bad Girls and Dirty Pictures: The Challenge to Reclaim Feminism*. Pluto, London.

Backett, Kathryn, 1982. *Mothers and Fathers*. Macmillan, London.

Badinter, Elisabeth, 1981. *The Myth of Motherhood*. London, Souvenir Press.

Bane, Mary Jo, 1976. *Here to Stay: American families in the Twentieth Century*. Basic Books, New York.

Banks, M., Bates, I., Breakwell, G., Bynner, J., Emler, N., Jamieson, J., Roberts, K., 1992. *Careers and Identities*. Open University Press, Milton Keynes.

Barker, Richard W., 1994. *Lone Fathers and Masculinities*. Avebury, Aldershot.

Barrett, Michèle and McIntosh, Mary, 1980. The family wage: some problems for socialist feminists. *Capital and Class*, 11, 51–72.

Barrett, Michèle and McIntosh, Mary, 1982. *The Anti-Social Family*. Verso, London.

Bauman, Zygmunt, 1987. *Legislators and Interpreters: On Modernity, Postmodernity and Intellectuals*. Polity Press, Cambridge.

Bauman, Zygmunt, 1990. Modernity and ambivalence. In Featherstone, 1990, 143–70.

Beck, Ulrich, 1994. The reinvention of politics: towards a theory of reflexive modernization. In Beck, Giddens and Lash (eds), 1–55.

Beck, Ulrich, Giddens, Anthony and Lash, Scott, 1994. *Reflexive Modernization: Politics, Tradition and Aesthetics in the Modern Social Order*. Polity Press, Cambridge.

Becker, Carol S, 1988. *Unbroken Ties: Lesbian Ex-Lovers*. Alyson, Boston.

Bell, Alan P. and Weinberg, Martin S., 1978. *Homosexualities: A Study of Diversity Among Men and Women*. Touchstone, New York.

Bell, Colin and Newby, Howard, 1976. Community communion, class and community action: the social sources of new urban politics. In Herbert D. J. and Johnson R. J. (eds) *Social Areas in Cities*. Wiley, London, 189–207.

Bell, Colin R, 1968. *Middle Class Families: Social and Geographic Mobility*. Routledge and Kegan Paul, London.

Bell, R., 1981. *Worlds of Friendship*. Sage, Beverly Hills.

Bellah, R. N., Madsen, R., Sullivan, W. M., Swidler, A., Tipton, S. M., 1985. *Habits of the Heart: Individualism and Commitment in American Life*. University of California Press, Berkeley.

Belotti, Elena, 1975. *Little Girls: Social Conditioning and its Effects on the Stereotyped Role of Women During Infancy*. Writers and Readers Publishing Cooperative, London.

Berger, Peter and Kellner, Hans, 1964. Marriage and the construction of reality. *Diogenes*, reprinted in Anderson, M. (ed.), 1980, 302–24.

Berger, Peter and Luckmann, Thomas, 1966. *The Social Construction of Reality*. Allen Lane, Harmondsworth, 1971.

Berk, Sarah, 1985. *The Gender Factory: The Apportionment of Work in American Households*. Plenum Press, New York.

Bittman, Michael, 1992. *Juggling Time: How Australian Families Use Time*. Australian Government Publishing Service, Canberra.

Bittman, Michael and Lovejoy, Frances, 1993. Domestic power: negotiating an unequal division of labour within a framework of equality. *Australian and New Zealand Journal of Sociology*, 29, 302–21.

Bjornberg, Ulla (ed.), 1992. *European Parents in the 1990s: Contradictions and Comparisons*. Transaction Publishers, New Brunswick and London.

Bjornberg, Ulla, 1995. Family orientation among men: fatherhood and partnership in the process of change. In Brannen and O'Brien (eds), 127–44.

Bleier, Ruth, 1991. Science and gender: a critique of biology and its theories on women. In Gunew, S. (ed.), 249–56

Blumstein, Philip and Schwartz, Pepper, 1983. *American Couples: Money, Work, Sex*. William Morrow, New York.

Bott, Elizabeth, 1964. *Family and Social Network: Roles Norms and External Relationships in Ordinary Urban Families*. Tavistock, London.

Boulton, M. G., 1983. *On Being A Mother: A Study of Women with Pre-School Children*. Tavistock, London.

Bourke, Joanna, 1994. *Working-Class Cultures in Britain 1890–1960: Gender, Class and Ethnicity*. Routledge, London.

Bowlby, John, 1953. *Child Care and the Growth of Love*. Penguin, Harmondsworth.

Bradshaw, J and Millar, J, 1991. *Lone Parent Families in the UK*. Her Majesty's Stationery Office, London.

Brake, Michael, 1985. *Comparative Youth Culture: The Sociology of Youth Cultures and Youth Subcultures in America, Britain and Canada*. Routledge and Kegan Paul, London.

Brannen, Julia and Collard, Jean, 1982. *Marriages in Trouble: the Process of Seeking Help*. Tavistock, London.

Brannen, Julia and Moss, Peter, 1991. *Managing Mothers: Dual Earner Households after Maternity Leave*. Unwin Hyman, London.

Brannen, Julia and O'Brien, Margaret (eds), 1995. *Childhood and Parenthood: Proceedings of the ISA Committee for Family Research Conference 1994*. Institute of Education, University of London, London.

Brannen, J., Dodd, K., Oakley, A. and Storey, P., 1994. *Young People, Health and Family Life*. Open University Press, Buckingham.

Broome, Richard, 1982. *Aboriginal Australia*. Allen and Unwin, London.

Brown, G. and Harris T., 1982. *Social Origins of Depression*. Tavistock, London.

Brown, Lyn and Gilligan, Carol, 1992. *Meeting at the Crossroads: Women's Psychology and Girls' Development*. Harvard University Press, Cambridge, Mass.

Brown, B., Burman, M. and Jamieson, L., 1993. *Sex Crimes on Trial: The Use of Sexual Evidence in Scottish Courts*. Edinburgh University Press, Edinburgh.

Brown, Beverley, 1992. Symbolic politics and pornography. *Economy and Society*, 21, 45–57.

Buck, N., Gershuny, J., Rose, D. and Scott, J., 1994. *Changing Households: The British Household Panel Survey 1990–1992*. ESRC Research Centre on Micro Social Change, University of Essex, Colchester.

Bulmer, Martin, 1986. *Neighbours: The Work of Philip Abrams*. Cambridge University Press, Cambridge.

Bulmer, Martin, 1987. *The Social Basis of Community Care*. Allen and Unwin, London.

Burgoyne, Jacqueline, 1991. Afterword: does the ring make any difference? Couples and the private face of a public relationship in post-war Britain. In Clark, D. (ed.), 235–56.

Burgoyne, Jacqueline and Clark, David, 1984. *Making a Go of It: A Study of Stepfamilies in Sheffield*. Routledge and Kegan Paul, London.

Burgoyne, O., Ormrod, R. and Richards, M, 1987. *Divorce Matters*. Penguin, Harmondsworth.

Busfield, Joan, 1987. Parenting and parenthood. In Cohen, G. (ed.) *Social Change and the Life Course*. Tavistock, London, 67–86.

Caldwell, M.A. and Peplau, L. A., 1982. Sex differences in same-sex friendship. *Sex Roles*, 8, 721–32.

Caldwell, Mayta A. and Peplau, Letitia Anne, 1984. The balance of power in lesbian relationships. *Sex Roles*, 10, 587–99.

Campbell, Beatrix, 1993. *Goliath: Britain's Dangerous Places*. Lime Trees, London.

Cancian, Francesca, 1984. Gender politics: love and power in the private and public spheres. In Rossi (ed.) *Gender and the Life Course*. Aldine, New York.

Cancian, Francesca M., 1986. The feminization of love *Signs*, 11, 692–709.

Cancian, Francesca M., 1987. *Love in America: Gender and Self-development*. Cambridge University Press, Cambridge.

Chambers, G. and Millar, A., 1986. *Prosecuting Sexual Assault: A Scottish Office Social Research Study*. Her Majesty's Stationery Office, London.

Chandler, Joan, 1991. *Women Without Husbands: An Exploration on the Margins of Marriage*. Macmillan, London.

Cheal, David, 1988. *The Gift Economy*. Routledge, London.

Cherlin, Andrew, 1992. *Marriage, Divorce, Remarriage*. Harvard University Press, Cambridge, Mass.

Cherlin, Andrew and Furstenberg, Frank, 1988. The changing European family: lessons for the American reader. *Journal of Family Issues*, 9, 291–7.

Chodorow, Nancy, 1978. *The Reproduction of Mothering*. University of California Press, Berkeley.

Chodorow, Nancy, 1994. *Femininities, Masculinities, Sexualities: Freud and Beyond*. University of Kentucky, Lexington, Kentucky.

Clark, David (ed.), 1991. *Marriage, Domestic Life and Social Change: Writings for Jacqueline Burgoyne* (1944–88). Routledge, London.

Clark, David, 1993. 'With my body I thee worship': the social construction of marital sex problems. In Scott, S. and Morgan D. (eds), 22–34.

Clarke, Lynda and Burghes, Louie, 1995. Cohabitation – a threat to family stability? *Family Policy Bulletin*, July, p. 4.

Clift, D., Stears, S., Legg, A., Memon, and Ryan, L., 1990. Blame and young people's moral judgements about AIDS. In Aggelton, P., Davies P., and Hart G. (eds) *AIDS, Individual, Cultural and Policy Dimensions*. Falmer Press, Lewes.

Cline, Sally, 1993. *Women, Celibacy and Passion*. Andre Deutsch, London.

Clunis, D. Merilee and Green, G. Dorsey, 1988. *Lesbian Couples*. Seal Press, Seattle.

Cochran, M., Larner, M., Riley, D., Gunnarsson, L., Henderson, C., 1990. *Extending Families: the Social Networks of Parents and their Children*. Cambridge University Press, Cambridge.

Cockburn, Cynthia, 1983. *Brothers: Male Dominance and Technological Change*. Pluto Press, London.

Collins, Patricia Hill, 1991. *Black Feminist Thought: Knowledge, Consciousness and the Politics of Empowerment*. Routledge, New York and London.

Coltrane, S, 1990. Birth Timing and the Division of Labour in Dual-Earner Families. *Journal of Family Issues*, 11, 157–81.

Connell, Robert W., 1987. *Gender and Power*. Polity Press, Cambridge.

Connell, Robert W., 1995. *Masculinities*. Polity Press, Cambridge.

Cooley, Charles H., 1909. *Social Organisations*. Schocken, New York.

Coontz, Stephanie, 1988. *The Social Origins of Private Life: A History of American Families 1600–1900*. Verso, London.

Coontz, Stephanie, 1992. *The Way We Never Were: American Families and the*

Nostalgia Trip. Basic Books, New York.

Corr, Helen, 1983. The school girl's curriculum and the ideology of the home 1870–1914. In Glasgow Women's Studies Group (eds) *Uncharted Lives*. Pressgang, Glasgow.

Corr, Helen, 1990. Politics of the sexes in English and Scottish teachers' unions 1870–1914. In Corr and Jamieson (eds), 186–205.

Corr, Helen and Jamieson, Lynn (eds) 1990. *Politics of Everyday Life: Continuity and Change in Work and the Family*. Macmillan, London, 74–97.

Cott, Nancy F. 1977. *The Bonds of Womanhood*. Yale University Press, New Haven.

Coveney, L., Jackson, M., Jeffreys, S., Kaye, L. and Mahony, P., 1984. *The Sexuality Papers: Male Sexuality and the Social Control of Women*. Hutchinson, London.

Cowan, Ruth Schwartz, 1989. *More Work For Mother*. Free Association Books, London.

Coward, Rosalind, 1982. Sexual violence and sexuality. *Feminist Review*, 11, 9–22.

Coward, Rosalind, 1983. *Patriarchal Precedents: Sexuality and Social Relations*. Routledge and Kegan Paul, London.

Craib, Ian, 1994. *The Importance of Disappointment*. Routledge, London.

Crow, Graham and Allan, Graham, 1994. *Community Life*. Harvester Wheatsheaf, Hemel Hempstead.

Crow, Graham and Allan, Graham, 1995a. Beyond 'insiders' and 'outsiders' in the sociology of community. Paper delivered to the British Sociological Association Conference, University of Leicester, April, 1995.

Crow, Graham and Allan, Graham 1995b. Community types, community typologies and community time. *Time and Society*, 4, 147–66.

Davidoff, Leonore, 1983. Class and gender in Victorian England. In Newton, J. et al. (eds).

Davidoff, Leonore, 1986. Mastered for life: servant and wife in Victorian and Edwardian England. In Thane, P. and Sutcliffe A. (eds) *Essays in Social History*. Oxford University Press, Oxford, 126–50.

Davidoff, Leonore and Hall, Catherine, 1987. *Family Fortunes: Men and Women of the English Middle-Class 1780–1850*. Hutchison, London.

Davies, Jon (ed.), 1993. *The Family: Is it Just Another Lifestyle Choice?* Institute of Economic Affairs: Health and Welfare Unit, London.

Davin, Anna, 1978. Imperialism and motherhood. *History Workshop Journal*, 5, 9–6

Day, Randal and Mackey, Wade, 1986. The role image of the American father. *Journal of Comparative Family Studies*, 3, 371–88.

de Beauvoir, Simone, 1972. *The Second Sex*. Penguin, Harmondsworth.

Delphy, Christine, 1984. *Close to Home: A Materialist Analysis of Women's Oppression*. Hutchinson, London.

Delphy, Christine and Leonard, Diana, 1992. *Familiar Exploitation: A New Analysis of Marriage in Contemporary Western Societies*. Polity Press, Cambridge.

D'Emilio, J. and Freedman, E. B., 1988. *Intimate Matters: A History of Sexuality in America*. Harper Row, New York.

Demos, John, 1982. The changing face of fatherhood: a new exploration in American family history. In Stanley H. Cath et al. (eds) *Father and Child: Developmental and Clinical Perspectives*. Little Brown, Boston.

Demos, John, 1986. *Past, Present, and Personal: The Family and the Life Course in*

American History. Oxford University Press, New York.

Denick, Lars, 1989. Growing up in the post-modern age: on the child's situation in the modern family and the family's situation in the modern welfare state. *Acta Sociologica*, 32, 155–80.

Dennis, Norman and Erdos, George, 1992. *Families Without Fatherhood*. Institute of Economic Affairs, Health and Welfare Unit, London.

Dennis, Norman, Henriques, Fernando and Slaughter, Clifford, 1969. *Coal is Our Life: An Analysis of a Yorkshire Mining Community*. Tavistock, London.

Deverson, Jane and Lindsay, Katharine, 1975. *Voices from the Middle Class: A Study of Families in Two Suburbs*. Hutchison, London.

Devine, Fiona, 1992. *Affluent Workers Revisited: Privatism and the Working Class*. Edinburgh University Press, Edinburgh.

Dinnerstein, Dorothy, 1976. *The Rocking of the Cradle, and the Ruling of the World*. Souvenir Press, London.

Dobash, Rebecca and Dobash, Russel, 1979. *Violence Against Wives: A Case Against the Patriarchy*. Free Press, New York.

Dobash, R. Emerson and Dobash, Russell, 1992. *Women, Violence and Social Change*. Routledge, London.

Duncombe, Jean and Marsden, Dennis, 1993. Love and intimacy: the gender division of emotion and emotion work. *Sociology*, 27, 221–241.

Duncombe, Jean and Marsden, Dennis, 1995a. Can men love? 'Reading', 'staging' and 'resisting' the Romance. In L. Pearce and J. Stacey (eds), 238–50.

Duncombe, Jean and Marsden, Dennis, 1995b. 'Workaholics' and 'whingeing women': theorising intimacy and emotion work: the last frontier of gender inequality? *Sociological Review*, 43, 150–69.

Duncombe Jean and Marsden, Dennis, 1996a. Whose orgasm is it anyway? 'Sex work' in long-term couple relationships. In J. Weeks and J. Holland (eds) *Sexual Cultures: Communities, Values and Intimacy*. St Martin's Press, New York, 220–38.

Duncombe, Jean and Marsden, Dennis, 1996b. Extending the social: a response to Ian Craib *Sociology*, 30, 155–8.

Duneier, Mitchell, 1992. *Slim's Table*. University of Chicago Press, Chicago.

Dunne, Gillian, 1997. *Lesbian Lifestyles: Women's Work and the Politics of Sexuality*. Macmillan, London.

Durham, Martin, 1991. *Sex and Politics: The Family and Morality in the Thatcher Years*. Macmillan, London.

Edgell, Stephen, 1980. *Middle Class Couple: A Study of Segregation, Domination and Inequality in Marriage*. George Allen and Unwin, London.

Edwards, Susan, 1986. Evidential matters in rape prosecution from 'first opportunity to complain' to corroboration. *New Law Journal*, 28, 291–3.

Edwards, M, 1981. *Financial Arrangements within Families*. National Women's Advisory Council, Canberra.

Ehrenreich, Barbara, 1983. *The Hearts of Men: American Dreams and the Flight from Commitment*. Anchor/Doubleday, Garden City, New York.

Ehrenreich, Barbara and English, Deirdre, 1979. *For Her Own Good: 150 Years of the Experts' Advice to Women*. Pluto Press, London.

Ehrenreich, Barbara, Hess, Elizabeth and Jacobs, Gloria, 1987. *Re-making Love: The Feminization of Sex*. Fontana (originally Anchor Books, 1986), London.

Ehrensaft, Diane, 1985. Dual parenting and the duel of intimacy. In Handel, G.

(ed.) *The Psychosocial Interior of the Family*. Aldine, New York.

Ehrensaft, Diane, 1987. *Parenting Together*. Free Press, New York.

Eisenhart, M. A. and Holland, D. C., 1983. Learning gender from peers: the role of peer groups in the cultural transmission of gender. *Human Organization*, 42, 321–3.

Eisenstein, Sarah, 1983. *Give Us Bread But Give Us Roses: Working Women's Consciousness in the United States, 1890 to the First World War*. Routledge and Kegan Paul, London.

Elder, Glen, 1977. *Children of the Great Depression: Social Change in Life Experience*. Chicago University Press, Chicago.

Elias, Norbert, 1978. *The Civilizing Process, Volume 1: The History of Manners*. Urizen, New York, and Basil Blackwell, Oxford.

Engels, Frederick, 1972. *The Origin of the Family, Private Property and the State*. Lawrence and Wishart, London.

Estrich, Susan, 1987. *Real Rape: How The Legal System Victimises Women Who Say No*. Harvard University Press, Cambridge, Massachusetts.

Everingham, Christine, 1994. *Motherhood and Modernity: An Investigation into the Rational Dimensions of Mothering*. Open University Press, Buckingham.

Evetts, J. 1988. Managing child care and work responsibilities. *Sociological Review*, 36, 503–31.

Faderman, Lillian, 1981. *Surpassing the Love of Men*. William Morrow, New York.

Faderman, Lillian, 1991. *Odd Girls and Twilight Lovers: A History of Lesbian Life in Twentieth-century America*. Penguin, New York.

Featherstone, Mike (ed.), 1990. *Global Culture: Nationalism, Globalization and Modernity*. Sage, London.

Finch, Janet, 1989. *Family Obligations and Social Change*. Polity Press, Cambridge.

Finch, Janet and Mason, Jennifer, 1990. Divorce, remarriage and family obligation. *Sociological Review*, 38, 219–46.

Finch, Janet and Mason, Jennifer, 1993. *Negotiating Family Responsibilities*. Routledge, London.

Finch, Janet and Summerfield, Penny, 1991. Social reconstruction and the emergence of companionate marriage, 1945–59. In Clark, D. (ed.), 7–32.

Fischer, Claude, 1982. *To Dwell among Friends: Personal Networks in Town and City*. Chicago University Press, Chicago.

Fischer, Claude, 1991. Ambivalent communities: how Americans understand their localities. In Wolfe, Alan (ed.) *America at Century's End*. University of California Press, Berkeley, 79–90.

Foucault, Michel, 1978. *The History of Sexuality, Volume 1: an Introduction*. Penguin, London.

Fox, M., Gibbs, M. and Auerbach, D., 1985. Age and gender dimensions of friendship. *Pyschology of Women Quarterly*, 9, 489–502.

Freud, Sigmund, 1924. The dissolution of the Oedipus complex, 1925: Some psychical consequences of the anatomical distinction. Reprinted in 1977. *The Pelican Freud Library. Volume 7: On Sexuality*. Penguin, Harmondsworth.

Furstenberg, Frank F., 1988. Good Dads – bad Dads: two faces of fatherhood. In Cherlin, A. J. (ed.) *The Changing American Family and Public Policy*. Urban Institute Press, Washington, DC, 193–218.

Furstenberg, Frank and Cherlin, Andrew, 1991. *Divided Families: What Happens to Children When Parents Part*. Harvard University Press, Cambridge, Mass.

Furstenberg, Frank F. and Nord, Christine W., 1985. Parenting apart: patterns of childrearing after maritial disruption. *Journal of Marriage and the Family*, 47, 893–904.

Gagnon, John H. and Simon, William, 1973. *Sexual Conduct*. Aldine, Chicago.

Gans, Herbert J., 1962. *The Urban Villagers: Group and Class in the Life of Italian-Americans*. The Free Press, New York.

Geerken, Michael and Gove, Walter, 1983. *At Home and At Work: The Family's Allocation of Labor*. Sage, Beverly Hills.

Gellner, Ernest, 1985. *The Psychological Movement or the Coming of Unreason*. Paladin Books, London.

Gershuny, Jonathan, Godwin, Michael and Jones, Sally, 1994. The domestic labour revolution: a process of lagged adaptation? In Anderson, M., Bechhofer, F. and Gershuny, J. (eds), 151–97.

Gershuny, Jonathan and Robinson, John P., 1988. Historical changes in household divisions of labour. *Demography*, 25, 537–54.

Gerson, Kathleen, 1985. *Hard Choices: How Women Decide about Work, Career and Motherhood*. University of California Press, Berkeley.

Gerson, Kathleen, 1993. *No Man's Land: Men's Changing Commitments to Family and Work*. Basic Books, New York.

Giddens, Anthony, 1990. *The Consequences of Modernity*. Polity Press, Cambridge, and Stanford University Press, Stanford, California.

Giddens, Anthony, 1991. Modernity and Self-identity: Self and Society in the Late Modern Age. Polity Press, Cambridge.

Giddens, Anthony, 1992. *The Transformation of Intimacy: Sexuality, Love and Eroticism in Modern Societies*. Polity Press, Cambridge.

Giddens, Anthony, 1994. Living in a post-traditional society. In Beck, U., Giddens, A. and Lash, S (eds), 56–109.

Giele, Janet Zollinger, 1974. Changes in the modern family: their impact on sex roles. In Coser, R. L. (ed.) *The Family Its Structures and Functions* (2nd ed). Macmillan, London, 460–70.

Gilbert, Lucia Albino, 1993. *Two Careers/One Family: The Promise of Gender Equality*. Sage, London.

Gilding, Michael, 1991. *The Making and Breaking of the Australian Family*. Allen and Unwin, Sydney.

Gilligan, Carol, 1982. *In a Different Voice: Psychological Theory and Women's Development*. Harvard University Press, Cambridge, Mass.

Gillis, John, 1985. *For Better, For Worse: British Marriages, 1600 to the Present*. Oxford University Press, New York.

Gittins, Diana, 1982. *Fair Sex: Family Size and Structure 1900–1939*. Hutchison, London.

Gittins, Diana, 1985. *The Family in Question; Changing Households and Familiar Ideologies*. Macmillan, London.

Glazer-Malbin, N. (ed.), 1976. *Old Family/New Family: Interpersonal Relationships*. Van Nostrand, New York.

Goldthorpe, J. H., Lockwood, D., Bechhofer, F. and Platt, J., 1969. *The Affluent Worker in the Class Structure*. Cambridge University Press, Cambridge.

Goodnow, J. and Bowes, J., 1994. *Men, Women and Household Work*. Oxford University Press, Melbourne.

Gordon, Linda, 1988. *Heroes of Their Own Lives: The Politics and History of Family*

Violence. Virago, London.

Gordon, Tuula, 1994. *Single Women*. Macmillan, London.

Gouldner, Alvin, 1960. The norm of reciprocity: a preliminary statement. *American Sociological Review*, 25, 161–78.

Gouldner, Helen and Strong, Mary Symons, 1987. *Speaking of Friendship: Middle-Class Women and Their Friends*. Greenwood Press, New York.

Grey, A., 1979. The working-class family as an economic unit. In Harris, C.C. (ed.) *The Sociology of the Family: New Directions for Britain*. University of Keele, Keele, 186–213.

Greer, Germaine, 1971. *The Female Eunuch*. New York, McGraw Hill.

Grieff, Geoffrey, 1985. *Single Fathers*. Lexington Books, Lexington, Mass.

Grieff, Geoffrey L., DeMaris, Alfred and Hood, Jane, 1993. Balancing work and single fatherhood. In Jane Hood (ed.) *Men Work and Family*. Sage, London, 176–94.

Griffin, Christine, 1985. *Typical Girls: Young Women From School to the Market*. Routledge and Kegan Paul, London.

Griffiths, Viv, 1995. *Adolescent Girls and Their Friends: A Feminist Ethnography*. Averbury, Aldershot.

Gunew, Sneja (ed.), 1991. *A Reader in Feminist Knowledge*. Routledge, London.

Haas, L. L. 1982. Determinants of role sharing behaviour: a study of egalitarian couples. *Sex Roles*, 8, 747–60.

Habgood, Ruth, 1992. On his terms: gender and the politics of domestic life. In Du Plessis, R. (ed.) *Feminist Voices: Women's Studies Texts for Aotearoa/New Zealand*. Oxford University Press, Oxford, 163–79.

Halson, J, 1991. Young women, sexual harassment and heterosexuality: violence power relations and mixed-sex schooling. In Pamela Abbott and Claire Wallace (eds) *Gender, Power and Sexuality*. Macmillan, London 97–113.

Hamilton, Roberta, 1978. *The Liberation of Women: A Study of Patriarchy and Capitalism*. George Allen and Unwin, London.

Hardey, Michael and Crow, Graham (eds), 1991. *Lone Parenthood: Coping with Constraints and Making Opportunities*. Harvester Wheatsheaf, Hemel Hempstead.

Hardyment, Christina, 1983. *Dream Babies: Childcare from Locke to Spock*. Cape, London.

Harlow, H., 1958. The nature of love. *American Psychologist*, 13, 673–85.

Harris, C. C., 1983. *The Family and Industrial Society*. George Allen and Unwin, London.

Hartmann, Heidi, 1979. Capitalism, patriarchy and job segregation by sex. In Zillah Eisenstein (ed.) *Capitalist Patriarchy and the Case For Socialist Feminism*. Monthly Review Press, New York, 206–47.

Haskey, John, 1995. Trends in marriage and cohabitation: the decline in marriage and the changing pattern of living in partnership. *Population Trends*, 80, 5–15.

Hays, Sharon, 1993. The cultural contradictions of contemporary motherhood: the social construction and paradoxical persistence of intensive child-rearing. Ph.D. thesis, University of California, San Diego.

Hays, Sharon, 1996. *The Cultural Contradictions of Motherhood*. Yale University Press, Yale.

Hendry, L. B., Shucksmith J., Love, J. G., Glendinning, A., 1993. *Young People's*

Leisure and Lifestyles. Routledge, London.

Henrique, J., Hollway, W., Urwin, C., Venn, C. and Walkerdine, V. (eds), 1984. *Changing the Subject*. Methuen, London.

Hertz, Rosanna, 1986. *More Equal Than Others: Women and Men in Dual Career Marriages*. University of California Press, Berkeley.

Hess, B. B., 1979. Sex roles, friendship and the life course. *Research on Ageing*, 1, 494–515.

Hewitt, R, 1988. *White Talk, Black Talk. Inter-racial Friendships and Communication among Adolescents*. Cambridge University Press, Cambridge.

Hey, Valerie, 1997. *The Company She Keeps: An Ethnography of Girls' Friendships*. Open University Press, Buckingham and Philadelphia.

Hite, Shere, 1976. *The Hite Report on Female Sexuality*. Dell, New York.

Hite, Shere, 1994. *The Hite Report on the Family: Growing Up Under Patriarchy*. Bloomsbury, London.

Hochschild, Arlie, 1975. The sociology of feelings and emotion: selected possibilities. In Milkman, R. and Kanter, (eds) *Another Voice*. Anchor, New York.

Hochschild, Arlie, 1983. *The Managed Heart: Commercialization of Human Feeling*. University of California Press, Berkeley and London.

Hochschild, Arlie, 1990. *The Second Shift: Working Parents and the Revolution at Home*. Piatkus, London.

Hochschild, Arlie, 1994. The commercial spirit of intimate life and the abduction of feminism: signs from women's advice books. *Theory Culture and Society*, 11, 1–24.

Hochschild, Arlie, 1995. Understanding the future of fatherhood. In Van Donegan, M., Frinking, G. and Jacobs, M. (eds) *Changing Fatherhood*. Thesis Publications, Amsterdam, 219–30.

Holland, Dorothy C. and Eisenhart, Margaret A., 1990. *Educated in Romance: Women, Achievement, and College Culture*. University of Chicago Press, Chicago.

Holland, Janet, Ramazanoglu, Caroline, Scott, Sue, Sharpe, Sue and Thomson, Rachel, 1991. *Pressure, Resistance, Empowerment: Young Women and the Negotiation of Safer Sex*. Tufnell Press, London.

Holland, Janet, Ramazanoglu, Caroline, and Sharpe, Sue, 1993. *Wimp or Gladiator: Contradictions in Acquiring Masculine Sexuality*. Tufnell Press, London.

Holland, Janet, Ramazanoglu, Caroline, Sharpe, Sue and Thomson, Rachel, 1994. Power and desire: the embodiment of female sexuality *Feminist Review*, 4, 21–38.

Hollway, Wendy, 1984a. Women's power in heterosexual sex. *Women's Studies International Forum*, 7, 63–73.

Hollway, Wendy, 1984b. Gender difference and the production of subjectivity. In Henrique et al. (eds.) 1984 and Jackson and Scott (eds) 1996, 84–100.

Hollway, Wendy, 1996. Recognition and heterosexual desire. In Richardson, D. (ed.) *Theorising Heterosexuality*. Open University Press, Buckingham, 91–108.

Hood, Jane (ed.), *Men, Work, and Family*. Sage, London.

Humphries, Jane, 1977. Class struggle and the persistence of the working-class family. *Cambridge Journal of Economics*, 1, 241–58.

Humphries, Jane, 1981. Protective legislation, the capitalist state, and working-class men: the case of the 1842 Mines Regulation Act. *Feminist Review*, 7, 1–33.

Hunt, Janet and Hunt, Larry, 1982. The dualities of careers and families: new integrations or new polarisations. *Social Problems*, 29, 499–510.

Hunt, Pauline, 1978. Cash transactions and household tasks. *Sociological Review*, 26, 555–71.

Hunt, Pauline, 1980. Gender and Class Consciousness. Macmillan, London.

Hutson, Susan and Jenkins, Richard, 1989. *Taking the Strain: Families, Unemployment and the Transition to Adulthood*. Open University Press, Milton Keynes.

Jackson, Margaret, 1987. 'Facts of life' or the eroticisation of women's oppression? Sexology and the social construction of heterosexuality. In Caplan, Pat (ed.) *The Cultural Construction of Sexuality*. Tavistock, London, 52–81.

Jackson, Margaret, 1994. *The Real Facts of Life: Feminism and the politics of sexuality*. Taylor and Francis, London.

Jackson, Stevi, 1982. *Childhood and Sexuality*. Basil Blackwell, Oxford.

Jackson, Stevi, 1994. *Theorizing Heterosexuality: gender, power and pleasure*. Strathclyde Papers on Sociology and Social Policy, University of Strathclyde, Glasgow.

Jackson, Stevi and Scott, Sue (eds), 1996. *Feminism and Sexuality: A Reader*. Edinburgh University Press, Edinburgh.

Jamieson, Lynn, 1983. A case study of the development of 'the modern family': urban Scotland in the early twentieth century. Unpublished Ph.D. thesis, Edinburgh University, Edinburgh.

Jamieson, Lynn, 1986. Limited resources and limiting conventions: working-class mothers and daughters in urban Scotland, 1890–1920. In Lewis, J. (ed) 46–69.

Jamieson, Lynn, 1987. Theories of family development and the experience of being brought up. *Sociology*, 21, 591–607.

Jamieson, Lynn and Corr, Helen, 1990. 'Earning your keep': self reliance and family obligation, ESRC 16–19, Initiative Occasional Papers. Social Statistics Research Unit, The City University, London, 30, 1–33.

Jamieson, Lynn and Toynbee, Claire, 1990. Shifting patterns of parental control. In Corr and Jamieson (eds) 86–113.

Jamieson, Lynn and Toynbee, Claire, 1992. *Country Bairns: Growing Up 1900–1930*. Edinburgh University Press, Edinburgh.

Jeffery-Poulter, Stephen, 1991. *Peers, Queers and Commons: The Struggle for Gay Law Reform from 1950 to the Present*. Routledge, London.

Jensen, An-Magritt, 1995. Paradoxes of fatherhood illustrated by the Norwegian case. In Brannen, J. and O'Brien, M. (eds), 146–56.

Jerrome, Dorothy, 1981. The significance of friendship for women in later life *Ageing and Society*, 1, 175–97.

Jerrome, Dorothy, 1983. Lonely women in a friendship club. *British Journal of Guidance and Counselling*, 11, 10–20.

Jerrome, Dorothy, 1984. Good company: the sociological implications of friendship. *Sociological Review*, 32, 696–781.

Jerrome, Dorothy, 1992. *Good Company: An Anthropological Study of Old People in Groups*. Edinburgh University Press, Edinburgh.

Johnson, Miriam M., 1988. *Strong Mothers, Weak Wives*. University of California Press, Berkeley.

Jones, Gill, 1995. *Leaving Home*. Open University Press, Buckingham.

Jowell, R., Witherspoon, S. and Brook, L., 1987. *British Social Attitudes: The 1987 Report*. Social and Community Planning Research, London.

Kappeler, Susanne, 1986. *The Pornography of Representation*. Polity Press, Cambridge.

Keller, Susan, 1968. *The Urban Neighbourhood: A Sociological Perspective*. Random House, New York.

Kelly, Liz, 1988. *Surviving Sexual Violence*. Polity Press, Cambridge.

Kelly, Liz, Burton, Sheila and Regan, Linda, 1996. Beyond victim or survivor: sexual violence, identity and feminist theory and practice. In Adkins L. and Merchant, V. (eds), *Sexualizing the Social: Power and the Organizing of Sexuality*. Macmillan, London, 77–102.

Kerr, Madeline, 1958. *People of Ship Street*. Routledge and Kegan Paul, London.

Kiernan, Kathleen and Estaugh, Valerie, 1993. *Cohabitation, Extra-Marital Childbearing and Social Policy*. Family Policy Studies Centre, London.

Kimball, G. 1983. *The 50–50 Marriage*. Beacon Press, Boston.

Kimmel, Michael S (ed.), 1987. *Changing Men: New Directions in Research on Men and Masculinity*. Sage, Beverly Hills.

Kinsey, Alfred C., 1948. *Sexual Behaviour in the Human Male*. W. B. Saunders, Philadelphia.

Kinsey, Alfred C. 1953. *Sexual Behaviour in the Human Female*. W. B. Saunders, Philadelphia.

Kitzinger, Celia, 1987. *The Social Construction of Lesbianism*. Sage, London.

Koedt, Anna, 1991. The myth of the vaginal orgasm. In Gunew, S. (ed.), 326–34.

Komarovsky, Mirra, 1962. *Blue Collar Marriage*. Vintage Books, New York.

Kurdek, Lawrence, 1993. The allocation of household labour in gay, lesbian, and heterosexual married couples. *Journal of Social Issues*, 49, 127–40.

Laing, R. D., 1960. *The Divided Self*. Tavistock, London.

Laqueur, Thomas, 1990. *Making Sex: Body and Gender From the Greeks to Freud*. Harvard University Press, Cambridge, Mass.

LaRossa, Ralph, 1989. Fatherhood and social change. *Family Relations*, 37, 451–7.

LaRossa, Ralph and LaRossa Maureen M., 1981. *Transition to Parenthood: How Infants Change Families*. Sage, Beverly Hills.

LaRossa, R., Gordon, B. A., Wilson, R. J., Bairan, A., Jaret, C., 1991. The fluctuating image of the 20th Century American Father. *Journal of Marriage and the Family*, 53, 987–97.

Lasch, Christopher, 1977. *Haven in a Heartless World*. Basic Books, New York.

Laumann, E., Michael R., Michaels, S. and Gagnon, J., 1994. *The Social Organization of Sexuality*. University of Chicago Press, Chicago.

Lazarsfeld, Peter and Merton, Robert, 1954. Friendship as social process. In Berger, M., Abel T. and Page, C. H. (eds) *Freedom and Control in Modern Society*. Van Nostrand, Princeton, New Jersey, pp. 18–66.

Lees, Sue, 1986. *Losing Out: Sexuality and Adolescent Girls*. Penguin, Harmondsworth.

Lees, Sue, 1989. Trial by Rape. *New Statesman and Society*, 24th November.

Lees, Sue, 1993. *Sugar and Spice: Sexuality and Adolescent Girls*. Penguin, Harmondsworth.

Lewin, Ellen, 1993. *Lesbian Mothers: Accounts of Gender in American Culture*. Cornell University Press, Ithaca and London.

Lewis, Charlie and O'Brien, Margaret (eds), 1987. *Reassessing Fatherhood: New Observations on Fathers and the Modern Family*. Sage, London.

Lewis, Jane, 1986. Anxieties about the family and the relationship between parents, children and the state in twentieth-century England. In Richards M. and Light, P. (eds) *Children of Social Worlds*. Polity Press, Cambridge, 31–54.

Lewis, Jane, 1994. *Women in Britain since 1945*. Blackwell, Oxford.

Lewis, S., Izraeli, D. and Hootman, H., 1992. *Dual Earner Families: International Perspectives*. Sage, London.

Litwak, Eugen and Szelenyi, Ivan, 1969. Primary group structures and their functions: kin, neighbours and friends. *American Sociological Review*, 34, 465–80.

Lobel, Kerry, 1986. *Naming the Violence: Speaking out about Lesbian Battering*. Seal Press, Seattle.

Luhmann, Niklas, 1986. *Love as Passion. The Codification of Intimacy*. Polity Press, Cambridge.

Luxton, M., 1980. *More Than a Labour of Love*. Women's Press, Toronto.

MacKinnon, Catharine A., 1982. Feminism, Marxism, method and the State: an agenda for theory. *Signs*, 7, 515–44.

MacKinnon, Catharine A., 1987. *Feminism Unmodified: Discourses on Life and Law*. Harvard University Press, Cambridge.

Mansfield, Penny and Collard, Jean, 1988. *The Beginning of the Rest of Your Life: a Portrait of Newly-Wed Marriage*. Macmillan, London.

Mark-Lawson, Jane and Witz, Anne, 1990. Familial control or patriarchal domination? The case of the family system of labour in 19th century coal mining. In Corr, H. and Jamieson, L. (eds), 117–40.

Marshall, Harriette, 1991. The social construction of motherhood: an analysis of childcare and parenting manuals. In Phoenix, A., Woollett, A. and Lloyd, E. (eds), 66–85.

Masters, William H. and Johnson, Virginia, E., 1966. *Human Sexual Response*. Bantam Books, New York.

Matoesian, Gregory M., 1993. *Reproducing Rape: Domination through Talk in the Courtroom*. Polity Press, Cambridge.

May, Elaine Tyler, 1988. *Homeward Bound: American Families in the Cold War Era*. Basic Books, New York.

May, Helen, 1992. *Minding Children, Managing Men: Conflict and Compromise in the Lives of Postwar Pakeha women*. Bridget Williams Books, Wellington, New Zealand.

McGuire, M., 1991. Sons and daughters. In Phoenix, A., Woollett, A. and Lloyd, E. (eds), 143–61.

McIntosh, Mary, 1968. The homosexual role. *Social Problems*, 16, 182–92.

McKee, Lorna and Bell, Colin, 1985. Marital and family relations in times of male unemployment. In Roberts, B., Finnegan, R. and Gallie, D. (eds), 387–99.

McKee, Lorna and O'Brien, Margaret (eds), 1982. *The Father Figure*. Tavistock, London.

McRae, Susan, 1993. *Cohabiting Mothers: Changing Marriage and Motherhood?* Policy Studies Institute, London.

McRobbie, Angela, 1978. Working class girls and the culture of femininity. In Centre for Contemporary Cultural Studies (ed.) *Women Take Issue: Aspects of Women's Subordination*. University of Birmingham, Birmingham, 96–108.

McRobbie, Angela, 1991. *Feminism and Youth Culture: From Jackie to Just Seventeen*. Macmillan, London.

McRobbie, Angela, 1994. *Post Modernism and Popular Culture*. Routledge, London.

McWhirter, D. P. and Mattison, A. M., 1984. *The Male Couple: How Relationships Develop*. Prentice Hall, Englewood Cliffs, New Jersey.

McWhirter, D. P., Sanders, S. A. and Reinisch, J. M. (eds), 1990. *Homosexuality/heterosexuality: Concepts of Sexual Orientation*. Oxford University Press, New York.

Mead, George Herbert, 1927, 1934. *Mind, Self and Society, from the Standpoint of Social Behaviourism*. Chicago University Press, Chicago.

Medrich, Elliott A., Roizen, J., Rubin, V. and Buckley, S., 1982. *The Serious Business of Growing Up: A Study of Children's Lives Outside of School*. University of California Press, Berkeley.

Meissner, M., Humphries, E. W., Meis, S. M. and Scheu, W. J., 1975. No exit for wives: sexual divisions of labour and the cumulation of household demands. *Canadian Review of Sociology and Anthropology*, 12, 24–39.

Milligan, Don, 1993. *Sex-Life: A Critical Commentary on the History of Sexuality*. Pluto Press, London.

Mintz, Stephen and Kellog, Susan, 1988. *Domestic Revolutions: A Social History of American Family Life*. Free Press, New York.

Morgan, David, 1990. No more heroes? Masculinity, violence and the civilising process. In Jamieson, L. and Corr, H. (eds) *State, Private Life and Political Change*. Macmillan, London, 13–30.

Morgan, David, 1991. Ideologies of marriage and family life. In Clark, D. (ed.), 113–38.

Morgan, Patricia, 1995. *Farewell to the Family?: Public Policy and Family Breakdown in Britain and the USA*. Institute of Economic Affairs, Health and Welfare Unit, London.

Morris, Lydia, 1984. Redundancy and patterns of household finance. *Sociological Review*, 32, 492–593.

Morris, Lydia, 1985. Renegotiation of the domestic division of labour in the context of redundancy. In Roberts B., Finnegan, R. and Gallie, D. (eds).

Morris, Lydia, 1987. Constraints on gender. *Work Employment and Society*, 1, 85–106.

Morris, Lydia, 1990. *The Workings of the Household*. Polity Press, Cambridge.

Morris, Lydia, 1994. *Dangerous Classes: The Underclass and Social Citizenship*. Routledge, London and New York.

Murray, Charles, 1984. *Losing Ground: American Social Policy 1950–1980*. Basic Books, New York.

Murray, Charles, 1990. *The Emerging British Underclass*. Institute of Economic Affairs, London.

Murray, Charles, 1994. *Underclass: The Crisis Deepens*. Institute of Economic Affairs, Health and Welfare Unit, London.

Naffine, N., 1990. *Law and the Sexes: Explorations in Feminist Jurisprudence*. Allen and Unwin, Sydney.

Nardi, Peter, 1992a. That's what friends are for: friends as family in the gay and lesbian community. In Plummer, K. (ed.) *Modern Homosexualities*. Routledge, London.

Nardi, Peter M., 1992b. Sex, friendship, and gender roles among gay men. In Nardi, P (ed.) *Men's Friendships*. London, Sage, 173–85.

Nestle, Joan, 1984. The fem question. In Vance, C. S. (ed.) *Pleasure and Danger: Exploring Female Sexuality*. Routledge and Kegan Paul, Boston, 232–41.

New, Caroline and David, Miriam, 1985. *For the Children's Sake*. Penguin, Harmondsworth.

Newson, John and Newson, Elizabeth, 1963. *Patterns of Infant Care in an Urban Community*. Penguin, Harmondsworth.

Newson, John, and Newson, Elizabeth, 1976. *Seven Year Olds in the Home Environment*. George Allen and Unwin, London.

Newton, J. L., Ryan, M. P. and Walkowitz, J. R. (eds), 1983. *Sex and Class in Women's History*. Routledge, London.

Nickols, S. Y. and Metzen, E. J., 1982. Impact of wife's employment upon husband's housework. *Journal of Family Issues*, 3, 199–217.

O'Brien, Margaret, 1992. Changing conceptions of fatherhood. In Bjornberg, U. (ed.).

O'Connor, Pat, 1992. *Friendships Between Women: A Critical Review*. Harvester Wheatsheaf, Hemel Hempstead.

O'Connor, Pat, 1991. Women's confidants outside marriage: shared or competing sources of intimacy. *Sociology*, 25, 241–54.

O'Connor, Pat, 1995. Understanding variation in marital sexual pleasure: an impossible task. *Sociological Review*, 43, 342–62.

Oliker, Stacey J. 1989. *Best Friends and Marriage: Exchange Among Women*. University of California Press, Berkeley.

Pahl, Jan, 1980. Patterns of money management within marriage. *Sociological Review*, 9, 313–35.

Pahl, Jan, 1983. The allocation of money and the structuring of inequality within marriage. *Sociological Review*, 13, 237–62.

Pahl, Jan, 1989. *Money and Marriage*. Macmillan, London.

Pahl, Ray E., 1984. *Divisions of Labour*. Blackwell, Oxford.

Parsons, Talcott, 1959. The social structure of the family. In Anshen, R. N. (ed.) *The Family, its Functions and Destiny*. Harper, New York, 241–74.

Parsons, Talcott, 1962. Youth in the context of American society. *Daedalus*, 91. Reprinted in Parsons, T., 1970, *Social Structure and Personality*. Collier Macmillan, New York.

Parsons, Talcott, 1964. *Essays in Sociological Theory*. Free Press, New York.

Parsons, Talcott and Bales, R. F. 1956. *Family Socialization and the Interaction Process*. Routledge and Kegan Paul, London.

Pateman, Carole, 1988. *The Sexual Contract*. Polity Press, Cambridge.

Patton, Cindy, 1985. *Sex and Germs: The Politics of AIDS*. South Press, Boston.

Peace, Helen, 1993. The pretended family: a study of the divisions of domestic labour in lesbian families. *University of Leicester, Discussion Papers in Sociology*, S93/3, Leicester.

Pearce, Lynne and Stacey, Jackie, 1995. *Romance Revisited*. Lawrence Wishart, London.

Pearsall, Ronald, 1969. *The Worm in the Bud: The World of Victorian Sexuality*. Weidenfeld and Nicolson, London.

Peplau, L. A. and Cochran, S. D. 1990. A relational perspective on homosexuality. In McWhirter, D. P., Sanders, S. A. and Reinisch, J. M. (eds).

Peplau, L. A., Cochran, S., Rook, K. and Padesky, C., 1978. Loving women: attachment and autonomy in lesbian relationships. *Journal of Social Issues*, 34, 7–27.

Phoenix, A., Woollett, A. and Lloyd, E., 1991. *Motherhood: Meanings, Practices and Ideologies*. Sage, London.

Pleck, Joseph, 1976. Man to man: is brotherhood possible? In Glazer-Malbin (ed.).

Pleck, Joseph, 1987. American fathering in historical perspective. In Kimmel, M. S. (ed.) pp. 83.

Plummer, Ken, 1995. *Telling Sexual Stories: Power, Change and Social Worlds*. Routledge, London.

Poster, Mark, 1978. *Critical Theory of the Family*. Pluto Press, London.

Prendergast, Shirley, 1994. *This is Time to Grow up: Girls' Experience of Menstruation*. Family Planning Association, London.

Price, C. D. 1974. *The Great White Walls are Built: Restrictive Immigration to North America and Australasia 1836–1888*. Australian Institute of International Affairs, Canberra.

Rafanell, Irene, 1995. Embodied inequality: an exploration of the body, sexuality and gender inequality. Unpublished M.Sc. dissertation, Edinburgh University, Edinburgh.

Rainwater, Lee, 1970. *Behind Ghetto Walls: Black Families in a Federal Slum*. Penguin, Harmondsworth.

Rainwater, Lee and Yancey, William, 1967. *The Moynihan Report and the Politics of Controversy*. Cambridge, Mass.

Rapoport, Rhona and Rapoport, Robert, 1971. *Dual-Career Families*. Penguin, Harmondsworth.

Rapoport, Rhona and Rapoport, Robert, 1976. *Dual Career Families Re-examined: New Integrations of Work and Family*. Martin Robertson, London.

Rapoport, Rhona and Rapoport, Robert (eds), 1978. *Working Couples*. Routledge and Kegan Paul, London.

Rapoport, R. N., Fogarty, M. P. and Rapoport, R., 1982. *Families in Britain*. Routledge and Kegan Paul, London.

Rawlins, William K. 1992. *Friendship Matters: Communication Dialectic and the Life Course*. Aldine De Gruyter, New York.

Raymond, Janice, 1991. *A Passion for Friends: Towards a Philosophy of Female Affection*. The Women's Press, London.

Reiger, Kerreen M., 1985. *The Disenchantment of the Home: Modernising the Australian Family 1880–1940*. Oxford University Press, Melbourne.

Ribbens, Jane, 1994. *Mothers and Their Children: A Feminist Sociology of Childrearing*. Sage, London.

Ribbens, Jane, 1995. Mothers' images of children and their implications for maternal response. In Brannen, J. and O'Brien, M. (eds), 60–78.

Rich, Adrienne, 1980. Compulsory heterosexuality and lesbian existence. *Signs*, 5, 631–60.

Richardson, Diane, 1993. *Women, Motherhood and Childrearing*. Macmillan, London.

Riley, David, 1990. Network influences on father involvement in childrearing. In Cochran et al. (eds).

Riley, Denise, 1983. *War in the Nursery: Theories of the Child and Mother*. Virago, London.

Rizzo, Thomas, 1989. *Friendship Development among Children in School*. Albex, Norwood, New Jersey.

Roberts, B., Finnegan, R. and Gallie, D. (eds), 1985. *New Approaches to Economic Life*. Manchester University Press, Manchester.

Roberts, Elizabeth, 1984. *A Woman's Place: An Oral History of Working-Class Women, 1890–1940*. Blackwell, Oxford.

Rosen, Ellen Israel, 1987. *Bitter Choices: Blue-Collar Women In and Out of Work*. University of Chicago Press, Chicago.

Ross, Ellen, 1983. Survival networks: women's neighbourhood sharing in London before World War I. *History Workshop*, 15, 4–27.

Rossi, Alice, 1984. Gender and parenthood. *American Sociological Review*, 49, 1–19.

Rothman, Ellen K, 1984. *Hands and Hearts: A History of Courtship in America*. Basic Books, New York.

Rubin, Lillian B., 1976. *Worlds of Pain: Life in the Working-Class Family*. Basic Books, New York.

Rubin, Lillian B., 1986. On men and friendship. *Psychoanalytical Review*, 73, 165–81.

Rubin, Lillian B., 1990. *Erotic Wars: What Happened to the Sexual Revolution?* Farrar, Strauss and Giroux, New York.

Rubin, Gayle, 1993. Misguided, dangerous and wrong: an analysis of anti-pornography politics. In Assiter, A. and Avedon, C. (eds), 18–40.

Ruble, D. N., Hackel, L. S., Fleming, A. S., Stagnor, C., 1988. Change in the marital relationship during the transition to first-time motherhood: effects of violated expectations concerning division of household labour. *Journal of Personality and Social Pyschology*, 55, 78–87.

Russell, Graeme, 1983. *The Changing Role of Fathers*. Open University Press, Milton Keynes.

Rutter, Michael, 1972. *Maternal Deprivation Reassessed*. Penguin, Harmondsworth.

Sahlins, Marshall, 1965. On the sociology of primitive exchange. In Banton, M. (ed.) *The Relevance of Models for Social Anthropology*. Association of Anthropology Monographs, London, 139–236.

Scanzoni, John, 1983. *Shaping Tomorrow's Family: Theory and Policy for the 21st Century*. Sage, Beverly Hills.

Scanzoni, J., Polonko, K., Teachman, J. and Thompson, L., 1989. *The Sexual Bond: Rethinking Families and Close Relationships*. Sage, Newbury Park, London.

Scheff, Thomas, 1990. *Microsociology, Discourse, Emotion and Social Structure*. University of Chicago Press, Chicago.

Schofield, Wendy, 1981. Complementary and conflicting identities: images of racial interacton in an interracial school. In Asher, S. and Gottman, J. (eds) *The Development of Children's Friendships*. Cambridge University Press, New York.

Schutz, Alfred, 1932. *The Phenomenology of the Social Word*. Reprinted 1972, Heinemann Educational Books, London.

Scott, John, 1995. *Sociological Theory: Contemporary Debates*. Edward Elgar, Aldershot.

Scott, Sue and Morgan, David (eds), 1993. *Body Matters: Essays on the Sociology of the Body*. The Falmer Press, London.

Scully, Diana, 1973/74. A funny thing happened on the way to the orifice: women in gynaecology text books. *American Journal of Sociology*, 78, 1045–9.

Scully, Diana, 1990. *Understanding Sexual Violence: A Study of Convicted Rapists*. Unwin Hyman, Cambridge, Mass.

Scutt, Jocelynne, 1983. *Even in the Best of Homes: Violence in the Family*. Penguin, Victoria.

Seabrook, Jeremy, 1982. *Working-Class Childhood: An Oral History*. Gollancz, London.

Sealey, J., Sin, R. Loosley, E., 1956. *Crestwood Heights*. University of Toronto Press, Toronto.

Seccombe, Wally, 1993. *Weathering the Storm: Working-class Families from the Industrial Revolution to the Fertility Decline*. Verso, London.

Segal, Lynne, 1990. *Slow Motion: Changing Masculinities, Changing Men*. Virago, London.

Segal, Lynne and McIntosh, Mary (eds), 1992. *Sex Exposed: The Sexuality and Pornography Debate*. Virago, London.

Seidman, Steven, 1992. *Embattled Eros: Sexual Politics and Ethics in Contemporary America*. Routledge, London.

Sennett, Richard, 1970. *Families Against the City: Middle-class Homes of Industrial Chicago*. Harvard University Press, Cambridge, Mass.

Sennett, Richard and Cobb, Jonathan, 1966. *The Hidden Injuries of Class*. Cambridge University Press, Cambridge.

Sharpe, Sue, 1976. *Just Like A Girl: How Girls Learn to be Women*. Penguin, Harmondsworth.

Sharpe, Sue, 1994. *Fathers and Daughters*. Routledge, London.

Shilts, Randy, 1987. *And the Band Played On: Politics, People and the AIDS Epidemic*. Penguin, Harmondsworth.

Silver, Allan, 1996. 'Two different sorts of commerce', or, Friendship and strangership in civil society. In Weintraub, J. and Kumar, K. (eds) *Public and Private in Thought and Practice: Perspectives on the Grand Dichotomy*. University of Chicago Press, Chicago.

Skolnick, Arlene, 1991. *Embattled Paradise: The American Family in an Age of Uncertainty*. Basic Books, New York.

Skolnick, Arlene, 1992. *The Intimate Environment: Exploring Marriage and the Family* (5th ed). Harper Collins, New York.

Smart, Carol and Smart, Barry, 1978. *Women, Sexuality and Social Control*. Routledge and Kegan Paul, London.

Smelser, Neil J. and Erikson, Erik H., 1980. *Themes of Work and Love in Adulthood*. Harvard University Press, Cambridge, Mass.

Smith, Adam, 1759. *The Theory of Moral Sentiments*. Reprinted by Clarendon Press, 1976, Oxford.

Smith-Rosenberg, Carroll, 1979. The female world of love and ritual: relations between women in nineteenth-century America. In Cott, N. F. and Pleck, E. H. (eds) *A Heritage of Her Own*. Simon and Schuster, Touchstone, New York.

Somerville, Jennifer, 1992. The New Right and family politics. *Economy and Society*, 21, 93–128.

Stack, Carol B., 1975. *All Our Kin: Strategies for Survival in a Black Community*. Harper Colophon Books, New York.

Stamp, P, 1985. Balance of financial power in marriage. *Sociological Review*, 33, 546–66.

Staples, Robert, 1982. *Black Masculinity: The Black Male's Role in American Society*. Black Scholar Press, San Francisco and New Beacon Books, London.

Staples, Robert (ed.), 1986. *The Black Family: Essays and Studies* (3rd edn).

Wadsworth, Belmont, California.

Stone, Lawrence, 1979. *The Family, Sex and Marriage in England 1500–1800*. Penguin, Harmondsworth.

Stone, Lawrence, 1993. *Broken Lives: Separation and Divorce in England 1660–1857*. Oxford University Press, Oxford.

Strathern, Marilyn, 1992a. *After Nature: English Kinship in the Late Twentieth Century*. Cambridge University Press, Cambridge.

Strathern, Marilyn, 1992b. *Reproducing the Future: Essays on Anthropology, Kinship and the New Reproductive Technologies*. Manchester University Press, Manchester.

Strauss, M. A., Gelles, R. and Steinmetz, S., 1980. *Behind Closed Doors: Violence in the American Family*. Doubleday, New York.

Swidler, 1980. Love and adulthood in American culture. In Smelser, N. and Erikson, E. (eds).

Temkin, J, 1987. *Rape and the Legal Process*. Sweet and Maxwell, London.

Thompson, John B., 1984. *Studies in the Theory of Ideology*. Polity Press, Cambridge.

Thompson, Linda and Walker, Alexis, 1989. Gender in families: women and men in marriage, work, and parenthood. *Journal of Marriage and the Family*, 51, 845–71.

Thompson, Paul, 1977. *The Edwardians: The Remaking of British Society*. Paladin, London.

Thomson, Rachel and Scott, Sue, 1991. *Learning about Sex: Young Women and the Social Construction of Sexual Identity*. Tufnell Press, London.

Thorne, Barrie, 1993. *Gender Play: Girls and Boys in School*. Rutgers University Press, New Brunswick, and Open University Press, Milton Keynes.

Tilly, Louise and Scott, Joan, 1978. *Women, Work and Family*. Holt Reinhart and Winston, New York.

Tolman, Deborah L., 1994. Doing desire: adolescent girls' struggle for/with sexuality. *Gender and Society*, 8, 324–42.

Toynbee, Claire, 1995. *His Work and Her Work*. University of Victoria Press, Wellington.

Trevarthen, C., 1993. The function of emotions in early infant communication and development. In Nadel, J. and Camaioni, L. (eds) *New Perspectives in Early Communicative Development*. Routledge, London, 48–81.

Uhlenberg, Peter, 1980. Death and the family. *Journal of Family History*, 5, 313–20.

VanEvery, Jo, 1995. *Heterosexual Women Changing the Family: Refusing to be a 'Wife'*. Taylor and Francis, London.

Vaughan, Daine, 1987. *Uncoupling*. Methuen, London.

Vigne, Thea, 1975. Parents and children 1890–1918: distance and dependence. *Oral History*, 3, 6–13.

Vogler, Carolyn, 1994. Money in the Household. In Anderson, M., Bechhofer, F. and Gershuny, J. (eds), 225–66.

Wajcman, Judy, 1991. *Feminism Confronts Technology*. Polity Press, Cambridge.

Walby, Sylvia, 1986. *Patriarchy at Work: Patriarchal and Capitalist Relations in Employment*. Polity Press, Cambridge.

Walby, Sylvia, 1989. *Theorising Patriarchy*. Basil Blackwell, Oxford.

Walby, Sylvia, 1990. Women's employment and the historical periodisation of patriarchy. In Corr H. and Jamieson L. (eds), 141–61.

Walby, Christine, 1990. *Who am I? Identity adoption and human fertilisation*. British

Agencies for Adoption and Fostering, London.

Walker, Karen, 1994. Men, women, and friendship: what they say, what they do. *Gender and Society*, 8, 246–65.

Walkerdine, Valerie and Lucey, Helen, 1989. *Democracy in the Kitchen: Regulating Mothers and Socialising Daughters*. Virago, London.

Walkowitz, Judith R., 1980. *Prostitution and Victorian Society: Women, Class, and the State*. Cambridge University Press, Cambridge.

Wallace, Claire, 1987. *For Richer For Poorer: Growing Up In and Out of Work*. Tavistock, London.

Wallerstein, Judith, S. and Blakeslee, Sandra, 1989. *Second Chances: Men, Women and Children a Decade After Divorce*. Ticknor and Fields, New York.

Wallerstein, Judith and Kelly, Joan B. 1980. *Surviving the Breakup: How Children and Parents Cope with Divorce*. Basic Books, New York.

Wallman, S., 1986. Ethnicity and the boundary process in context. In Rex, J. and Mason D. (eds) *Theories of Race and Ethnic Relations*. Cambridge University Press, Cambridge, 226–45.

Watney, Simon, 1987. *Policing Desire: Pornography, AIDS and the Media*. Comedia/Methuen, London.

Weber, Max, 1904. (1968 edition, edited by Gunther Roth and Claus Wittich) *Economy and Society: An Outline of Interpretive Sociology, Vol 1*. Chap. 1. Bedminster Press, New York.

Weeks, Jeffrey, 1981. *Sex, Politics and Society: The Regulation of Sexuality Since 1800*. Longman, New York.

Weeks, Jeffrey and Holland, Janet (eds) 1996. *Sexual Cultures: Communities, Values and Intimacy*. Macmillan, London.

Weiss, Robert, 1985. Men and the Family. *Family Process*, 24, 49–58.

Wellings, Kaye, Field, Julia, Johnson, Anne M. and Wadsworth, Jane, 1994. *Sexual Behaviour in Britain: The National Survey of Sexual Attitudes and Lifestyles*. Penguin, London.

Weston, Kath, 1991. *Families We Choose: Lesbians, Gays, Kinship*. Columbia University Press, New York.

Wheelock, Jane, 1990. *Husbands at Home: The Domestic Economy in a Post-Industrial Society*. Routledge, London.

Wight, Daniel, 1993a. Constraint or cognition? Young men and safer heterosexual sex. In Aggleton, Peter, Davies, Peter, and Hart, Graham (eds) *Aids: Facing the Second Decade*. Falmer Press, London, 41–60.

Wight, Daniel, 1993b. *Workers Not Wasters. Masculine Respectability, Consumption and Unemployment in Central Scotland: A Community Study*. Edinburgh University Press, Edinburgh.

Wight, Daniel, 1994. Boys' thoughts and talk about sex in a working-class locality of Glasgow. *Sociological Review*, 42, 702–37.

Wight, Daniel, 1996. Beyond the predatory male: the diversity of young Glaswegian men's discourses to describe heterosexual relationships. In Adkins, L. and Merchant, V. (eds), 145–73.

Wilcock, R. C. and Franke, W. H., 1963. *Unwanted Workers*. Free Press, Glencoe, New York.

Willmott, Peter, 1987. *Friendship Networks and Social Support*. Policy Studies Institute, London.

Willmott, Peter and Young, Michael, 1976. *Family and Class in a London Suburb*.

The New English Library, London.

Wilson, William J., 1993. *The Ghetto Underclass: Social Science Perspectives*. Sage, Newbury Park, California.

Wolf, Naomi, 1993. *Fire with Fire: The New Female Power and How it Will Change the Twenty-First Century*. Chatto and Windus, London.

Wood, Julian, 1984. Groping toward sexism: boys' sexual talk. In McRobbie, A. and Nava, M. (eds) *Gender and Generation*. Macmillan, London, 58–84.

Woollett, Anne and Phoenix, Ann, 1991. Psychological views of mothering. In Phoenix, A., Woollett, A. and Lloyd, E. (eds), 28–46.

Wright, P. H., 1978. Towards a theory of friendship based on a conception of self. *Human Communication Research*, 4, 196–207.

Wright, P. H., 1988. Interpreting research on gender differences in friendship: a case for moderation and a plea for caution. *Journal of Social and Personal Relationships*, 5, 367–73.

Wyness, Michael, 1992. Schooling and the normalisation of sex talk within the home. *British Journal of Sociology of Education*, 13, 89–103.

Young, Michael and Willmott, Peter, 1957. *Family and Kinship in East London*. Penguin, Harmondsworth.

Young, Michael and Willmott, Peter, 1973. *The Symmetrical Family*. Penguin, Harmondsworth.

Index